Doug Grow

University of Minnesota Press
Minneapolis · London

Published by the University of Minnesota Press
111 Third Avenue South, Suite 290
Minneapolis, MN 55401-2520

http://www.upress.umn.edu

Library of Congress
Cataloging-in-Publication Data

Grow, Douglas.
We're gonna win, Twins! / Doug Grow.
      p.   cm.
ISBN 978-0-8166-5621-9 (hc : alk. paper)
1. Minnesota Twins (Baseball team)—
History. I. Title.
GV875.M55G76 2010
796.357′6409776579—dc22

                          2009054309

Design and production by Mighty Media, Inc.
Text design by Chris Long

Printed in the United States of America
on acid-free paper

The University of Minnesota is an equal-opportunity educator and employer.

17 16 15 14 13 12 11 10
10 9 8 7 6 5 4 3 2 1

For my dad, Bill, who loved writing and playing catch in the backyard, and for Uncle Duke, who always had time to take a kid to a ballgame

Contents

Celebrate Good Times

The Minnesota Twins were exhausted as their flight approached the Twin Cities on October 12, 1987. So there was a small groan when the pilot announced that there were "a few thousand" fans at the Metrodome to greet them.

Hours earlier, the Twins had defeated the Detroit Tigers in the American League playoffs, winning the chance to go to the World Series. As thousands of Detroit fans had watched sullenly, the Twins had danced around the field, jumping into each other's arms and shouting, "We did it! We did it!" And then they'd jumped and shouted some more before entering the cramped clubhouse in ancient Tiger Stadium, where they had poured champagne and beer over each other while hugging and screaming, "Can you believe it?"

On the plane, they were emotionally drained and quiet. The pressure of the last weeks of the season, the intensity of the playoffs, the improbability of the triumph over the favored Tigers, the joyful outburst following their 9–5 victory, which had finished off a best-of-seven series in just five games, and the excitement over the thought of playing in the World Series had wrung the last energy from the players. The party was over; it was time to go home.

But there was one more stop to make—at the Hubert H. Humphrey Metrodome—before they'd be free to go home and collapse. The players boarded buses and, escorted by police cars, headed from the airport, where they'd been greeted by a few hundred fans, to the Dome. Slowly, the players awakened from their stupors as they became aware that something strange was happening around them.

It was almost ten o'clock on a Monday night and yet there was activity everywhere. There were people on the overpasses waving banners. And the closer the buses got to the Dome, the more people there were.

The buses made it to the loading dock area behind the Dome. There were people, yelling and waving.

"Why aren't they inside?" Twins first baseman Kent Hrbek asked a security man on the bus.

"There's no room inside, Herbie," the security man said.

The buses pulled into the stadium. The players got off and headed toward the right field entrance to the playing surface of the Dome. The doors to the field opened, and the players were overwhelmed by the sight and sound of 60,000 people.

"We walked onto the field and you could see the Dome wasn't fully lighted," recalled catcher Tim Laudner. "There was a bank of lights on over third base and a bank of lights on maybe in right center. So it was half light, half dark. Almost eerie. I looked toward home plate and I said to whoever was near me, 'there's no aisles!' There were just people everywhere and the most incredible cheers."

The players were stunned.

"They opened the door in the tunnel, I looked out and I thought, 'Oh, oh, here come the tears,'" said third baseman Gary Gaetti. "I bawled the whole time."

Others, like Kirby Puckett and Bert Blyleven, laughed and waved. "What are we doing here? What are we doing here?" Blyleven kept asking.

Then there was Juan Berenguer, also known as Señor Smoke and El Gasolino. He was a passionate, usually reliable, relief pitcher. He strolled around the field wearing a long trench coat, which he had purchased at a shop on Nicollet Mall when he had come to Minnesota as a member of the Twins at the start of the 1987 season. This coat was topped by a large fedora, presented to him by his friend, former Twins star Tony Oliva.

"I thought it would look beautiful on him," Oliva said.

The Twins players had laughed when they first saw Berenguer in the getup. "They called me Pancho Villa," said Berenguer. "They would say, 'Hey Pancho, where'd you park your horse?'"

Berenguer, with his sweepdown mustache, loved the villainous imagery. But he didn't look threatening on this night. He was almost regal as he strolled around the field toting a briefcase with one arm, waving with the other.

Berenguer always carried the briefcase because it contained things most important to him, such as family pictures, including several of his father, who had died when Berenguer was a child in Panama. There was also a doll, presented to him by a fellow Panamanian when Berenguer signed his first professional contract in 1975 with the New York Mets. He was twenty years old and didn't speak a word of English. The doll, which he called Little Smoke, traveled with him through the minor leagues and to major-league stops in New York, Kansas City, Toronto, Detroit, and San Francisco before he arrived in Minnesota before the '87 season.

Before every game, Señor Smoke and Little Smoke would have a conversation: "Be ready, Little Smoke. I may need you tonight." On this night, Señor Smoke waved, while Little Smoke remained in the briefcase.

Watching over this eruption of wild Minnesota joy were Dave Moore and Mark Weber of the Twins' marketing department, and Bill Lester, who had become executive director of the Metrodome in June of 1987. They had thrown together the homecoming over a 48-hour period. But they hadn't expected this. In fact, they would have been terrified had they known 60,000 people would show up.

It had happened like this: The Twins had won the first two games of the playoff series against the Tigers in Minnesota, 8–5 on October 7 and 6–3 on October 8. The two wins were only a mild surprise, because even though most in baseball assumed that the Tigers were the superior team, the Twins had been monstrous in the Dome all season long, compiling a 56–25 record, the best home record in baseball. But on the road they had been dismal, winning just 29 of 81 games.

True to form, the Twins lost, 7–6, to the Tigers when the playoff series resumed in Detroit on October 10. But then, on Sunday, October 11, the Twins did the unthinkable—they defeated the Tigers 5–3. One more victory and they'd be headed to the World Series.

"It dawned on us," recalled Weber. "They could win it in Detroit. What should we do if they did?"

Moore, who was in Detroit with the team, and Weber and Lester, who were back in Minnesota, started having conversations about what should happen if the Twins were to win the playoff series in Detroit. All three were small-town guys. All three thought in terms of a small-town high school basketball team winning the state championship and being welcomed home with a motorcade and a rally in the high school gym. They wanted something like that for the Twins.

"These were still the simplest and most innocent times," said Lester. "This was long before 9-11. There was no al-Qaeda. You didn't have to deal with Homeland Security. We were just this little city in the Midwest. We were the

Waltons. The biggest problem you had to concern yourself with was people drinking too much."

The three decided that if the Twins did win in Detroit, they'd throw open the doors to the Dome, have a couple of high school bands on the field, let the players wave, and call it a night. There was a pool in the Twins' office as to how many people would show up for such an event. High guess: 17,000.

October 12, 1987 became a small-town night in the big city. Fans filled the Metrodome to welcome home the American League champion Twins after their upset victory over the Tigers in Detroit. Juan Berenguer (aka El Gasolino, Señor Smoke, and Pancho Villa) waves to the massive crowd. PHOTO BY BRIAN PETERSON. COPYRIGHT 2009 *STAR TRIBUNE*/MINNEAPOLIS–ST. PAUL.

Lester did have some moments of trepidation when he went for a jog Monday morning. "I was running along and it suddenly dawned on me, 'We don't have an event. There's not going to be a game. We're going to have people in the Dome who have had all afternoon and most of the evening to drink.'"

But by then, it was too late to make changes in the plan. Lester made sure that there were enough people available to staff a few concession stands. The Twins made arrangements to have enough security personnel on hand to manage a crowd of up to 20,000.

"When they told me about the homecoming plan," said Jerry Bell, who had become the Twins' president at the start of the season, "I had my doubts. I said make sure you put all the fans in the sections behind home plate and put the TV cameras out by second base. I wanted to be sure that on TV it looked like there were some people there."

On Monday afternoon, October 12, during the telecast of the Twins' game against the Tigers, a crawl ran across the bottom of the screen: "If the Twins win, there will be a welcome-home celebration at the Dome. Gates will open at seven o'clock." The possible celebration was also mentioned by announcers during the broadcast. That was the extent of the marketing.

The Twins did win, 9–5, and a wave of euphoria rolled across the Twin Cities. "Actually, it had been building up for the last month of the season," Weber said. "But nobody could have predicted this. When you look back, I don't know if something like that night could ever happen again. Everything was special. The fans had seen the nucleus of this team grow up together. Remember, we still hadn't come to the era of multimillion-dollar contracts. There was a connection between fans and players that probably can never exist again."

Weber was in his office, deep in the basement of the Dome, when people started arriving by the hundreds, then by the thousands, for the celebration. They kept coming and coming.

"There were thousands of people with their kids," said Lester. "That's what saved us. Everybody was well behaved because there were so many kids. The ushers would open up one section of the Dome and as soon as that filled up, they'd open the next section. They just kept filling it up. There were a few drunks. But by the end of the night I think the only damage done was a broken sink in one of the men's rooms. The bill to fix it was $85."

When the players arrived, a roar filled the Dome that would continue on through the World Series against the St. Louis Cardinals. The players had heard ovations in the final weeks of the regular season, but nothing like this. They kept looking up from the field into the wall of noise and people. There were a few speeches. There was more roaring and waving.

For one night, Minneapolis was the world's biggest small town. For one night, everyone in Minnesota was a fan. For one night, all the politics and bottom-line business of major-league baseball was not just forgiven, but forgotten.

Juan Berenguer looks back at the night in the Dome as the most incredible of his baseball life. Sometimes he still gets goose bumps thinking about it. And sometimes he slips on the long coat and the big fedora and starts heading for the front door of his home in the Twin Cities suburbs. "But my kids always stop me," he said. "They say, 'Leave it home, Dad.'"

Tim Laudner has talked about that night to schoolkids and Kiwanis clubs for years. And every time he talks about the event, it gets to him. His throat tightens, his eyes moisten. "The emotion of the fans and the players was genuine," he said. "To share that moment with those guys and those fans still gives me the chills. It was as good as it gets."

1961

Twins Territory

The World: Soviet cosmonaut Yuri Gagarin becomes the first human in space. The trial of Hitler henchman Adolf Eichmann begins in Israel. His attorney, Dieter Wechtenbruch said Eichmann was showing "a philosophical interest in the afterlife." Eichmann was found guilty and hanged in the spring of 1962.

The Nation: John F. Kennedy becomes the country's first Roman Catholic president. The Peace Corps is formed. The CIA-backed invasion of Cuba turns into a debacle. The federal minimum wage is raised from $1 an hour to $1.15.

The State: The state legislature passes a bill making the common loon the state's official bird. The Vikings play their first NFL game and a rookie quarterback, Fran Tarkenton, comes off the bench and throws four touchdown passes in a 37–13 Vikings win over the Chicago Bears.

Pop Culture: Grammy Song of the Year: "Moon River," by Henry Mancini. Best Picture: *West Side Story*. Best Seller: *The Agony and the Ecstasy*, by Irving Stone. Top-Rated Television Show: *Gunsmoke*.

The Season: The Twins finish in seventh place in the ten-team American League, thirty-eight games behind the New York Yankees. This is the season of the great home run derby between Roger Maris and Mickey Mantle to see if either can surpass Babe Ruth's magical 60 home runs. Mantle is the sentimental favorite of the nation, but it's Maris who breaks Ruth's record on the final game of the season.

Cookie Lavagetto and Billy Gardner found themselves driving across North Dakota. It was December 1960 and their destination was Rugby, a town at the geographic center of North America. A few months earlier, Calvin Griffith had announced that he was moving the Washington Senators to Minnesota, where the team was to be known as the Twins, a name designed to prevent any hard feelings in either Minneapolis or St. Paul.

Now Lavagetto, the team's manager, and Gardner, its veteran second baseman, were on a baseball mission to a father-and-son banquet at Rugby's First Lutheran Church. That a couple of big-leaguers were coming was a big deal in Rugby. Photos of Gardner and Lavagetto had been placed in the entry of the church a month before the event.

Snow was falling and the wind was blowing as the two advanced slowly up Highway 2. The heater in their car was failing. Gardner, who had played with the New York Giants, Baltimore, and Washington, and Lavagetto, who had played in Brooklyn and Pittsburgh, were startled by the remoteness around them and were growing more skeptical about their trip with each passing mile.

They stopped frequently to call the church, informing event organizers of their growing concerns about the weather conditions. The last call came from the lounge at the Elks Club in Devils Lake, North Dakota, still sixty miles southeast of Rugby. "Our socks are frozen to our feet," Gardner said. The big league emissaries said they couldn't—they wouldn't—drive farther. To the disgust of the people of Rugby, Lavagetto and Gardner went home the next day.

Welcome to Twins Territory.

After years of hope and weeks of hype, the first major-league baseball game in Minnesota, held April 21, 1961, was almost anticlimactic. It wasn't so much that the Twins lost their first home game at Metropolitan Stadium to their Washington successors, it was that they lost before a crowd of 24,606 on a surprisingly pleasant Friday afternoon.

The *Minneapolis Tribune* understated the disappointment of 6,000 empty seats, reporting on the front page of the paper that fans "had flocked to Met Stadium." The Upper Midwest's dominant newspaper also excitedly reported that this was the largest crowd ever to gather at the Met.

But Griffith never was good at spin. "I was disappointed in the crowd, but the game was all right," Griffith told reporters.

The *Minneapolis Star*'s influential sports editor, Charlie Johnson, who had pulled so many strings to bring a major-league team to the Twin Cities, saw the empty seats as a black eye. "Naturally, the Twin Cities of Minneapolis and St. Paul and the Upper Midwest didn't fare too well prestige-wise when the park was not completely sold out for the first major-league game played in this area," he wrote.

That people didn't rush to Met Stadium, which was still a work in progress, probably shouldn't have come as a surprise. Five days before the home opener, there was a snow and ice storm in the Twin Cities in which four people died. Because of the storm, some of the parking lots at the Met had not been coated with asphalt, so many people who did attend the game had to walk through mud to get to the stadium.

But there were big-picture factors at play, too. Though Twin Cities' boosters were trying to sell the idea that major-league baseball would make the area big-league, there were a lot of Minnesotans who weren't so sure. Sports fans had felt the callous side of pro sports. The Minneapolis Lakers had left the city a year earlier for Los Angeles, just as the team, behind super rookie Elgin Baylor, had begun to show signs of resurgence. And the region already had the University of Minnesota football team to rally around. The Gophers were declared national champions at the conclusion of the 1960 regular season, before losing to Washington in the Rose Bowl.

But the biggest problem was that the team that was supposed to make the Twin Cities "big-league" represented the dregs of professional sports. The Senators were a longtime laughingstock summed up in the phrase, "Washington, first in war, first in peace, last in the American League."

So synonymous were the Washington Senators with failure that Douglass Wallop's 1954 novel, *The Year the Yankees Lost the Pennant*, was made into the long-running hit musical, *Damn Yankees*. In the story, a beleaguered Senators fan makes a Faustian deal with the devil and becomes star player Joe Hardy, who carries Washington past the hated Yankees.

That was Broadway. In reality, the Senators remained awful even as the musical received a Tony Award. The Senators of 1955 lost 101 of 154 games. To make matters more dismal, the beloved old owner of the team, Clark Griffith, died that year, passing the team on to his adopted son, Calvin, and Calvin's sister, Thelma Haynes. Under this new generation of Griffiths, the team remained abysmal, finishing last in 1957, 1958, and 1959. This was the team Minnesota had "won."

Results of the *Minneapolis Tribune*'s Minnesota Poll taken a few weeks before the start of the 1961 season showed the team could expect to draw 1.2 million fans in its first season, a dramatic improvement over the 743,000 fans Griffith's Senators had attracted in its last season in Washington.

But responses to the poll showed coolness toward pro sports. Half of the respondents showed some interest in baseball, but only 19 percent indicated "great interest." As the season opened, just four in ten respondents could even identify the team.

The players seemed as skeptical as the fans about the move. In their final season in Washington, the Senators had finally made positive things happen. Only a seven-game losing streak at the end of the 1960 season dashed the team's hopes of a .500 season. Still, the Senators managed to finish fifth in the eight-team American League, and the team did have a young star, Harmon Killebrew.

Killebrew liked playing in D.C. "It was fun to be in the nation's capital. It was hard to leave. None of us knew what to expect."

That doubt about leaving Washington continued up to opening day at the Met. When the team arrived in Minnesota for the first time, following a successful three-city road trip to open the 1961 season, there were 3,000 people waiting to greet the players at Wold-Chamberlain Field, which later would be renamed Twin Cities International Airport.

"We're happy to see them here," Jim Lemon, a slugger who was nearing the end of his career, told a gaggle of reporters. "Of course, it is a nice evening. But this is still a good sign."

That fell a little short of an it's-great-to-be-in-Minnesota sentiment.

Excited about it or not, the Senators were the Twins. In the meantime, in Washington, an expansion team was thrown together to be the new Washington Senators, a team that would continue the historic futility of the old Senators and later move to Texas and become the Texas Rangers.

The pursuit of a major-league team had begun in earnest almost ten years before that first game in Minnesota. In *Stadium Games,* a book about Minnesota's tortured history with its professional sports teams and the buildings they play in, Jay Weiner pinpoints a 1952 lunch at the Minneapolis Athletic Club as the beginning of the effort to bring baseball to the Twin Cities. The meeting involved Charlie Johnson, the *Trib's* sports editor, Gerald Moore, a sales manager of a storage and moving company, and Norm McGrew, who worked for the Minneapolis Chamber of Commerce. At that lunch, they decided that the Twin Cities, a metro area of a million people, needed a baseball team, but to attract a team a stadium would first have to be built. The three men didn't realize how hard this project would be. And they couldn't have anticipated how their stadium struggle would come to represent baseball in the state.

Making the idea of major-league baseball in Minnesota seem possible was that baseball franchises, after a half-century of being anchored, were moving. In 1953, the Braves left Boston, moving to Milwaukee, which had County Stadium, a new, publicly-built ballpark. In 1954, the Browns left St. Louis and headed to Baltimore, where the newly-named Orioles had a publicly-built stadium ready for them to move into.

Clearly, a ballpark was needed if the region was going to attract a major-league team. Neither Nicollet Park, home of the minor-league Minneapolis Millers, nor Lexington Park, home of the minor-league St. Paul Saints, was adequate for a major-league franchise. Those two old parks were no longer even adequate for the American Association teams that called them home.

There was no Mall of America, no Thunderbird Hotel, no Ikea. Cornfields and melon patches were torn up when the political fighting ended and construction began on Metropolitan Stadium in 1955.
MINNEAPOLIS STAR JOURNAL PHOTO. COURTESY OF THE MINNESOTA HISTORICAL SOCIETY.

Given the need for only one major-league baseball stadium, boosters in St. Paul and Minneapolis did what comes naturally to them—they feuded and went their separate ways. St. Paulites demanded a St. Paul site for the ballpark, eventually building Midway Stadium. The Minneapolis boosters wanted the new park to be in Paul Gerhardt's melon patch in Bloomington.

The first bulldozers started turning farmland into Met Stadium in the summer of 1955, the funding coming from $500 bonds sold to 2,600 people who saw the purchase as a civic gesture. There were no guarantees that a major-league team would come to the park, which was to be built in installments, starting with a 20,000-seat stadium that cost $4.5 million. The Millers were the first tenants, moving into the new ballpark in 1956.

Met Stadium did stir the big-league talk. The first to make Minnesota believe that major-league baseball could become a reality was Horace Stone-

Calvin Griffith *(right)* brought the Washington Senators history with him in the form of a huge painting of Walter "Big Train" Johnson, the Senators' grandest star. COURTESY OF THE *ST. PAUL PIONEER PRESS.*

ham, owner of the New York Giants. Stoneham gushed about the stadium, a unique, triple-deck structure with no pillars to block the view. "It is the finest minor-league park in the country and there are only two in the majors that are better," he said.

But in the spring of 1957, Stoneham broke hearts in New York and Minnesota when he announced that he was taking the Giants to San Francisco in a package deal with Walter O'Malley, who was taking his Brooklyn Dodgers to Los Angeles. The Cleveland Indians showed interest, but backed off because of legal entanglements in Ohio.

That set the stage for Griffith. But he—and Minnesota baseball boosters had a problem. Major League Baseball didn't want to ruffle the feathers of Congress, which allowed baseball special antitrust exemption. The members of the Congress wanted the national pastime played in the nation's capital. To mess with Congress meant messing with the game's monopoly status.

Bobbleheads have a long history in baseball, but this one is rare. The first handful of Twins dolls were labeled "Minneapolis" Twins. At the time, the club hadn't been officially named the Minnesota Twins and the team had been incorporated as the "Minneapolis Baseball Club." FROM THE COLLECTION OF CLYDE DOEPNER; PHOTO BY ROBERT FOGT.

The flirtations with Griffith began in 1958. He was in, out, in again. Expansion on Met Stadium, with the public's money at risk, was begun. Much of the flirting was played out in public and led to colorful sports writing. Shirley Povich of the *Washington Post,* for example, called Minneapolis "a shameless hussy" because of its efforts to lure Griffith to the melon patch.

With the threat of a new major baseball league, the Continental League, hanging over its head, Major League Baseball decided to expand for the 1961 season. The National League would have a New York team again, the expansion Mets, and a team in Houston. In the American League, Griffith would be allowed to move his team to Minnesota, an expansion team would be formed in Washington, and Los Angeles would get a team, the Angels.

ACCURATE TV LISTINGS FOR CHANNELS ② ④ ⑤ ⑨ ⑪
WEEK OF APRIL 8-14
15c

TV TIMES

SPECIAL!
TV Score Card
Lineups - Statistics
Season TV Schedule

Minnesota
Twins
Debut on
Channel 11

LA VAGETTO

KILLEBREW

GRIFFITH

SCOTT   WOLFF

A local TV guide promoting the arrival of big-league baseball to Minnesota. The original broadcast and telecast crew featured Bob Wolff, Ray Scott, and Halsey Hall. Wolff had been the team's radio voice in Washington but he didn't understand the magic of Hall and left the team after one year, replaced by a young talent from Baltimore, Herb Carneal. FROM THE COLLECTION OF CLYDE DOEPNER; PHOTO BY ROBERT FOGT.

In October 1960, the announcement was made that the Twins were coming to Minnesota. Griffith, who claimed to have only $25,000 in the bank when he arrived in the state, received $250,000 from Twin Cities businessmen so he could pay a compensation fee to the Boston Red Sox and the Los Angeles Dodgers for their loss of minor-league rights to Minneapolis (Boston) and St. Paul (Los Angeles). According to Major League Baseball rules, the Red Sox and Dodgers had to move their minor-league franchises elsewhere. Griffith also received 90 percent of concessions at Met Stadium, including during Vikings games. He got a $600,000 radio and television deal, double what he'd had in Washington. In return, he was to pay 7 percent of net ticket receipts as rent to the Stadium Commission. (A season ticket could be purchased for $40.) No rent would be required in years the Twins drew fewer than 750,000 fans.

Griffith, perceived as a buffoon by so many in both Washington and Minnesota, showed a sophisticated understanding of the region he was moving to. Griffith went out of his way to make sure that he purchased half of his office furniture and carpeting in St. Paul, the other half in Minneapolis. The Twins became the first team in pro sports to be named after a region, not a city. That showed that Griffith saw the potential of marketing to an entire region. He courted sportswriters in Rochester, Duluth, and Sioux Falls as carefully as he did the Twin Cities scribes. He sent players and coaches on mission trips to places like Rugby, North Dakota.

The Twins started the 1961 season on the road, in Yankee Stadium. Starting pitcher Pedro Ramos, who throughout spring training had said he just might go off and fight with anti-Castro forces, was brilliant, outdueling Whitey Ford. The Twins won, 6–0, and came to their new home after the road trip with a 5–1 record. The only downer in the opening week of the season was that Killebrew pulled a hamstring in Baltimore and had to miss the home opener.

The *Tribune* was filled with breathless hype as the Twins prepared for their first home game. Business would boom because of major-league baseball. "Cities that made the switch from bush to big time in the past decade all

Twins schedules popped up everywhere, including this season-opening schedule—of home games only—on matchbooks. Twins ashtrays and cigarette lighters were also common at a time when smoking was socially acceptable. FROM THE COLLECTION OF CLYDE DOEPNER.

A ticket for the first ever Twins home game. Although tickets at the Metrodome carried the rain check provision, younger Twins fans who never experienced outdoor baseball at the Met may need to acquaint themselves with the policy at Target Field. FROM THE COLLECTION OF CLYDE DOEPNER.

report rather startling income heights," claimed one story, noting that a Milwaukee study showed out-of-town fans spent $11 a day in Milwaukee when in town for a Braves game.

The society pages ran stories about the players' wives and the eligible bachelors on the team. The "gay bachelors," reported Barbara Flanagan, included Ray Moore, Dan Dobbek, Pedro Ramos, and Billy Consolo. The Cuban players were seen as especially exotic. Ramos was described as "The Gay Caballero" who loved to mambo and rumba but not cha-cha. Camilo Pascual's wife, Raquel, was described as "a dark-eyed Spanish beauty. Mrs. Pascual has pale skin and shuns a suntan."

The *Tribune* was packed with hotel ads for fans coming from afar. "When in Minneapolis, head for the Hotel Pick-Nicollet. Air-conditioned room. Breakfast in bed. Dinner for two in the famous Waikiki Room and free parking. $25.30, including tips."

There was even a story about how women should dress for big-league baseball. "You should dress casually and comfortably," said Mrs. James Robertson (wife of Twins vice president Jimmy Robertson). "But you should wear a dress to the park. Baseball's big league and high class." (A decade later, the Twins would introduce "Halter Top Day" to Minnesota, and beer-swilling men would slobber, "Put it on, baby.")

The first season would be filled with more downs than ups. There was a nasty 12-game losing streak that started in late May. During that streak, the Twins fell to ninth in the league and Griffith ordered his manager, Lavagetto, to take "a leave of absence." He was on leave for seven games, returned in mid-June and was fired on June 23, replaced by Sam Mele. "I never said that the manager is sure of his job," Griffith said. "A manager's job is always in jeopardy."

There were highlights, too, the most momentous of those coming from the opposition.

On May 3, Roger Maris hit his second home run of the season—and his only Met Stadium homer of the year—off Pedro Ramos in the seventh inning. The 18,158 people at the game had seen what would turn out to be one of a record-breaking 61 hit by Maris that season. (He hit three other homers—numbers 16, 17, and 41—against the Twins in '61, but all of them in Yankee Stadium.)

And then there was a seemingly minor deal made on June 1. Griffith sent infielder Billy Consolo to the Milwaukee Braves for a broken-down second baseman, Billy Martin. Martin instantly became a fan favorite, despite the fact that he batted just .246 and committed 17 errors in what would prove to be his final season as a player. What the fans loved was the fact that Martin had once been a star player for the New York Yankees. And they loved that he was filled with fire, which was both his great strength and fatal weakness.

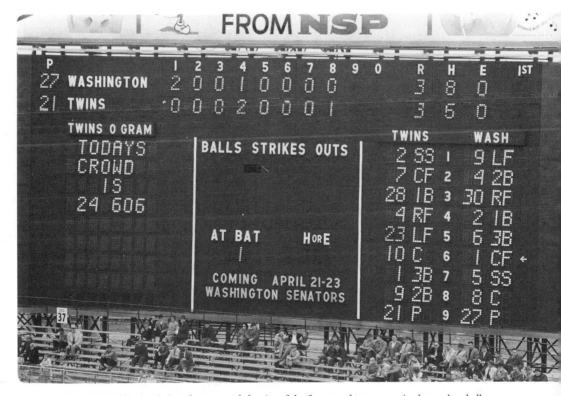

The amazing "Twins O Gram" announced the size of the first crowd to see a major-league baseball game at Metropolitan Stadium. It was a disappointment to Calvin Griffith and team boosters who had worked so hard to make Minnesota "big league." PHOTO BY JOHN CROFT. *MINNEAPOLIS STAR TRIBUNE* NEWS NEGATIVE COLLECTION, MINNESOTA HISTORICAL SOCIETY.

But it was the first home game that was the precursor to what was ahead. After Governor Elmer Andersen threw out the first ball, the new Twins and Washington were tied 3–3 entering the ninth, when the Senators scored twice against Ray Moore, who had replaced starting pitcher Pascual.

In the home half of the ninth, Bob Allison reached first on an error and, with one out, advanced to third on a single by Earl Battey. Pinch hitter Elmer Valo walked, loading the bases. But Hal Naragon popped to short and pinch hitter Pete Whisenant struck out.

Minnesota's team had lost its first home game, but the region was officially "big-league" and its sports culture would never be the same again.

1962

Holy Cow!

The World: The Cuban missile crisis comes to a dramatic conclusion on October 28 when the Soviet Union's Nikita Khrushchev agrees to dismantle nuclear missiles that had been erected in Cuba. President John Kennedy is heralded as the man who made Khrushchev blink.

The Nation: On February 20, John Glenn, aboard Friendship 7, becomes the first American to orbit the earth and is welcomed home with a tickertape parade in New York. Actress Marilyn Monroe, 36, is found dead in her home in Brentwood, California.

The State: Walter Mondale wins his first political race, for Minnesota's attorney general, a position he'd been appointed to two years earlier. The Trashmen form in Minneapolis and, a year later, release their one and only hit, "Surfin' Bird."

Pop Culture: Billboard's #1 Song: "Stranger on the Shore," by Mr. Acker Bilk. Best Picture: *Lawrence of Arabia.* Best Seller: *Ship of Fools,* by Katherine Anne Porter. Top-Rated Television Show: *The Beverly Hillbillies.*

The Season: Camilo Pascual wins 20 games, Harmon Killebrew leads the league in home runs (48) and RBI (126), and the Twins become the talk of baseball by finishing second, by five games, to the mighty Yankees.

When the Twins returned to their old hometown in 1962, catcher Earl Battey had a chance to shake the hand of President John Kennedy. Presidents and baseball have a rich history, dating back to 1910 when Clark Griffith enticed President William Howard Taft to throw out the first pitch for the Senators' home opener. The promotion was such a success that most years, the president throws out the opening pitch to officially kick off the new season. In 1953, President Dwight Eisenhower was to throw out the first pitch, but let it be known that he was going to skip the opener to attend the Masters Golf Tournament. He instead sent Vice President Richard Nixon to do the honors. Former president Harry Truman, no fan of Nixon's, wrote a letter to Griffith, warning the Senators owner that Nixon might "throw a curve ball." Nixon's pitch selection became a nonfactor when the game was rained out and Eisenhower was available for the makeup game. COURTESY OF THE MINNESOTA TWINS.

The 160-acre Skogen farm in Otter Tail County was like thousands of others in Minnesota in the early 1960s. It had a two-story white house with a porch on the south side, a faded red barn, and a herd of thirty-six cows that were milked morning and night.

In the kitchen and the barn, there were radios always tuned to KBRF-AM out of Fergus Falls. The station offered weather, news, agriculture reports, obituaries—and Minnesota Twins baseball, featuring Harmon Killebrew and the biggest star of them all, color commentator Halsey Hall.

"None of us knew the man, but everyone could imitate his voice," said Dan Skogen, who grew up milking cows and listening to Hall's commentary of Twins games. "When you heard that voice and heard his stories, you envisioned a guy with cigar burns on his clothes and maybe a shot of booze close by."

The vision was on the mark. Hall was a devoted family man, but he was addicted to cigars, loved a good drink, and devoured green onions in bunches. He was a great storyteller and a pungent broadcast partner.

Herb Carneal, the Twins' legendary play-by-play announcer, was once asked what it was like sitting next to Hall.

"There's a lot to be said for an open-air booth," he said.

Hall was sixty-two years old when Griffith brought the team to Minnesota and was already well known in the Twin Cities as a sportswriter for the *Minneapolis Tribune* and sportscaster on WCCO Radio. As was the custom of his era, Hall didn't cover sports as a journalist; he befriended sports figures. He was a homer.

In *Holy Cow! The Life and Times of Halsey Hall*, Stew Thornley wrote of Hall's relationship with the University of Minnesota football team. Hall was a Gopher motivator when he wasn't broadcasting the team's games, sending letters of support to players in hard times. For example, in 1973, when the Gophers lost successive games to Ohio State, Kansas, and Nebraska, Hall wrote a letter to the team's captains, Darrel Bunge and Jeff Gunderson.

"You have faced some of the behemoths of football. You never quit. You have improved with every game, regardless of the score.... Keep your chin up, boys. Better times will come."

It was Hall who is said to have come up with the name "Golden" Gophers when, in 1934, coach Bernie Bierman sent his squad on the field in gold uniforms.

Gopher football—in golden and hard times—was Hall's first love. But it was Twins baseball, and the team's huge radio network, that turned him into a regional icon. In that first season, Hall was teamed in the broadcast booth with Ray Scott, best known as the voice of the Green Bay Packers, and Bob Wolff, who had been the Senators' longtime play-by-play voice in Washington.

Off the air, the chemistry of this trio was awful. "Wolff was an East Coast guy," said Larry Jagoe, longtime producer of Twins broadcasts. "He just didn't seem to like Midwesterners. He was professional enough not to let it show on the broadcasts, but when he wasn't on the air he was vicious."

Wolff would stand at the back of the booth ridiculing Hall, whom he saw as an unprofessional, Midwestern rube.

This went on for weeks until Scott snapped. During a commercial break, Scott got out of his chair, turned to Wolff and said, "If this keeps up, somebody's going to lose their fucking teeth."

For the rest of the 1961 season, Wolff kept his opinions of Hall and the Midwest to himself. After the last game of the season, he accepted a job with Madison Square Garden in New York and was replaced in the booth by Carneal, who had been broadcasting Baltimore Orioles games. Carneal was available because Hamm's Brewery, which had been the sponsor of Orioles games as well as Twins games, lost sponsorship rights in Baltimore.

Carneal would remain the calm, reassuring voice of the Twins until his death before opening day in 2007. Ultimately, Carneal would be an even bigger symbol of the Twins than Hall. But in the 1960s, the booth, and the region, belonged to Hall.

Herb Carneal (*left*) joined Halsey Hall (*center*) and Ray Scott in 1962. Carneal would become the voice of summer in the Upper Midwest. COURTESY OF THE MINNESOTA TWINS.

In 1962, this new broadcast team got to tell one of baseball's most refreshing stories. The Twins, who came to Minnesota with their roots embedded in last place, spent the season in hot pursuit of the Yankees. Their 92 victories was the most by a Griffith-owned team in three decades.

Killebrew was marvelous. "Our Paul Bunyan," said pitcher Jim Kaat of Killebrew, who led the American League in home runs and runs batted in. Kaat, who was only twenty-three years old but already in his fourth big-league season, won 18 games for the Twins in 1962 and the first of 16 consecutive Gold Glove awards for his defensive skills. Camilo Pascual won 20 games. Jack Kralick pitched the first no-hitter in the team's history, defeating the Kansas City A's 1–0 on August 26.

The team also was energized by Vic Power, an effervescent first baseman whom the Twins acquired for Pedro Ramos just as the season began. He batted .290, won his fifth Gold Glove, and won fans over with his style.

Power was a man ahead of his time. He deserves to be remembered as a significant stereotype-buster during the long, painful transition period between baseball's color barrier being broken by Jackie Robinson in 1947 and genuine acceptance of players of color.

Puerto Rican by birth, Power was stunned when he first encountered the bigotry in the United States. Though often labeled as a "showboat" and a "troublemaker," he refused to betray himself so that he could better fit the strict limitations placed on black players in the 1950s.

In 1954, he would have been, along with Elston Howard, the first player of color on the mighty Yankees. But just before the season, ownership decided that Power's personality didn't "fit the Yankee image." He was traded before the start of the '54 season to the Philadelphia Athletics.

During the seasons of spring training in the South, he constantly ran into segregation. Sometimes, he laughed at it.

"We don't serve Negroes," he was told by a waitress in the South.

"That's okay," he replied. "I don't eat Negroes. I want some rice and beans."

When, in 1955, the A's moved from Philadelphia to Kansas City, Power was a constant target of Kansas City cops who were offended that this black man not only drove a flashy Cadillac convertible, but was also often in the company of white women.

Sportswriters saw him as a "showboat" because he caught the baseball with one hand, often with a sweeping flourish. But the simple fact was he could play.

"He was one of the best fielding first baseman of all time," pitcher Jim

"Mudcat" Grant was quoted as saying of Power, who was his teammate in Cleveland and Minnesota. "I remember once when he missed a popup down the right field line. After the game, he took his glove into the clubhouse and cut it into little bitty pieces. He said, 'I don't need that glove anymore.'"

Power would make a breathtaking play, or Killebrew would hit a ball out of sight and Hall would yell, "Holy cow!" And fans throughout the Upper Midwest would smile. On the other hand, if Hall muttered "holy cow" quietly, or in disgust, listeners instantly knew that Bob Allison had struck out or an ump had blown a call.

New Yorkers claim that the Yankees' Hall of Fame shortstop, Phil Rizzuto, was the first to use the "holy cow" expression when he became a Yankee broadcaster in 1957. Harry Caray, the most famous of all baseball broadcasters—with the Cardinals, White Sox, and Cubs—insisted he was the first to use the expression. He said he "holy cowed" into a microphone while broadcasting a baseball game in Battle Creek, Michigan, in the 1940s.

But Hall said he was the first broadcaster to use the phrase, claiming to have used it back when he was broadcasting the minor-league games of the Minneapolis Millers in the 1930s.

There are mixed views about just who was wise enough to place Hall in the Twins' broadcast booth. Griffith, in his later years, said Hall was his choice. He'd known Hall years before he'd moved the team to Minnesota and, he told Thornley, he'd been impressed.

"He interviewed me and when it was over I thought, 'This man is a master. He has a vocabulary as good as Mr. Churchill's and he knows how to use it.' When it came time to make a decision on the final member of the broadcast crew, I recommended Halsey."

Rob Brown, who ran wcco's marketing department from 1962 to 1970, said many around Griffith in the Twins' organization were not fans of Halsey. At times, Griffith was on the verge of caving to internal pressure and dumping Hall.

"They didn't understand the glory of Halsey," Brown said. "There were some who were always fighting having him on the broadcast team."

Wise heads prevailed. Hall stayed in the booth through the 1972 season, when wcco made the decision that, at age seventy-four, Hall could no longer handle the rigors of travel and dropped him from the broadcast team.

Hall died at his home on December 30, 1977, a bottle of Scotch that he had received for Christmas in his hand. The stories about him still linger, such as the one in which a cub reporter asked Hall why he always carried his own supply of liquor when he was on the road with the Twins.

"Don't all the hotels have bars?"

"My boy," said Hall, "you never know when you might run into a local election."

Hall's voice was carried over a vast radio network that made the Twins the hometown team of people as far away as Denver. In their first season in Minnesota, Twins games were carried on sixty stations across the region, a network second only to that of the St. Louis Cardinals.

At the center of this network was WCCO Radio, which dominated its market like no other radio station in the country. When the Twins arrived in Minnesota, WCCO had more listeners than all other Twin Cities stations combined. *The Arthur Godfrey Show*, a nationally syndicated, powerhouse CBS show, had more listeners in the Twin Cities than any other market in the country, meaning more people were listening to Godfrey on WCCO than were listening in huge markets such as New York, Los Angeles, and Chicago. According to local legend, pilots landing in the Twin Cities could see lights go off across the region at precisely 10:15 each night. That's when Cedric Adams, a newspaper and radio star, signed off on his nightly newscast.

There was never a doubt that WCCO would be the flagship station of the Minnesota Twins. Working with WCCO, WTCN-TV, and the Hamm's Brewery, which owned the rights to the Twins' broadcasts and telecasts, Griffith received a $600,000 broadcast deal, more than double what he'd received in Washington.

Seldom was heard a discouraging word about the team on this vast network, though Griffith complained frequently of WCCO's fixation on the weather. "Jesus Christ, you're costing me tickets," Griffith bellowed whenever WCCO announcers would mention even a possibility of rain.

In the early years, Griffith's team received constant, friendly coverage on the radio and in the daily newspapers. The sportswriters were kind not only because they were so happy to be covering major-league baseball and because the team was better than expected, but because Griffith was a generous host. In the Twins Room at Metropolitan Stadium, food was bountiful and liquor flowed for the media. Writers also received gifts at Christmas and frequent free dinners at fine establishments when the team was on the road.

Griffith didn't just cater to the needs of the Twin Cities media. He saw to it that sportswriters from smaller markets were also treated as big-leaguers. There were permanent seats in the press box for sportswriters from Rochester, Duluth, St. Cloud, and Sioux Falls. Sportswriters from the smallest of towns were seldom turned down when they requested media credentials.

"He was awfully good to us," said John Egan, longtime sports editor of the

Sioux Falls *Argus Leader.* "I thanked him one time for all he did for those of us from smaller markets and he said, 'Go out to the parking lot and look around. There are a lot of North Dakota and South Dakota license plates out there.'"

Griffith understood he was getting something in return for his gracious hosting. Space that once might have gone to the local bowling team or the high school basketball team was now going to the Minnesota Twins. Egan said that the extensive exposure quickly changed the habits of people in the smaller markets around the region.

"The sophisticated fan started making two or three trips a year to Twins games," he said. "It wasn't cool to go to the local games anymore."

Even kids noticed adult behavior changing. "My Grandma Peterson was the type of person who never shushed us," said Skogen. "But the one exception to that was when the Twins were on the radio. If the Twins were about to rally and we were making noise, she'd say, 'Shssh, we need to listen to the game now.'"

Skogen grew up planning to follow his father's footsteps on the farm. But he got a harsh farming lesson when he was a junior in high school. He had contracted with some neighbors to farm a few hundred acres for them.

"It turned out to be one of those years we had a terrible drought," Skogen said. "I did all that work and ended up with nothing. I knew then I needed a Plan B."

So he got into radio. Most of the farms like the Skogen place are gone now. But small-town radio thrives. Skogen serves as a cohost on the morning shows on KWAD AM and FM in Wadena, Minnesota. He's also a state senator. And he is a sports broadcaster, calling play-by-play for as many as one hundred high school games a year.

Just like Halsey Hall?

"Nobody was like Halsey," he said.

1963

One-Season Wonder

The World: The United States, the United Kingdom, and the Soviet Union sign a nuclear test ban treaty.

The Nation: On November 22, President John F. Kennedy is assassinated while riding in a motorcade in Dallas, and within hours vice president Lyndon Johnson is sworn in as president. Two days after being arrested for killing the President and a Dallas police officer, Lee Harvey Oswald is shot and killed by Dallas nightclub owner Jack Ruby. Martin Luther King Jr. delivers his "I Have a Dream" speech in Washington. Civil rights worker Medgar Evers is murdered in Jackson, Mississippi. George Wallace is sworn in as governor of Alabama saying, "Segregation now, segregation tomorrow, segregation forever."

The State: After recounts and court challenges, it is determined that DFL candidate Karl Rolvaag has defeated incumbent governor Elmer L. Andersen by 91 votes, in a race in which 1.3 million votes were cast.

Pop Culture: "I Want to Hold Your Hand" and "I Saw Her Standing There" are the first singles by the Beatles to be released in the United States. Best Picture: *Tom Jones.* Best Seller: *The Shoes of the Fisherman,* by Morris L. West. Top-Rated Television Show: *The Beverly Hillbillies.*

The Season: A rookie outfielder, Jimmie Hall, joins an already powerful Twins lineup, hitting 33 home runs and driving in 80. Camilo Pascual is a 20-game winner for the second year in a row. Earl Battey and Zoilo Versalles are starters on the American League All-Star team.

During the seventh inning, Bill Dailey would start to stir down in the Twins' bullpen. Come the eighth, he'd jump into a red convertible, take the short ride from the bullpen to the Twins' dugout, get out of the car, carefully step over the first base chalk line, wet his fingers, and make the sign of the cross in the dirt. "Superstitious, not religion," he explained.

All the while, the organist would be playing "Bill Bailey Won't You Please Come Home." Except at Met Stadium in 1963, the title and words were changed to "Bill Dailey Won't You Please Come In." A *Minneapolis Tribune* sportswriter, Bill McGrane, rewrote the lyrics:

> Won't you come in, Bill Dailey,
> Won't you come,
> We blew a three-run lead.
> You do the pitchin', baby, we'll get 'em back,
> We like your sidearm speed.
> Remember last Tuesday evening,

For one remarkable season, Bill Dailey would travel from the Met Stadium bullpen via a red convertible with the song "Bill Dailey Won't You Please Come In" playing in the background. PHOTO BY JOHN CROFT. *MINNEAPOLIS STAR TRIBUNE* NEWS NEGATIVE COLLECTION, MINNESOTA HISTORICAL SOCIETY.

You bailed us out,
With nothing but an infield hit.
Camilo's to blame, ain't it a shame,
Bill Dailey, won't you please come.

Dailey was a classic baseball story. A Virginian with a country drawl, he'd been purchased by the Twins from the Cleveland Indians a couple of days before the start of the season. It was a ho-hum deal. Dailey, 28, had spent a couple of nondescript seasons with the Indians and there was nothing for Twins fans to get excited about—until a few weeks into the season when it became clear that the lanky right-hander was getting everybody out.

There were questions about whether the team's 1962 success had been a fluke. But as the 1963 season moved on, it was clear the Twins were the real deal. What a time to be in the Twin Cities! Everything seemed possible. Not only did the cities have two major professional sports teams, the Guthrie Theater opened on May 7 with a production of *Hamlet*. Theater critics from across the country were impressed by both the bold architecture and artistic visions of the Guthrie.

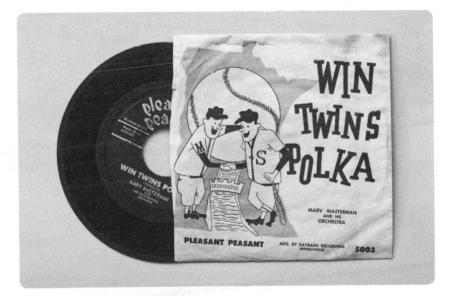

The Twins have had ballplayers inducted into the Hall of Fame, but musicians have flourished because of Twins baseball, too. Accordionist Marv Masterman, creator of "Win Twins Polka," was inducted into the Ironworld Polka Hall of Fame in Chisholm in 2005. FROM THE COLLECTION OF CLYDE DOEPNER; PHOTO BY ROBERT FOGT.

The left field bleachers at the Met became home to millions of memories. PHOTO BY GERALD BRIMA-COMBE. *MINNEAPOLIS STAR TRIBUNE* NEWS NEGATIVE COLLECTION, MINNESOTA HISTORICAL SOCIETY.

Additionally, the Cooper Theater—a technological wonder—had opened in St. Louis Park, one of three such futuristic movie theaters in the country. In March 1963, a movie spectacle, *How the West Was Won*, opened at the Cooper. People from throughout the five-state area ordered tickets in advance to see this wonder on the 105-foot-wide screen that curved 146 degrees.

"It was one of the few films I went to where the audience applauded when the drapes in front of the screen started to open all the way," recalled Joel Thom, who later managed the Cooper, in an interview with the *Star Tribune.* "It was thrilling, just absolutely tingling to have that experience." The movie ran for eighty-eight weeks.

But Met Stadium was the place to be. The Twins had been embraced by the region.

William Leggett, a *Sports Illustrated* writer, arrived in midseason to see what all the buzz was about. He was impressed, reporting that 250 planes had come into the Twin Cities for a Twins "fly-in" promotion. "Every boy in the state seems to be wearing a Twin cap and a Twin jacket."

And why not? This team, Leggett reported, was the one team in the American League good enough to beat the Yankees.

In the end, they weren't good enough to beat the Yanks, falling to third in the ten-team American League, thirteen games behind New York and three behind the Chicago White Sox. But the Twins—with Killebrew hitting 45 homers, Bob Allison hitting 35, rookie Jimmie Hall hitting 33, and Earl Battey hitting 26—out-homered the Bronx Bombers, 225–188. And they outdrew the Yankees, attracting a league-leading 1.4 million fans.

The team also figured it had its bullpen anchored for years to come with Dailey, who for one season was unhittable. But nothing is so fickle as the life of a professional athlete. In the twelfth game of the 1964 season, the Twins were playing the Cleveland Indians at the Met. The organist played "Bill Dailey Won't You Please Come In." The convertible delivered Dailey to the first base line. He stepped across the chalk line, wet his fingers, made a cross in the dirt, and headed to the mound.

Max Alvis of the Indians hit a slow roller between the mound and third base. The grass was damp. Dailey slipped as he fielded the ball. With his body falling, he fired, awkwardly, toward first. Alvis was safe. Dailey felt something in his shoulder. He went back to the mound, but suddenly his control, so good in 1963, was gone.

The stats tell the story: In 1963, Dailey pitched 108 innings in 66 games. He had 21 saves and compiled a 6–3 record. In that incredible season, he walked just 19 batters while striking out 72.

But in 15 innings in the early days of the 1964 season, he walked 17 batters, hit 4, threw 3 wild pitches, and struck out only 6.

"My arm was just hanging there," said Dailey. "Even when I was warming, nobody was safe standing anywhere near me. I had no idea where the ball was going."

The Twins tried shooting him up with cortisone. He'd get a shot, try to pitch, fail, and get another shot. He said he had eighteen cortisone shots in his aching shoulder before the Twins shipped him to the minor leagues in June to "work out" his problems. The club was convinced that his issues were mental, not physical; that he'd lost confidence and, in the process, messed up his pitching mechanics.

But even in the minors, he couldn't find his control and his right shoulder ached. Finally, he went to a specialist to see what was wrong with his shoulder. "They put some dye in there and took some pictures," Dailey said. "The doctor said my rotator cuff was held together by a string."

The Twins held events ranging from Halter Top Day to a day for nuns where players, in this case Camilo Pascual, handed out autographs and accepted blessings. COURTESY OF THE MINNESOTA TWINS.

The two had a brief conversation.

"What can you do?" Dailey asked the doc.

"I can operate," the doc said.

"If you operate, what are the chances I'll pitch again?" Dailey asked.

"About 100 to 1," the doc said.

"I figure knives are for gutting deer and cleaning fish anyway," Dailey said. "If the chances are 100 to 1 I'll pitch again, I'm going home."

Dailey never threw a pitch again. For a few years, he worked for the Hamm's breweries in Minnesota and Colorado. But then he and his wife, Anne, returned home to Virginia. In a conversation in the fall of 2008, Dailey said he never bemoaned what might have been.

"As soon as I knew I couldn't pitch, I said to myself, 'I could be a horse's butt and feel bad about what had happened.' I'd seen that happen with a lot of guys. Plus, we'd seen a lot of couples get divorced, mess up their lives, when they couldn't play anymore. My feeling was, when it's over, it's over."

In his seventies, Dailey, who had been paid $14,000 during his one glorious season, was still working as a security guard at a munitions plant in Virginia.

He doesn't watch major-league baseball games.

"I can't stand to watch those millionaires cry like babies," he said. "We played because we loved the game. I remember one time, I'd pitched in seven games in six days because of a doubleheader, and I heard (bullpen coach) Hal Naragon say, 'No matter what happens we don't get Dailey up today.' I said, 'Hal, don't be saying that. This is what I do for a living.'"

For one short summer, nobody did it better.

1964

The Cuban Connection

The World: Nelson Mandela, a leader of the African National Congress, is sentenced to life in prison in South Africa on charges of being a terrorist.

The Nation: The Gulf of Tonkin Resolution is approved by Congress, granting President Lyndon Johnson the authority to "take all necessary measures" to repel any attacks against U.S. forces in South Vietnam. The resolution allows Johnson to wage war against North Vietnam without receiving a declaration of war from Congress. Johnson easily defeats Barry Goldwater in the presidential election. Ford Motor Company begins manufacturing the Mustang.

The State: The Rolling Stones come to Minnesota and draw just 283 people to Excelsior Park's Danceland. Construction of the I-35W bridge over the Mississippi near downtown Minneapolis begins. The bridge would open in 1967 and collapse in 2007.

Pop Culture: Billboard's #1 Song: "I Want to Hold Your Hand," by the Beatles. Best Picture: *My Fair Lady*. Best Seller: *The Spy Who Came In from the Cold*, by John Le Carré. The Beatles appear on television's *The Ed Sullivan Show*.

The Season: The Twins get a new right fielder, Tony Oliva, who ends up being an All-Star and the league's Rookie of the Year and batting champion. They slipped to seventh in the standings, but on May 2 became the third team in major-league history to hit four successive homers in the same inning: Oliva, Bob Allison, Jimmie Hall, and Harmon Killebrew all homered against Kansas City pitching in a 5–4 Twins win.

Harmon could hit 'em anywhere in any conditions, including in the snow on this tour of Alaska following the 1964 season in which he hit 49 homers and drove in 111 runs for the Twins. COURTESY OF THE MINNESOTA TWINS.

Twins baseball and Cuba are forever intertwined. On the day before the Twins' first-ever home game in 1961, a ragtag army of rebels stormed Cochinos Bay—the Bay of Pigs—in what turned out to be a CIA-backed effort to drive Fidel Castro from power.

Early reports of that invasion were positive in the U.S. media. Castro was on the ropes, the reports said. The revolutionaries had established a beachhead. Castro was reported by the Associated Press to have suffered either a mental or physical breakdown because of the assault. On the sports pages, Twins pitcher Pedro Ramos, who frequently carried a gun, was reported to be ready to return to his homeland to help drive Castro from power.

Most of the reports turned out to be bogus. The invasion was a miserable failure, an embarrassment to the Kennedy administration. Castro stayed healthy for decades. Ramos didn't leave the team until he was traded to Cleveland in 1962 for first baseman Vic Power and pitcher Dick Stigman.

On the field, the team that Minnesota inherited had at times in its history been called the "Cuban Senators" because of all the Cuban players Clark Griffith had employed. The team that arrived from Washington in 1961 included more Cuban players than any other team in baseball: pitchers Ramos and Camilo Pascual, first baseman Julio Becquer, and shortstop Zoilo Versalles. And in 1964, the greatest Cuban player of them all, Tony Oliva, arrived at Met Stadium.

Like all of the other Cuban players, Oliva was signed by Joe Cambria, an Italian immigrant who ran a laundry in Baltimore until meeting up with Sen-

Because of his color and woeful fielding, Tony Oliva barely hung on in the Twins' minor-league organization. But, in Charlotte, and everywhere else, Oliva could always hit. He took over in right field for the team in 1964 and became the American League's Rookie of the Year and batting champion. He also later became a superior fielder. COURTESY OF THE MINNESOTA TWINS.

ators owner Clark Griffith in the 1930s. In a twenty-six-year period, Cambria signed 400 Cubans to play in the Senators system.

Griffith loved Cambria's work because the Cuban players were talented and they worked cheap. Through the late 1930s and into the 1940s, the Cubans signed by Cambria were white. After Jackie Robinson broke the color barrier, Cambria was free to wander the island nation signing Cubans of all colors.

There are two views of Cambria, who was known in Cuba as Papa Joe. The negative view is that he exploited young Cubans, signing them in bulk for little or no money and not preparing them for the segregation and competition they would face in the United States.

But those players who survived and made it to the big leagues don't share that view. They say Cambria was a father figure, an adviser, a friend.

There was nothing unique about the signing of Oliva. He was named after his father, Pedro Oliva, and grew up on a farm in Pinar del Río, a province in the western portion of the country. Oliva's father loved the game so much he built a field on a portion of his farm. From the first time he picked up a bat when he was seven years old, little Pedro could hit.

Oliva kept moving up through a series of Cuban leagues until, at nineteen, he was spotted by Roberto Fernandez, who played in the Senators organization. Fernandez called Cambria in Havana and told him about Oliva,

"If you think he is that good, you sign him to a contract," Cambria is said to have told Fernandez.

Oliva received nothing when he signed with the Twins in February of 1961. His teammates took up a collection to buy him clothes for his trip to the United States and to help him pay for a passport.

Young Pedro immediately ran into difficulties. He couldn't get a passport in time to report to the Twins' minor-league facility in Fernandina Beach, Florida. So he borrowed the passport of his brother, Antonio. Thus, Pedro Oliva became Tony Oliva. (A few years after arriving in the United States, he had his name legally changed.)

Then, when he arrived in Fernandina Beach, he was faced with segregation for the first time in his life. He had come with twenty other Cubans. The fifteen white Cubans were welcome at the town's only hotel. The six black Cubans were hauled, by station wagon, to a large rooming house in the "colored" section of the community.

Oliva was stunned, but he also was totally focused on being a major-league baseball player. He accepted the customs of this new land. "The way I looked at it, if you don't want me in your house, I don't want to be there," he said years later.

Four days into his first minor-league camp, after getting seven hits in ten trips to the plate, he was called into an office, along with several other black Cubans. They were given documents to sign. Oliva assumed he was being assigned to a minor-league team until one of the Cubans, who could read English, explained what the document said. "They're giving us our release. We're supposed to go home now."

In retrospect, Oliva believes the Twins had run into a racial numbers problem. The organization had two Class D minor-league teams, one in Erie, Pennsylvania, the other in Fort Walton Beach, Florida. Blacks couldn't play in Fort Walton Beach and the Erie roster already was full. The Twins were keeping only one of the six black Cubans who had come to the United States.

Oliva was crushed, but Cambria kept working. The day after Oliva and the others were released, he took Oliva and two others to Jacksonville, Florida, to work out with the Pittsburgh Pirates. The Pirates weren't interested.

Cambria had one more idea. He had a friend, Phil Howser, who was general manager of the Twins' AA Class minor-league team in Charlotte, North Carolina. Howser, Cambria thought, might be able to find spots on Class D teams near Charlotte. Howser tried to get the three players on three different

Hamm's Beer, the Hamm's Bear, and Minnesota Twins baseball were inseparable when the team arrived in 1961. In fact, incentives from Hamm's, as well as other sponsors, helped Calvin Griffith make the decision to move from Washington to Minnesota. FROM THE COLLECTION OF CLYDE DOEPNER; PHOTO BY ROBERT FOGT.

teams in the Western Carolinas League, but all three teams rejected the players because they were "colored."

Howser asked the players if they wanted to return to Cuba or keep trying. Only Oliva wanted to keep trying to find a baseball home. Howser gave Oliva a hotel room in Charlotte and three dollars a day for expenses while he continued searching for a place for Oliva to play. While he waited, Oliva worked out with the Charlotte Hornets. And while he waited, the Bay of Pigs Invasion unfolded.

The skinny, knock-kneed young ballplayer paid no attention at the time to this fiasco, but the invasion would have huge impact on the rest of his life. The invasion cut off virtually all relations between Castro and the United States. Oliva was among the last players to legally leave Cuba, and it would become difficult to go home again. Because of U.S. policies, it was difficult to even send money home to his family.

But in 1961, young Tony Oliva was only interested in making it in baseball. Finally, in June, Howser found a spot for Oliva on the roster of the Class D team in Wyeville, Virginia, in the Appalachian League. There, people quickly learned three things about Oliva: (1) He couldn't judge a fly ball; (2) he had a tremendous arm, but no idea where the ball was going when he threw it; and (3) he could hit. In a 68-game season, Oliva committed 14 errors, but he hit .410, the highest average in all of organized baseball.

He went to work on his fielding and he kept on hitting as he moved up through the Twins' organization. He was promoted to the Twins for September of 1962 and had four hits in nine at bats. He was called up again in September of 1963 and had three hits in seven at bats.

He stayed with the Twins and was the right fielder in 1964, living in the Hotel Maryland in downtown Minneapolis. Manager Sam Mele, Oliva's biggest fan, communicated with Oliva through pitcher/interpreter Camilo Pascual. The Twins were a disappointment in that season. But Oliva wasn't. He was a starter in the All-Star Game, the American League Rookie of the Year, and the American League batting champion.

Everything about Oliva was—and remains—star quality. Only his knees betrayed him, shortening his career by years. But Oliva, who remained in Minnesota after his career ended, never stopped smiling. In 2006, he was brought in for a fitness day at a Minneapolis inner-city school. Most of the kids were immigrants, likely unfamiliar with baseball so surely they'd never heard of Tony Oliva. But within moments, it didn't matter. Oliva's smile lit up the whole gym and soon a couple hundred kids were laughing and exercising with him.

Those kids weren't the only ones who don't know the name Tony Oliva. Even for the greatest players, fame is a fleeting thing.

Twins general manager Bill Smith tells the story of Oliva working with a young Twins prospect during batting practice in spring training in 2005. Oliva, whose English can be challenging, was trying to make a point. The kid wasn't getting it. Finally, out of frustration, the sixty-seven-year-old Oliva grabbed the kid's bat, jumped into the batting cage, and started hitting line drives all over the park. The kid was amazed.

"Did you used to play?" he asked.

"Did I used to play!?" said Oliva, laughing.

1965

Integration, the Beatles, and Triumph

The World: Cosmonaut Aleksei Leonov becomes the first person to take a walk in space, leaving his craft for twelve minutes. Cigarette advertising is banned on British television.

The Nation: President Lyndon Johnson unveils his "Great Society" program in his State of the Union address. The first U.S. combat troops—3,500 Marines— land in South Vietnam and the first "teach-in" opposing the war is held at the University of Michigan. Malcolm X is assassinated in New York. The 630-foot Gateway Arch is completed in St. Louis.

The State: Six tornadoes touch down in the Twin Cities and six people are killed; Fridley is the hardest hit area.

Pop Culture: Billboard's #1 Song: "Wooly Bully," by Sam the Sham and the Pharaohs. Best Picture: *The Sound of Music.* Best Seller: *The Source,* by James A. Michener. Top-Rated Television Show: *Bonanza.*

The Season: Twins clinch the pennant on September 26 in Washington, D.C., with a 2–1 victory over the Senators. The World Series isn't the only big baseball event held in the Twin Cities; the All-Star Game also is played at the Met, and a grandstand seat costs six dollars.

Pennant fever swept the region throughout the magical summer of 1965. This banner hanging in St. Paul in September, written in Spanish, cheered the team on: "Tony [Oliva], Zee [Zoilo Versalles], Sandy [Valdespino], and all of the Twins: Let's Go to the World Series!" COURTESY OF THE *ST. PAUL PIONEER PRESS.*

Walter Alston, manager of the Los Angeles Dodgers, plodded to the mound. It was the third inning of the first game of the World Series. It was sixty degrees and sunny on this October 6 afternoon and Vice President Hubert Humphrey, who had thrown out the first pitch, was in his box seat, cheering loudly with the rest of the record Met Stadium crowd of 47,797.

The Twins, once baseball's laughingstock, had jumped on Dodger pitcher Don Drysdale. Frank Quilici, the Twins' second baseman, had started the third inning with a double down the left field line. Pitcher Jim Grant's sacrifice bunt attempt had been fumbled, putting two Twins runners on when shortstop Zoilo Versalles stepped to the plate. The third pitch he saw ended up deep in the bleachers in left field for a three-run homer.

And the Twins kept hitting. Left fielder Sandy Valdespino doubled, Harmon Killebrew singled, and catcher Earl Battey drove home both with a single. Quilici tied a World Series record, getting his second hit of the inning, driving home Battey.

That's when Alston went to the mound.

"Bet you wish I was Jewish," Drysdale is said to have uttered, as he handed the ball to Alston and headed to the bench.

His comment was an acknowledgement of the fact that baseball's best pitcher, Sandy Koufax, was at the Saint Paul Hotel observing Yom Kippur as the Twins were beating up Drysdale. To gentiles—at least young, baseball-loving gentiles in the Midwest—the decision was incredible. "What's the day of atonement compared to Game 1 of the World Series?"

Even Twins players were getting a lesson in Judaism because of Koufax's decision not to play. "I don't think most of us had ever heard of Yom Kippur before that game," said Twins pitcher Jim Kaat.

Around the country, Jewish leaders still use the story of Koufax in talking about the meaning of faith. Koufax has always shrugged off his decision.

"There was never any decision to make because there was never any possibility I would pitch," he wrote in a 1966 biography. "The club knows I don't work that day."

The first letter requesting World Series tickets was drawn by Helen Teawalt (*left*) and Helen Levander from the mailbags containing letters from thousands of fans hoping for tickets. The lucky guy was Clayton Larson of Edina, who purchased four sets of box seats for $193.00. COURTESY OF THE *ST. PAUL PIONEER PRESS*.

So with Koufax at the hotel, the Twins defeated the Dodgers, 8–2, and people celebrated all over the region.

At the start of the season no one, including the players, had expected the Twins to be in the World Series. Most assumed the Yankees would win the pennant because the Yankees always won the pennant. Dating back to 1949, the Yanks had only twice failed to reach the World Series (1954 and 1959). But in 1965, Mickey Mantle and Roger Maris were hurt more than they were healthy and New York collapsed, failing to play .500 baseball for the first time since 1925.

"Johnny Klippstein was my roomie," said Kaat, "and he kept telling me, 'Jim, we've got enough talent here to win.' We finally started to believe in ourselves about halfway through the season."

The Yankees mortality and the strength of the rising Twins was proven with a single swing of the bat on July 11, the day before the Twins were to be hosts of baseball's All-Star Game. The Twins had won two of the first three games of a four-game series against the Yankees at the Met. But in the final game of the series, the Yankees had taken a 5–4 lead over the Twins in the top of the ninth. Wasn't this the way it always was in games against the Yankees?

Still, the home team had three more outs. With one out, third baseman Rich Rollins drew a walk from Yankee reliever Pete Mikkelsen. Then Tony Oliva made the second out of the inning on a fly to center.

Killebrew stepped to the plate. On a 3–2 pitch, Mikkelsen threw a fastball, inside. Killebrew swung and the from the left field bleachers to the first base box seats, 35,263 fans screamed. From Sioux Falls to Des Moines to Duluth there was delirium as Halsey Hall bellowed, "Holy cow!" The ball soared into the left field stands and the Twins were 6–5 winners heading into the All-Star Game.

At that moment, everyone in the Upper Midwest dared believe that the first-place Twins were the real deal. Until Kirby Puckett took his mighty swing in the sixth game of the 1991 World Series, this was the Twins' most meaningful home run.

To make everything sweeter about this remarkable summer was the fact that the All-Star Game was played at the Met and six members of the Twins— Battey, Killebrew, outfielders Jimmie Hall and Oliva, Grant and, of course, Versalles—were on the American League roster.

The National League, considered superior at the time, was coming to Met Stadium with a team that could represent a wing of baseball's Hall of Fame: Willie Mays, Hank Aaron, Roberto Clemente, Ernie Banks, Juan Marichal, Drysdale, Koufax, and Bob Gibson.

Killebrew, who had homered in the fifth inning of the game, struck out against Gibson in the ninth inning with the tying run on second. The American League lost, but it didn't matter. Minnesota had been host to an All-Star Game. Minnesotans had seen the giants of baseball before their own eyes. This was a summer of magic for the area.

On August 21, the Beatles came into Met Stadium, an event that was preceded by a press conference during which a reporter asked a question that reflected the conflicting combination of old Midwest values and generational change.

Reporter: "How can you sleep at night with your long hair?"
John: "Well, when you're asleep at night, you don't notice."

Paul: "True. True. That told him."

George: "How do you sleep with your arms and your legs attached? It's the same."

Ringo: "You get used to it."

George: "Maybe that's why we've been up every night."

Paul: "Maybe that's why we have parties. That's it. We can't sleep with this long hair."

The Beatles relaxed in the Twins' clubhouse before performing, Ringo sitting in Killebrew's chair. They raced onto the field to the stage, set up around the pitcher's mound. There were 25,000 people in the stands, the top ticket price was just five dollars. It was the only show on their U.S. tour that wasn't sold out.

The Beatles left and the Twins became the compelling story of the summer again, clinching the pennant on September 26 in Washington, the city they'd left five seasons earlier. Only 8,302 people were on hand for the clincher, a 2–1 victory in a game in which the Twins had just three hits.

Battey, among the players who had been reluctant to leave D.C. for Minnesota, referred to the irony of where the Twins had clinched the pennant.

"I wish we could have done this while we were in Washington," he told writers after the clinching game. "A lot of us who played in Washington wish the town could get some kind of credit."

By season's end, the Twins won a franchise record 102 games and finished seven games ahead of the White Sox, and a whopping twenty-five games ahead of the Yankees.

Not everything had been smooth for the Twins. Griffith, not manager Sam Mele, hired new coaches; Billy Martin to coach at third and work with infielders; Jim Lemon to work with hitters; and John Sain, brilliant, but independent, to be the team's pitching coach. Martin and Sain did not get along.

Martin would tell reporters, off the record, of course, that he believed Sain was undermining the authority of the manager. That seemed ironic, given that most in baseball assumed that Martin had been hired to take over for Mele should the Twins get off to a bad start in 1965.

Martin was jealous of the fact that Griffith was paying Sain, who had been an immensely successful coach with the Yankees, the princely sum of $25,000 a year to work with Twins pitchers. Additionally, Martin didn't like the idea that Sain's opinions about how the game should be played were at least as strong as his own.

Among his pitchers—and Sain did view himself as the chief executive officer of the pitching staff—he was beloved. Sain believed in the power of

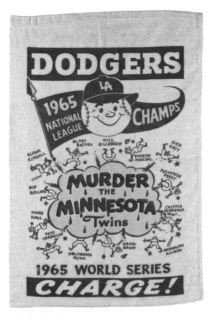

This Los Angeles Dodgers poster was a little less than sophisticated. FROM THE COLLECTION OF CLYDE DOEPNER; PHOTO BY ROBERT FOGT.

positive thinking. He didn't believe in having his pitchers run. He didn't second-guess. And wherever he went, he was successful. In 1965, Grant had his best season, compiling a 21–7 record. Whitey Ford had his best record as a Yankee, 25–4, when Sain was his pitching coach. After Sain was fired by Mele following the 1966 season, he went to Detroit and Denny McLain won 31 games. Clearly, the man knew how to work with pitchers.

But Martin was as important to the team as Sain. He worked constantly—and always patiently—with Versalles, who had his one great, MVP season.

And Mele, despite an underlying distrust of Sain, was successful in preventing the personality clashes of Sain and Martin from being a negative among the players. At season's end, Mele was effusive in his praise of both coaches.

Perhaps the big reason that the clashes of the coaches didn't negatively affect the Twins is the fact that the real leaders in major-league clubhouses aren't the coaches or even the manager. Star players, for better or worse, are the leaders. And the Twins were blessed with stars who didn't act like stars.

"No one was cocky or expected special treatment on the team because guys like Harmon Killebrew and Bob Allison didn't expect special treatment," said Quilici, a rookie second baseman in 1965. "I remember coming to spring training and Harmon came over and introduced himself, 'Hi, I'm Harmon Killebrew. Welcome to the club.' You don't know how good that makes a rookie feel. After Harmon came over, it was Allison, then Jim Kaat, and then Earl Battey. I don't know if anybody appreciates what a special guy Earl Battey was. He was a great athlete and the most stable guy in the world."

And, as the major black voice on the team, he was a remarkable diplomat at a time of evolving race relations.

The subject of race and the Twins didn't start with Griffith's 1978 speech in Waseca, Minnesota. It arrived with the team in 1961. Like many of the teams, the Twins stayed in segregated hotels during spring training in Florida. The white players stayed at Orlando's luxurious Cherry Plaza, players of color were at the much less grand Sadler Hotel in the black section of what was then a quiet little town.

Segregation in the south seemed to go virtually unnoticed by players of all races. But this did not mean that players of color were insensitive to racial inequality. For example, following their first season in Minnesota, both Battey and outfielder Lenny Green stormed out of a midwinter baseball banquet in Minnesota when Rosy Ryan, the former general manager of the Minneapolis Millers minor-league baseball team, told an inappropriate story in which he referred to black players as "blackbirds."

Battey and Green both received criticism from Bill Bond, the executive editor of the *St. Paul Pioneer Press and Dispatch,* for their walkout. While chastising the two players, Bond praised Ryan for "his use of the vernacular."

According to University of Wisconsin–Eau Claire professor, Charles Beehauser, who did a study of the desegregation of baseball's training camps, this moment served as a racial wakeup call in Minnesota. Blacks were outraged by Bond's words and white liberals were activated. Two governors, Elmer Andersen and Karl Rolvaag, and a young attorney general, Walter Mondale, all became active in a fight to force the Twins to address the segregation issue in Florida.

While he was governor, Andersen wrote letters to both Griffith and Frank Flynn, the general manager of the Cherry Plaza, pressuring the team to move to a different hotel or the hotel to integrate.

"Our state has a very fine tradition relative to good relationships between people of different creeds, color, national origin, etc," Andersen wrote. "I have deep convictions about this personally...."

In one of his letters, Flynn shocked Andersen with this response: "... Let us rejoice together that, in our great country, we are still entitled to freedom of thought and expression."

Andersen wrote to Griffith, "You are off to a good start in Minnesota. You're making money. The public is with you. But ..."

Griffith responded with letters that would include phrases such as: "My views on segregation are well known, but the fact is, the people of Minnesota don't have the right to tell the people of Florida how to act."

He continued to stall. The Twins remained segregated and in 1964 they were baseball's only team staying in segregated hotels. Battey became more forceful, saying that Griffith's slowness was starting to affect team morale.

Even the vendors at the Met seemed big-league, displaying the two-bottle pour during the World Series. PHOTO BY DWIGHT MILLER. *MINNEAPOLIS STAR TRIBUNE* NEWS NEGATIVE COLLECTION, MINNESOTA HISTORICAL SOCIETY.

It was also increasing the outrage in Minnesota. The NAACP and other groups grew more agitated. Mondale informed Rolvaag, who had succeeded Andersen in 1963, that there were hotels in Orlando that would accept the entire Twins team. Media pressure grew.

The 1964 season began with NAACP-led protesters outside the Met, decrying the situation. Even Floridians were starting to feel the pressure and in 1965, the Twins' spring training quarters were integrated. Finally, even in spring training, the Twins were one team. Surely, that was a factor in the season that followed.

Battey, as ever, was thoughtful about what the change would mean. He was concerned that integration would be harmful to black businesses in Orlando. Through all of this, Battey was a positive influence on the field. Though limited by injuries, he still managed to hit .297 and drive in 60 runs for the Twins in their pennant-winning season.

While the Twins breezed through the season, the Dodgers struggled. They were 4½ games out of first—behind the San Francisco Giants and Pittsburgh Pirates—in mid-September. But down the stretch, the Dodgers became unstoppable, winning 15 of their last 16 games and clinching the pennant on the next-to-the-last day of the season. Their team batting average, .245, was the lowest ever for a National League pennant winner. But Koufax was the equalizer. He was simply unhittable, finishing the year with a 26–8 record, a 2.04 earned run average, and 382 strikeouts in 336 innings. He completed 27 games.

"I stood on the sideline watching him throw," said Kaat. "The ball just went 'whoosh.' I kept wondering, 'Who can hit this guy?'"

There was, of course, considerable hype in the days leading up to Minnesota's first World Series.

There were the usual economic impact stories in the local media. The Twins predicted that 45 percent of the people for the first two games of the Series would be "out-of-towners," spending $2.2 million in "new money" in the region.

That "new money" flowed into bars and restaurants after the first game victory. But there was trepidation among those celebrating. With the Jewish holiday past, the Twins had to face the unbeatable foe, Koufax, in the second game of the Series, when Koufax and Kaat squared off. But the game is remembered mostly for the diving catch Bob Allison made, a catch that is forever a part of Twins lore.

The game was tied, 0–0, in the fifth. Before the inning began, Kaat turned to Sain and said, "If I give up a run, it's over."

Sain merely smiled.

In the fifth, the Dodgers' Ron Fairly singled to right. Jim Lefebvre stepped to the plate and smoked a line drive between the foul line and Allison, the Twins' left fielder. It had rained the night before and the field still was wet. Allison took off, the ball curving away from him. Lefebvre's smash was going to be a run-scoring double for sure. Allison stretched, reached out, and somehow caught the ball a foot off the ground as he slid twenty feet across the foul line.

There was shocked silence, then bedlam. Kaat leaped on the mound. Fairly retreated back to first base, barely ahead of Allison's throw. People still talk of what might have been, for after Allison's catch Wes Parker singled. What if that had given the Dodgers a 2–0 lead?

But Allison's catch had ended the Dodgers' best scoring opportunity and the half-inning ended with both teams scoreless. The Twins, capitalizing on errors by Los Angeles third baseman Jim Gilliam in what he described as his "worst game ever," managed to score two runs in the sixth inning and end up with a 5–1 victory over Koufax.

They were brimming with confidence as they headed to Los Angeles. But the confidence was wiped out quickly as the Dodgers won three straight, 4–0, 7–2, and 7–0 (with Koufax throwing a four-hitter).

Grant assured the Twins there would be a seventh game with his arm and his bat. On just two days' rest, he pitched a complete game and hit a three-run homer in the Twins' 5–1 Game 6 victory. The basepaths at the Met had been layered with loose dirt for the game, a groundskeeping strategy designed to slow down the Dodgers, who had stolen eight bases during the three games in Los Angeles.

Marion Nines vowed she would walk the eighteen miles from Nisswa to her Brainerd home if the Twins lost the World Series. Sandy Koufax shut out the Twins in Game 7, and Nines, who was sixty-six years old, walked. COURTESY OF AP IMAGES.

In Game 7, once more it was Koufax versus Kaat, both pitching on two days' rest. The Dodgers' Lou Johnson broke a 0–0 tie in the fourth inning with a homer and that's all LA needed. The Dodgers won, 2–0. The Twins, shut out just three times all season, had twice been shut out by Koufax.

Still, spirits were high among the Twins and their fans. "Wait 'til next year," everybody was saying.

Next year didn't happen for twenty-two seasons.

1966
Zoilo's Pain

The World: Indira Gandhi is elected prime minister of India. The Soviet Union's Venera 3 crashes on Venus, becoming the first spacecraft to "land" on another planet's surface.

The Nation: Ronald Reagan is elected governor of California. The average income in the United States is $6,900, and the Dow Industrial Average closes the year at 785. Sniper Charles Whitman kills fourteen and wounds thirty-one from his perch atop a tower at the University of Texas.

The State: Little-known Republican Harold LeVander is elected governor, defeating incumbent Karl Rolvaag. The first International Snowmobile race from Winnipeg to St. Paul is held; the annual event sputtered out in 1982.

Pop Culture: Grammy Song of the Year: "Michelle," by the Beatles. *Doctor Zhivago*, starring Omar Sharif and Julie Christie, receives five Oscars. Best Seller: *Valley of the Dolls*, by Jacqueline Susann. The first episode of *Star Trek* is aired on NBC.

The Season: Jim "Mudcat" Grant holds out in spring training for a $50,000 contract. "He's not getting it from me," said Calvin Griffith. Grant eventually signs, but wins only 12 games. Jim Kaat becomes the ace of the pitching staff, winning a career high 25 games but the Twins fall to second place, nine games behind the pitching-rich Baltimore Orioles, who go on to sweep the Dodgers in a low-scoring World Series.

The rapid decline of Zoilo Versalles began following his greatest season. It was a decline that didn't end until he was found dead in his Bloomington apartment in 1995, alone and broke. He'd lost his home to foreclosure. His family to separation. He sold his Most Valuable Player trophy and his All-Star rings and his Gold Glove award to try to remain solvent. A bad back and his

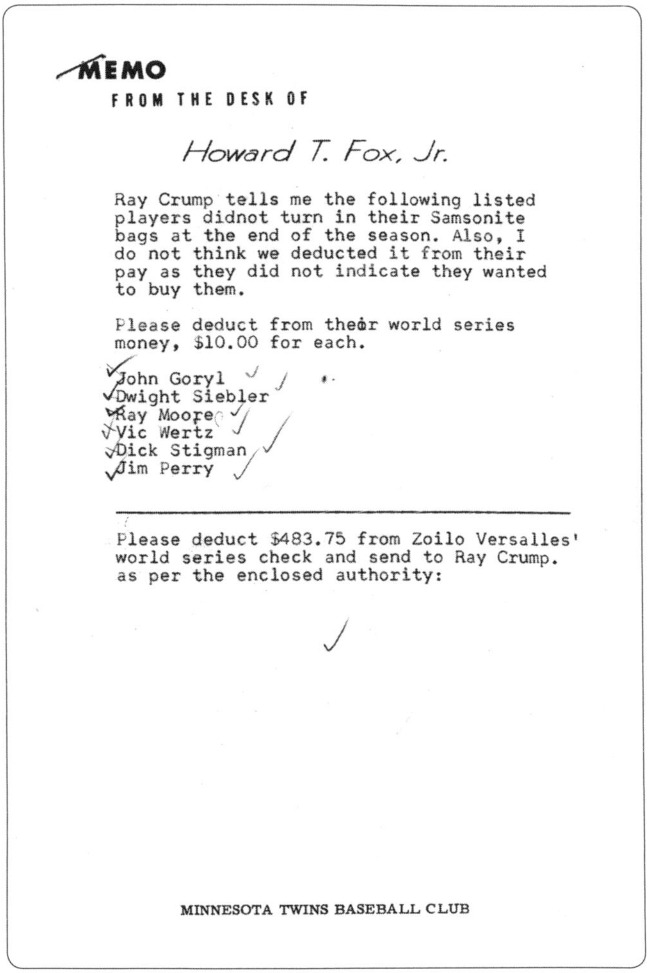

MEMO

FROM THE DESK OF

Howard T. Fox, Jr.

Ray Crump tells me the following listed
players didnot turn in their Samsonite
bags at the end of the season. Also, I
do not think we deducted it from their
pay as they did not indicate they wanted
to buy them.

Please deduct from their world series
money, $10.00 for each.

John Goryl
Dwight Siebler
Ray Moore
Vic Wertz
Dick Stigman
Jim Perry

Please deduct $483.75 from Zoilo Versalles'
world series check and send to Ray Crump.
as per the enclosed authority:

MINNESOTA TWINS BASEBALL CLUB

Twins owner Calvin Griffith was noted for his frugality, as evidenced by this memo from Griffith's longtime right-hand man, Howard Fox. The memo also underscores the fact that Zoilo Versalles was constantly in debt. In this case, he owed clubhouse dues. Players pay dues for all the services—shoe polishing, uniform laundering, food and beverages—taken care of by the clubhouse manager. FROM THE COLLECTION OF CLYDE DOEPNER.

inability to either read or write in English made it almost impossible for him to find work. Unlike many old ballplayers who keep a close relationship with the Twins, Versalles separated himself from his old team and most of his old teammates. He was fifty-five at the time of his death.

An autopsy showed that he had died from heart disease. But it could also be said that he died from a broken heart.

Baseball statisticians have not been kind to Versalles' memory. The Internet is filled with the Web sites of stat freaks who claim that Versalles, who in 1965 became the first Latin player ever to be MVP, was the worst player ever to win the award.

Statistically that may be true.

But people who see the game only through the prism of statistics never appreciate that the game is about so much more than numbers. For one season, the twenty-five-year-old Versalles played better than he'd ever played before—and better than he ever played again. For one season, he changed the personality of the Twins from being a slow-footed team that relied on the home run, to a team that dared to take the extra base, a team that could come up with the clutch-fielding play.

"Anybody who thinks that Zoilo didn't deserve to be MVP in 1965 doesn't know baseball; they're just a fan," said Frank Quilici, who was a rookie second baseman teamed with Versalles in '65.

How important was Versalles to the Twins in the year they won the pennant? Look at what happened in 1966, when Versalles came down to earth. His batting average dropped by 24 points. In 1965 he led the league in doubles with 45, but only hit 20 in 1966. He fell from a league-leading 12 triples in 1965, to 6 in 1966. His RBIs went from 77 to 36. Due to injuries he played in 23 fewer games in 1966 than he'd played in 1965. He assisted in 36 fewer double plays and stole 17 fewer bases.

A lesser Versalles in 1966 meant the Twins fell back, too. Despite the fact that Jim Kaat won 25 games and Harmon Killebrew and Tony Oliva were as splendid as always, the 1966 Twins won nine fewer games than they'd won in '65 and fell to second, nine games behind the Baltimore Orioles.

The 1966 drop-off was the start of a long slide for Versalles. Following the 1967 season, in which he hit just .200, even Twins owner Calvin Griffith, who had always been the young shortstop's greatest fan, gave up on him. Versalles was traded, along with pitcher Mudcat Grant, to the Los Angeles Dodgers for catcher John Roseboro and pitchers Ron Perranoski and Bob Miller.

"That killed him," said his countryman, Oliva. "He didn't expect that. He always belonged here."

His decline accelerated. After one awful season, in which he further injured an always brittle back and batted .196, the Dodgers dropped him. He showed up in Cleveland, Washington, the Mexican League, and Atlanta, but was out of baseball by the time he was thirty-two.

What happened to Zoilo?

Quilici believes it was a combination of problems, beginning with a bad back.

"Zoilo had a really bad back, but a lot of people didn't believe him," said Quilici. "They thought he was faking it. So Zoilo started taking painkillers for some relief. He wasn't an educated man, you know, so I doubt he followed the prescriptions. He just knew the painkillers helped. Plus, back then, there were amphetamines in every clubhouse. It wasn't until 1966 until baseball banned them. I think Zoilo was probably using those, too. He just wanted to feel okay."

Kaat has thought a lot about his old teammate over the years, though because of language barriers, they were never particularly close.

"Zoilo was a really pleasant guy and he played hard," said Kaat. "You loved to have him out there behind you. But I always felt bad for him. He didn't come from a stable background like so many of us did. He was always sending money back home. He had so many responsibilities. I've always believed that it actually hurt him when he won the Most Valuable Player award. If Tony [Oliva] had won it, I think Tony could have handled it. But Zoilo won it and he came back the next year and tried to play like Superman. It was just one more thing for him to have to deal with."

Oliva, it should be noted, finished second in the MVP voting in 1965. He did have a wonderful season, leading the league in hitting

The "*new* major-league baseball stadium" promotion found on the beer cups for the 1966 season is a reference to the completion of a double-deck structure in left field, which raised capacity at the Met for baseball games to 45,900. In reality, the structure was added to benefit the Vikings. FROM THE COLLECTION OF CLYDE DOEPNER; PHOTO BY ROBERT FOGT.

(.321) while driving in 98 runs. But there was no doubt among the baseball writers of the era who was the MVP: Versalles received nineteen of the twenty first-place votes, with Oliva receiving the other one.

In an interview with the *Star Tribune*'s Tom Briere prior to the 1965 World Series, Versalles himself seemed to understand what he most needed: A kind, firm hand to help him through what was always a difficult life. The Twins had that support system for him, in the person of third base coach Billy Martin.

Martin had a special affinity for players from tough backgrounds, probably because, growing up poor and fatherless in Oakland, he could identify so closely with them.

"Billy knows all the problems," Versalles said in that interview. "He understands. He talks to me in a nice way. He tells me what I do good and when I do something bad; he doesn't jump all over me. He only says, 'No more of that now, this is the right way to do it.'"

Versalles' relationship with Martin was so close, it almost backfired on him.

In a spring training game in 1965, Twins manager Sam Mele, a hard-nosed traditionalist, angrily yanked Versalles from a game for what he saw as "lackadaisical effort" in going after a ground ball.

"I'll play for Billy, not for you," Versalles shouted at Mele when he came into the Twins' dugout.

"That'll cost you $100," Mele yelled.

"Make it $200," Versalles responded.

"Okay, $200," said Mele.

"Why not make it $300?" said Versalles.

"That's what it is," said Mele.

This outburst got huge play back in Minnesota. Mele made it clear he wanted a different shortstop.

But Martin wasn't Versalles's only supporter. Calvin Griffith seemed to empathize with him, too. Perhaps, deep down, Griffith could identify with Versalles because before he was adopted by his uncle, Griffith, too, had come from poverty.

Griffith did force Versalles to apologize to Mele before the season began. But he also refused to trade him. The Twins' owner tried hard to toss his shortstop lifelines. When Versalles got into financial tight spots, which were constant because Zoilo was always buying new cars and new clothes and sending money home, Griffith would advance him money.

The Twins tried to make Minnesota feel like home to the homesick

Zoilo Versalles on Father's Day, 1966, with two of his kids, Juanita and Grant. COURTESY OF THE ST. PAUL PIONEER PRESS.

player. For several months, Versalles lived in the south Minneapolis home of a wealthy couple. Griffith helped cut through red tape to get Versalles's young wife out of Cuba in 1961. Later, they would be joined by other members of Zoilo's family.

Still, Versalles always yearned for Cuba, a destination that became increasingly difficult to reach as tensions rose between the U.S. government and Fidel Castro.

Griffith had hoped the 1965 season would make life easier for his short-stop. He even doubled Versalles's salary from $20,000 to $46,000 for the 1966 season.

"Versalles always had the potential," Griffith told the *Tribune*'s Briere. "They used to call Versalles all kinds of names, but he's human, just like any-one else. All he needed was a little patient handling, understanding, and con-sideration."

Kaat makes the point that ballplayers are no different from the rest of us. We all are products of our backgrounds and make decisions based on how we were taught.

Versalles had been a seventeen-year-old kid with a second-grade edu-cation when he was signed by the Twins out of Veldado, Cuba in 1958. He'd never traveled. He'd never had any money. He couldn't speak a word of Eng-lish and yet, suddenly he was in the United States where young players were expected to sink or swim on their own. It takes considerable self-confidence to be able to survive in that environment. Versalles always seemed to be in danger of sinking.

Zoilo appears ready to nab this greased pig, being chased by a horde of kids at the Met. COURTESY OF THE MINNESOTA TWINS.

With the possible exception of Martin, few managers or coaches understood Versalles. People even struggled pronouncing his name. He received the nickname "Zorro" because in 1961, a baseball card company mistakenly printed that name on his card.

Stereotypical labels—"moody" and "hotdog"—were stuck on him by writers, fans, and others in baseball. His problems with money became almost a standing joke among frugal Midwesterners.

In his book on the Twins' pennant-winning season, *Cool of the Evening*, author Jim Thielman points out that even as a minor-leaguer, Versalles found managing money nearly impossible. When he was given a television set by fans in minor-league Charleston, he sold it to a teammate. When with the Twins in 1961, he tried to sell his beloved hi-fi player to a teammate because he needed cash to get "home."

But what Quilici always will remember about Versalles is his empathy.

"In spring training in 1966, we were going to Houston for a game," recalled Quilici. "[Manager] Sam Mele pulls me off the bus and says, 'We gotta send you back to the minors, but I'll get you back as soon as I can.' Zoilo saw me outside the bus and he says, 'Where you going?' I tell him I'm headed back to the minors. Zoilo says, 'No, no, they can't do that.' And I said, 'That's the way baseball is, Zoilo.' He keeps saying, 'No, no' and puts his arm on me. I tell him, 'You're the greatest shortstop in baseball, Zoilo. Keep playing hard.' He said, 'I'll have you back as soon as I can.' He was really sad for me."

But when Versalles lost baseball, the one thing that had always saved him, he was lost. Oliva noted that it was far more difficult for Hispanics in the 1960s and '70s to find any meaningful work outside the game than it was in later decades.

When his playing days were over, Versalles returned to Minnesota and he continued to make decisions that hurt him. Because he could neither read nor write in English, job opportunities were limited. His bad back made custodial jobs difficult.

He rejected the one thing that might have renewed him. Many old Twins players spend time with each other at Twins games and functions. Versalles refused to do that, feeling he'd been rejected by the team.

"A guy like Zoilo could have been a good coach," said Oliva, "but nobody offered him that chance. The only thing he knew was baseball. He felt like there was no place for him."

1967

The Great Race

The World: Israel is victorious in the six-day war against Arab states. Greek King Constantine II is deposed by a military junta. Che Guevara is killed in Bolivia.

The Nation: More than 7,000 National Guard troops are called into Detroit to halt riots. Thurgood Marshall is named the first black Supreme Court justice and the Supreme Court rules that interracial marriage is constitutionally protected. Minimum wage is raised from $1.25 to $1.40. Green Bay defeats Kansas City, 35–10, in the first Super Bowl.

The State: Rioters break windows and start fires along Plymouth Avenue in North Minneapolis. Senator Eugene McCarthy begins his candidacy for president, saying, "I am concerned this administration has set no limits" in the war in Vietnam.

Pop Culture: Billboard's #1 Song: "To Sir With Love," by Lulu. Several great movies are released, including *The Graduate, Bonnie and Clyde, Cool Hand Luke,* and *Guess Who's Coming to Dinner.* Best Seller: *The Arrangement,* by Elia Kazan. Top-Rated Television Show: *The Andy Griffith Show.* The first production of *Hair* opens off-Broadway.

The Season: The Twins, the Boston Red Sox, the Detroit Tigers, and the Chicago White Sox stage the most compelling pennant race in baseball history, with the Twins being the final team to fall to Boston on the final game of the season. Boston's Carl Yastrzemski wins the triple crown, though he ends up tied with Harmon Killebrew for the home run title with 424.

To this day, members of the '67 Twins say they can hear the "pop!" in Jim Kaat's left elbow. With that sound, they knew they were in trouble.

The greatest race in the history of major-league baseball was down to the second-to-last day. The Twins had come into Boston on September 29 to prepare for the final two-game series of the season. They held a one-game lead over the Red Sox and Kaat was scheduled to pitch. Though he had only a 16–13 record, he had been baseball's best pitcher in September, winning game after game as the Twins, Red Sox, Detroit Tigers, and Chicago White Sox fought for the pennant.

This was the era when pitchers dominated the game, as evidenced by the feebleness of the White Sox. They were contending despite the fact that they batted only .225 as a team and hit a total of 87 home runs all season.

Even the Twins struggled in 1967, hitting only 131 homers and batting a collective .240. But some struggled more than others. Harmon Killebrew hit 44 homers. Bob Allison, nearing the end of his career, had 25 homers. Tony Oliva had a "down" year by his standards but still had a .289 average and 17 home runs.

The Twins also had added a rookie second baseman to the lineup, Rod Carew, who was ordered onto the major-league roster at the end of spring training by Calvin Griffith, over the objections of manager Sam Mele. Griffith had been watching Carew closely from the time he'd finished second in the rookie league in hitting in 1965. Mele thought Carew needed another year in the minors; there was a uniform in the locker room at the Twins' top farm club in Denver with Carew's name on it.

Things turned out better for Carew than Mele. Fifty games into the season, the Twins were playing only .500 ball. Mele was fired and replaced by Cal Ermer, much to the distress of Twins fans. They didn't care so much about Mele being fired. They wanted the team's third base coach, Billy Martin, to take over as manager instead of Ermer, a longtime manager in the Twins' minor-league system.

Carew, after a slow start, was batting over .300 and headed for the All-Star Game, despite the fact that his season was constantly being interrupted by weekends spent on Marine reserve duty. He missed two weeks of the Great Race in August to meet his requirement of Marine training.

This was one of the realities of the summer of '67—young men were either being drafted and sent to Vietnam, fleeing to Canada, or joining the reserves.

Another of the realities of the summer were race riots across the country, including on Plymouth Avenue in North Minneapolis, which over two days and nights was forever changed.

With the celebration of the Minneapolis Aquatennial in full swing in downtown Minneapolis, rioting broke out along the 1800 block of Plymouth Avenue on the city's north side on Wednesday, July 20, and continued on Thursday. Mayor Arthur Naftalin requested the governor to send in the National Guard and by Friday, more than 600 troops were called in to calm the city.

People throwing Molotov cocktails had set fires in a number of small businesses along Plymouth Avenue. A lumberyard in south Minneapolis was burning. Firefighters were being pelted with rocks. Newspapers and Naftalin clearly were shocked at the behavior of "roving bands of Negroes."

Naftalin, known for his liberal policies and empathy to the black population, which he said had too long been oppressed, was angry.

"The reason for this lawlessness is not related to deficiencies or neglect," he said. "These people are beyond our reach."

Sam Newlund, a reporter for the *Minneapolis Tribune,* watched as a National Guard lieutenant, Todd Horness, addressed about sixty of his troops who were about to be dispatched.

"Gentlemen, don't blow your cool," he told them. "The sharper we look, the more respected we're going to be by these disorganized groups," Horness said. "Troops will remain silent. If you get into a jawing match, the first thing you know you're going to be swinging a rifle butt and the whole thing will go to hell."

What was happening here? No one could understand, including newspaper editors. The stories of the riots shared top billing in the newspaper with Aquatennial Queens and Aqua Jesters.

The results of the rioting lasted decades after the last fire had been put out. Most of the businesses that had been damaged by fire or rock-throwing never reopened. The last of the Jewish families—north Minneapolis once had been home of a large Jewish community—moved.

All the while, the games went on.

The Twins hadn't really become a factor in the Great Race until late June. Met Stadium was their launching pad, delightfully described by *Sports Illustrated*'s William Leggett:

> It was not until just before the All-Star break that the Twins began to make efficient use of their own ballpark, Metropolitan Stadium, and the way they have used it has pushed them to where they are today.

The Met, as Twin fans call it, is a somewhat psychedelic contraption seemingly built by piling one afterthought on another. Unlike most of the newer stadiums in the major leagues, it has a bizarre charm: hitters have a genuine chance there. The omnipresent threat of the home run causes good pitchers to bear down almost all the time and bad ones to cry. Beginning on June 23, the Twins, in three home stands, won 23 of 29 games.

As late as September 27, there was the possibility of a four-way first-place tie in the American League. For the players on the contending teams, every day at the ballpark was a thrill.

"Every day felt like the World Series," recalled Kaat. "Every day you'd come to the park knowing the game was so important. The energy was incredible."

On September 29, the White Sox became the first team to fold, losing a 1–0 game to the Washington Senators.

While the White Sox were losing, the Twins were holding a team meeting. But they weren't talking about their crucial two-game series. Rather, the talk was of how World Series shares should be divided when they won the pennant. The discussion turned ugly. Several of the players didn't want Mele to

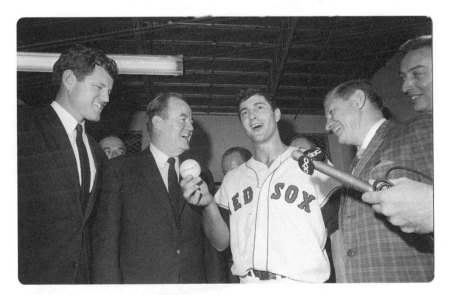

Was Hubert Humphrey really smiling inside? Along with Senator Ted Kennedy, Humphrey, a die-hard Twins fan, chatted with Carl Yastrzemski after Yaz's three-run homer led the Red Sox into a first-place tie with the Twins on the next-to-last day of the season. COURTESY OF AP IMAGES.

receive any money, not even a partial share. Other players argued that if Mele was to receive no money, Ermer shouldn't get a share, either. In the end, it was decided that Ermer should receive a full share and Mele should get nothing.

That unpleasant business settled, the Twins set out to meet the Red Sox, Kaat facing Jose Santiago, the Red Sox's second-best pitcher, on a lovely Saturday afternoon.

The fans at Fenway were in a frenzied state. This season had come as an unexpected delight in New England, where fans were talking about the race as "The Impossible Dream." This wasn't hyperbole. The Red Sox hadn't been to the World Series since 1946, and in 1966, the team had finished a dismal ninth. Baseball was all but dead in the region. Red Sox Nation? It wasn't even Red Sox County. In 1966, the Red Sox had attracted only 811,000 fans, ranking eighth (of ten) in the American League. Attendance more than doubled in the year of the Great Race.

As the game began, fans were waving "Yaz for President" signs and screaming at the top of their lungs. Despite the atmosphere in Boston, the Twins were confident. Kaat was at the top of his game the last quarter of the season. In his nine starts prior to this huge game, he'd gone 7–0, with six complete games. He'd struck out 65, walked only 6 and had a 1.51 earned run average. Never before and never again would he have a stretch like this.

With each batter he faced, he seemed to gain stride and the Twins took a 1–0 lead into the third inning. Then came the "pop."

The Twins' pitcher, known for durability, had to leave the game, his left arm limp at his side, a torn ligament in his left elbow. Boston scored 6 runs off three Twins relief pitchers, Jim Perry, Ron Kline, and Jim Merritt.

The Twins and Red Sox were tied for first. The Detroit Tigers were still alive, needing a doubleheader sweep of the California Angels. For the Twins, the season now was down to 20-game winner Dean Chance against Boston's key pitcher, Jim Lonborg.

Chance had come to the Twins in one of the big deals Calvin Griffith always seemed to be making. He'd given up pitcher Pete Cimino, first baseman Don Mincher, and the fading outfielder, Jimmie Hall, for Chance and shortstop Jackie Hernandez.

Chance had won the Cy Young Award with the Angels in 1964. But he was best known for two things: roaming the LA streets with his pal, Bo Belinsky, and his mouth. As a successful, but young, pitcher with the Angels, Chance was publicly blunt about the play of his teammates.

For example, after one game in which he struck out 12, he had this to say: "I had to strike 'em out. I didn't dare let 'em hit the ball to anyone."

The great race of 1967 meant that four teams—the Twins, the Boston Red Sox, the Detroit Tigers, and the Chicago White Sox—had to be prepared for the World Series. On the final day of the season, the Twins lost to Boston, meaning all of the Twins World Series preparation was for naught. Lapel pins are traditionally given to media and special guests at the World Series. Calvin Griffith was disgusted at having spent money on pins that weren't used in 1967. He solved the wasted pin money in 1969 when the Twins would have been in the Series had they been able to get past the Baltimore Orioles in the playoffs: ordered pins without dates so they could be used in any season. FROM THE COLLECTION OF CLYDE DOEPNER; PHOTO BY ROBERT FOGT.

His teammates quickly grew weary of his insults, at one point filling his locker with garbage that was topped with a sign reading: "I'm not naturally stupid, I'm just practicing."

By the time he got to the Twins, he'd become wiser. He also became the team's biggest winner, compiling a 20–13 record entering the season's final game. But he was facing Lonborg, who was magic for the Red Sox.

Chance and the Twins did hold a 2–0 lead entering the bottom of the sixth, but Lonborg led off with a bunt single. Later in the fateful inning, Yastrzemski, who went 7-for-8 in the two games, hit a two-run single and Twins relief pitcher Al Worthington entered the game and threw two run-scoring wild pitches. The Red Sox won, 5–3, and the Twins were finished for the year.

But the Great Race wasn't over. Detroit was playing a doubleheader against California and, after winning the first game, was just a half-game behind the Red Sox. A second game victory for the Tigers would force a play-off with the Red Sox.

The Twins pondered what might have been.

"After a season like that," said Quilici, "you never stop thinking of all the games you might have won."

The Red Sox sat in their locker room, listening to the Tigers–Angels game. It wasn't until California had defeated the Tigers in the second game of the doubleheader that the Red Sox could celebrate their impossible dream.

Years later, after his long career was over, Kaat was riding his bike along a beach in Florida.

"Hey Kaat," he heard someone yell. "If you wouldn't have gotten hurt we never would have beat you."

Kaat looked toward the sound. It was Carl Yastrzemski.

1968
Harmon's Stretch

The World: Warsaw Pact forces march into Czechoslovakia, crushing a series of reforms that had been made under the leadership of Alexander Dubček. In Vietnam, U.S. troops kill 347 villagers in My Lai, creating worldwide outrage.

The Nation: Martin Luther King Jr. is assassinated in Memphis, Tennessee. Senator Bobby Kennedy is assassinated in Los Angeles, California, as he was about to speak to supporters following his victory in the California presidential primary.

The State: Minnesota Senator Eugene McCarthy, critic of the Vietnam War, finishes a close second to President Lyndon Johnson in the New Hampshire primary, leading Johnson to announce nineteen days later that he would not seek a second presidential term. Another Minnesotan, vice president Hubert Humphrey, ultimately wins the Democratic Party's nomination, but loses the November election to Richard Nixon.

Pop Culture: Billboard's #1 Song: "Hey Jude," by the Beatles. Best Picture: *Oliver!* Best Seller: *Airport,* by Arthur Hailey. Top-Rated Television Show: *Rowan and Martin's Laugh-In.*

The Season: Twins finish seventh, twenty-four games behind the Detroit Tigers, who had Denny McLain, the first pitcher since Dizzy Dean to win 30 games. Following the season, Cal Ermer is fired and replaced by Billy Martin. Tony Oliva leads the team in hitting (.289, 68 RBI).

It was the st-reeeeetch heard 'round Twins territory. In the 1968 All-Star Game, Killebrew made a stretch to grab a throw and ended up being carried off the field with a torn hamstring, missing two months of the season. COURTESY OF AP IMAGES.

"No, Harmon, no!" The sense of horror, the pleading, was shared by Twins followers across the Midwest. The 1968 All-Star Game was being played in Houston. Harmon Killebrew was the American League's first baseman. In the third inning he stretched to reach for a throw from California Angels short-stop, Jim Fregosi.

As one, Twins fans shouted their warnings of peril at their television screens. "No, Harmon, no!" But Killebrew kept stretching and stretching until he was doing the splits on the Houston turf. All Twins fans knew that Kille-brew was not built to do the splits. Something had to give within Killebrew's massive thighs. Turned out it was his right hamstring.

"I heard it split like a rubber band," Killebrew said.

He'd hadn't done anything so unusual, he said. He'd just stretched for a wide throw as he always did. "And the clay gave away under my spikes."

He missed the next two months of a season that was dismal for the Twins and baseball and, for that matter, the country. In the midst of national tumult—the assassinations of Martin Luther King Jr. and Bobby Kennedy; an emotion-packed presidential campaign featuring two Minnesotans, Eugene McCarthy and Hubert Humphrey—baseball was being written off as a quaint game from a different place in American history.

There were hundreds of articles like this one from the July 26, 1968 issue of *Time* magazine:

> Interest in baseball has been falling off for years as people discover how exciting other sports and forms of leisure activity can be. Compared with the violence and sophistication of pro football, the frenetic pace of hockey and basketball, baseball seems elementary, antiquated and soporific. It still draws more fans in total than other pro sports teams. But that is only because there are 1,620 big league baseball games each season (v. 182 pro football games). Attendance per game has actually dropped by 2,639 fans over the past 20 years. Donald Deskins, a social scientist at the University of Michigan, says the big problem is that baseball simply is out of step with the times. "It's too slow," says Deskins. "It's not action oriented."

Certainly, the last thing the game needed in the summer of '68 was losing Killebrew. Killebrew could generate excitement and scoring with one swing of the bat.

The All-Star Game in which Killebrew was injured was indicative of the

In the pre-bobblehead, pre-Dome era, Bat Days were the big promotion to lure fans to the Met. COURTESY OF THE MINNESOTA TWINS.

game's problem. The National League won, 1–0. This was the summer of zero. The summer that the Dodgers' Don Drysdale pitched 58 consecutive scoreless innings; the Cardinals' Bob Gibson had an ERA of 1.12; Cleveland's Luis Tiant had and ERA of 1.60, tops in the American League; Detroit's Denny McLain won 31 games; Carl Yastrzemski hit a meager .301 and still won the A.L. batting championship; and teams averaged a combined 5.9 runs per game. To put that in perspective, the 2008 Twins averaged 5.1 runs per game. The 2008 Twins and their opponents combined averaged 9.6 runs per game.

Not surprisingly, baseball attendance was sliding. In 1968, nine major-league teams drew fewer than one million fans. The Washington Senators, Cincinnati Reds, Pittsburgh Pirates, and Philadelphia Phillies all drew fewer than 800,000 spectators. But Minnesota was one of baseball's few bright spots. Despite a dismal season on the field and falling to seventh place, the team attracted 1.1 million fans, fourth-highest in the American League.

Pro football, with all of its brutality and militaristic jargon, was becoming the country's national pastime, ironic given the massive peace movement in the streets. Though the Twins' public relations director, Tom Mee, did not allow football game telecasts to be on in the Twins' press box during Sunday afternoon baseball games, even Calvin Griffith often watched NFL games while his Twins were on the field.

Following the 1968 season, major-league owners would make changes designed to make hitting easier and, therefore, the games more exciting for the fans. The height of the pitching mound was lowered from 15 inches to 10 inches and the height of the strike zone was raised. They also came up with the designated hitter rule, although it would not be implemented until 1973, when the American League adopted it on "an experimental basis." The experiment and the debate continue.

When Killebrew did his unintentional splits in the All-Star Game, Griffith knew the Twins' season was a washout. He was in the dressing room with his star slugger following the game, muttering, "Nothing's going right this year."

The single highlight for the Twins came on September 22 during the final home game of the season. In the hopes of generating some fan interest, the Twins announced that Cesar Tovar would be the starting pitcher against the Oakland A's and play all nine positions. In fact, this would be no great feat for the incredible athlete from Venezuela. Over his career, he played all positions, except pitcher, catcher, and first base, on a routine basis.

Only 11,340 people came to the Met to watch Tovar became the second player to show off his versatility. In 1965, Bert Campaneris, playing for

Kansas City, had done the same thing. The Kansas City franchise moved to Oakland at the start of the '68 season, and Campaneris was the first batter Tovar faced. The A's shortstop popped out to third. Tovar walked a batter, Danny Cater, and also balked, moving Cater to second. But he struck out mighty Reggie Jackson, his teammates roaring with incredulity on the bench, and got Sal Bando to foul out to first.

It was when Tovar strapped on the catcher's gear that his teammates started guffawing. He looked like a kid in the backyard, the gear hanging on his 5-9, 155-pound frame.

The laughter got louder when Tovar crouched behind the plate to catch for pitcher Tommy Hall. Everyone in the ballpark could see Tovar's signals. He might as well have shouted, "Throw a fastball!"

Somehow, though, Hall got through the inning without allowing a run. Tovar's teammates pounded their catcher on the back when he returned to the dugout. Hall was smiling with relief. He'd survived the inning despite the fact that every A's hitter had to know what every pitch would be.

The Twins ended up winning the game, 2–1, with Tovar playing errorless ball and contributing a hit and a run to his multipurpose effort. For one day, the Twins had been able to laugh.

While the season was being played out in Minnesota, a more dramatic story was unfolding 700 miles to the west. In May, the Twins' top farm team, the Denver Bears, had gotten off to a 7–22 start. Griffith approached the Twins' third base coach, Billy Martin, and offered him a choice: He could stay with the Twins or he could take over as manager of the Bears.

Martin agonized over the decision. Was Griffith just trying to get rid of him? Should he really leave the big leagues? In the end, he made the move. He thrilled the fans in Denver. In one lopsided game in which the Bears were being pounded and Martin was being heckled, he climbed into the stands, drank beer, and chatted with the spectators. Mostly, though, he lit a fire under the team, which went 58–28 in 1968 under his guidance. Given the lethargy of the Twins and the success of the Bears, Griffith was backed into a corner. He had no choice but to fire Cal Ermer and name Martin as manager of the Twins.

1969
Billy Ball!

The World: The lunar module Eagle, carrying astronauts Neil Armstrong, Michael Collins, and Edwin "Buzz" Aldrin, lands on the moon on July 20. As he steps on the moon's surface, Armstrong says, "That's one small step for man, one giant leap for mankind."

The Nation: Fewer than 20,000 people were expected but more than 400,000 showed up at Max Yasgur's dairy farm near Woodstock, New York, to hear such artists as Jimi Hendrix, Joan Baez, Joe Cocker, The Who, and The Grateful Dead.

The State: Garrison Keillor accepts a job with Minnesota Public Radio. Five years later, his first *Prairie Home Companion* show aired. Joe Kapp led the Minnesota Vikings to a 12–2 record and playoff victories over the Los Angeles Rams and Cleveland Browns, before the Vikings were upset in the Super Bowl by Kansas City, 23–7.

Pop Culture: Billboard's #1 Song: "Sugar, Sugar," by The Archies. Best Picture: *Midnight Cowboy.* Best Seller: *Portnoy's Complaint,* by Philip Roth. Top-Rated Television Show: *Rowan and Martin's Laugh-In.*

The Season: The major leagues are subdivided into divisions. The Twins, under Billy Martin, win the American League West by nine games over Oakland, only to be swept by the Baltimore Orioles in the first round of baseball's new playoff format. Harmon Killebrew leads the majors in home runs (49)

Calvin Griffith was reluctant to hire the popular, but explosive, Billy Martin to manage the Twins. But once he decided, Griffith was not reluctant to use Martin in all sorts of promotions, including this poster-sized home schedule. FROM THE COLLECTION OF CLYDE DOEPNER; PHOTO BY ROBERT FOGT.

and RBI (140) and is the league's MVP. Rod Carew is batting champion and Jim Perry and Dave Boswell each win 20 games. But the big story in baseball is the Amazin' Mets, who beat the Orioles 4–1 in the World Series.

This was baseball during Billy Martin's one season as manager of the Twins: Harmon Killebrew stole 8 bases in the 1969 season. In the rest of his 21 seasons in the big leagues combined, he stole 11 bases. This was Billy Ball: Cesar Tovar stole a career high 45 bases and Rod Carew stole home seven times. This was Billy Ball: The Twins flourished, easily winning the newly formed American League West Division, and attendance at Met Stadium increased by almost 20 percent over the previous season.

But this also was Billy Ball: Martin threw Hubert Humphrey out of the clubhouse after a loss. "Mr Vice President, I'm trying to teach these guys that losing is hard to take and I just don't want you to go around shaking hands and having them smile, because they're taking the loss hard and that's the way it should be." Humphrey said he understood. Calvin Griffith was embarrassed.

And this was Billy Ball, too: On August 6, after a 3–1 victory over the Detroit Tigers, Martin and several players were drinking at the Lindell A.C., a legendary sports bar only a few blocks from Tiger Stadium. Art Fowler, Martin's pitching coach and drinking companion, told Martin that star pitcher Dave Boswell had refused to run his twenty laps—foul line to foul line—prior to the game.

"You go back to the hotel and I'll handle Boswell tomorrow at the ballpark," Martin told Fowler.

Things got ugly quickly in the version of the story Martin told Peter Golenbock in the Martin biography *Wild, High, and Tight.*

When Fowler left, Boswell approached Martin.

"Art told you about my running, didn't he," Boswell said to Martin.

"That's his job," said Martin. "He's a good pitching coach."

"Well, I'm going back to the hotel and kick his butt," said Boswell.

"Bozy, you're not going to do anything like that," said Martin. "Number one, Art only has one eye and number two, you're not going to kick his butt."

Dave Mona, a kid reporter covering the Twins for the *Minneapolis Tribune* in 1969, says that Boswell and Martin were cut from the same cloth. They were both highly competitive and both totally unpredictable when they drank, which they did often.

At the Lindell A.C., Bob Allison saw a problem about to become a disaster. Allison, 6 feet 4 inches and 220 pounds, tried to intervene.

"If you're going to be tough about this, why don't you hit me?" Allison said to Boswell. The two went outside the club.

The mistake Allison made was that he was wearing western cut pants, which were popular at the time. The trousers had deep pockets and Allison, according to most accounts, had his hands in those pockets.

Boswell, 6 feet 3 inches and 185 pounds, sized up his advantage and took a big swing at Allison.

"The word was that he hit him so hard that Bob ripped both pockets off his pants," said Twins first baseman Rich Reese.

At this point, Martin jumped in. In his version, he grabbed a chain Boswell was wearing around his neck and started throwing punches.

"Must have hit him forty times until I heard him grunt," said Martin. "Then I backed off and punched him three or four times in the face and he bounced off the wall. I hit him again and when he hit the ground, he was out."

Most players believe that Martin, at least at the beginning of his assault, must have had some help.

Either way, Boswell was sent to a hospital for observation. "The doctors at the hospital asked me, 'Who hit you with a pipe?'" Boswell later told reporters.

He needed twenty stitches in his face to close the cuts; Martin needed stitches on the knuckles of his right hand.

After being released from the hospital, Boswell was sent home to Baltimore. Because no reporters had been at the club, the Twins hoped the public would never find out about the fight. The official word was that Boswell had been sent home to recover from a blister on his pitching hand.

It took four days before word got back to the Twin Cities media that Boswell was recovering from more than a blister. In those media blackout days, Griffith met with Martin and with his brain trust over what to do.

"Why'd you hit him so many times?" Griffith asked Martin.

"Because he's bigger than me," Martin replied.

Some of Griffith's advisors, including vice president Howard Fox, who'd been punched by Martin in an incident in 1966, wanted Martin fired, or at least suspended.

But Griffith, mindful of the fact that the Twins were playing well, didn't want to disrupt a good thing. Martin was not suspended.

When reporters finally did learn of the incident, it was huge news. There was a front-page story in the *Minneapolis Tribune*. Boswell was vilified as a gun-toting, hair-trigger-tempered talent.

"They're making me out to be a bad wolf," Boswell said.

Over the years, Boswell had different versions of the brawl. At the time, he said he'd run most of his laps. Years later, he told Dean Urdahl, author

Billy Martin lit a fire under the Twins and lit into umpires—and some of his own players—during his one season as the team's manager. COURTESY OF THE *ST. PAUL PIONEER PRESS*.

of *Touching Bases with Our Memories,* that the reason he hadn't run his laps is that someone had given him a "hot foot" while he was playing cards in the clubhouse prior to the August 6 game. (A "hot foot" is a classic baseball prank in which a player sticks a match in an unsuspecting player's spikes, lights the match and then watches as the victim hops around, trying to put out the fire.) In this version of his story, Boswell said, he'd actually received a burn on his foot and couldn't run laps.

But the incident did pass. Boswell and Martin made up. The Twins kept rolling and easily won the division.

Many from the era believe this was the best Twins team ever. Griffith had traded pitcher Jim Merritt to the Cincinnati Reds for shortstop Leo Cardenas following the disappointing 1968 season. Cardenas played splendidly, filling a hole that had been created when the team had traded a fading Zoilo Versalles and Jim Grant to the Dodgers for catcher John Roseboro, super reliever Ron Perranoski, and pitcher Bob Miller before the 1968 season.

Killebrew, alternating between third base and first, was at the top of his game and was named the league's Most Valuable Player. Rod Carew won his first batting title. There were two 20-game winners on the staff, Jim Perry and Boswell.

And then there was Martin.

"We would have been good without Billy, but he made us better," said Reese, who had a career year (.322, 16 homers, 69 RBI), playing first when Killebrew played third.

Twins fans had loved Martin from the moment he'd arrived in Minnesota in June of 1961 in a trade to Milwaukee for Billy Consolo. Martin had been a sparkplug on the great New York Yankee teams of the 1950s, and his arrival in Minnesota brought big-league legitimacy to the Twins.

"We were the prairie rubes, and anything or anybody associated with the Yankees was big time in our minds," said Mona of why a trade involving journeymen players meant so much. "Besides, Billy appealed to the blue-collar guy. He played hard and he rebelled against all authority."

Martin seemed to warm to Minnesota, too. After his one partial season as a player with the Twins, he retired from the game and accepted two jobs: One as a scout and troubleshooter for the team, the other as a public relations person for Grain Belt Beer. His popularity with blue-collar fans only grew. As a Grain Belt guy, Martin said there wasn't a bar in Minnesota, the Dakotas, and Iowa that he hadn't been in. He was everybody's pal.

Fans loved the fiery side of Martin.

But there was a sensitive side of him the fans didn't see. Charley Walters, now a sports columnist with the *St. Paul Pioneer Press,* was a kid pitcher from Minneapolis in the Twins system when Martin came up and tapped him on the shoulder during spring training in 1969.

Walters's first thought was dread. "I was afraid he was going to tell me I was being sent down," he said.

But Martin had a different message. "He said, 'Hey kid, call your folks. Tell them you're coming north with the club.'"

When the team arrived in Minnesota, there was more good news for Walters. At Met Stadium, a local car dealer had furnished brand new Fords for the Twins players to use during the season.

"Pick one," Walters was told by a Twins official.

"What?" said Walters, astonished.

"Any one you want," he was told.

He picked a red Ford Torino.

Every day Walters was a big-leaguer it was like living on a cloud, though there were moments of confusion for a kid pitcher, in part because under Martin, the Twins had two pitching coaches. There was the legendary Early "Gus" Wynn, Griffith's choice to be the pitching coach, and then there was the manager's pal, Fowler.

"Gus would work real patiently with you," said Walters. "He'd go over all the mechanics, release points, all of those things. Then Fowler would call you over. 'What did Gus tell you?' So I'd tell him all of this stuff that Gus was teaching me and Art would say, 'Fuck all that. Throw the ball hard and over the plate.'"

The end came too quickly for Walters. About six weeks into the season, Walters got a tap on the shoulder from clubhouse manager Ray Crump.

"Billy wants to see you," Crump said.

Walters went to Martin's office. "Kid, we're sending you down to Denver so you can work a little on the curveball," Martin said. Martin's voice was gentle. He gave Walters a pat on the shoulder.

Walters returned to his locker, feeling bad, but hopeful.

"I was sitting there wondering, 'What am I going to tell my parents?'" Walters said, "and I get a tap on the shoulder again. It's Crump. He says, 'Hey kid, give me the keys to the Torino.' So in one day, I go from $10,000 salary with a nice car to $5,000 and no car."

To make matters worse, Walters wasn't shipped to Triple A Denver. Instead, the Twins brass sent him to Double A Charlotte. Martin was furious, believing his credibility had been undermined.

"Those guys don't know anything about players," he told the *Tribune*'s Sid Hartman. "Why didn't they ask me?"

Now it was Griffith's turn to be upset. A meeting was called with Griffith, Griffith's brother, Sherry Robertson, who headed the farm system, and Rob-

Calvin Griffith quickly learned that it was not a good idea to play home games on the weekend of the Minnesota fishing opener. But, a fisherman himself, he staged fishing promotions, this one involving (*from left*) Bob Allison, Jim Perry, Billy Martin, Rich Rollins, and Early Wynn. COURTESY OF THE MINNESOTA TWINS.

ertson's assistant, George Brophy. Martin apologized but a day later popped off again to Twin Cities reporters.

"If he [Brophy] had been a young man, I would have punched his lights out," he said.

All of this over a twenty-two-year-old kid who never would make it back to the majors.

But it was a classic example of why many players loved Martin. He was looking out for them. Latin and black players had a special affinity for Martin.

"Billy always saw himself as the underdog," said Carew, "and we were the underdogs. Playing for Billy was intense, but it was also fun. The only thing he wouldn't tolerate was an alibi. If you made a mistake and owned up to it, you never had a problem with Billy."

The Twins made few mistakes on the field in 1969. Hopes were high as they headed to Baltimore for the first-ever League Championship Series. The Orioles broke their hearts.

In the first game in Baltimore on October 4, the Twins held a 3–2 lead entering the ninth inning. But Boog Powell tied the game when led off the ninth with a homer off starting pitcher Jim Perry. In the bottom of the twelfth, the Orioles scored the game-winning run without getting a ball out of the infield. Shortstop Mark Belanger got an infield single, moved to second on a sacrifice bunt, to third on a groundout, and scored when Paul Blair dropped down a bunt for a hit.

There was more misery in Game 2. The Twins managed just three hits off Oriole starter Dave McNally and Baltimore scored the game's only run in the bottom of the eleventh when Curt Motton hit a two-out single, scoring Powell.

After two close losses in Baltimore, the Twins returned to the Met, convinced they could bounce back. But Martin pulled a stunner. He chose journeyman Bob Miller, who had a 5–5 record as a spare-part pitcher during the regular season, to start the third game instead of Jim Kaat.

Fighting a nagging hamstring injury, Kaat had not been his best in 1969, finishing the season with a 14–13 record. "I felt like I was pitching on a leg and a half," he said.

The Twins' mainstay also had several run-ins with both of the team's pitching coaches—not to mention a few confrontations with Martin. Though Kaat liked the fact that Martin believed in sticking with starters, he did not like the fact that Martin often second-guessed the pitch selections of his staff. He also didn't like the fact that under Martin, the job of the pitching coach was to do Martin's bidding, not work closely with pitchers.

"Sometimes Fowler would come to the mound and say, 'I've got nothing to tell you,'" Kaat recalled. "'The only reason I'm here is that Billy sent me.'"

Still, with so much riding on one game, why would Martin turn to a journeyman like Miller over Kaat?

Kaat's theory: "I think what happened is that before the series started, Billy asked Calvin, 'Who would you start?' Calvin said, 'I'd go with Boswell, Perry, and Kaat.' I think Martin just had to show Calvin he wasn't going to take orders from anyone, no matter the situation."

Whatever Martin's reasoning, it backfired. Miller was bad and the Orioles laughed their way to an 11–2 victory.

Two days after the season ended, Griffith called for a meeting with Martin.

"Why'd you start Miller?" he asked.

"Because I'm the manager," said Martin.

Two days after that meeting, he wasn't the manager anymore. Griffith fired Martin, saying Martin "is like sitting on a keg of dynamite."

Minnesota fans never forgave Griffith.

1970
Bill Ball

The World: Chile's Salvador Allende becomes the first elected Marxist president in the Americas (he would be killed in a coup in 1973). Soviet dissident and author Aleksandr Solzhenitsyn is awarded the Nobel Prize in literature.

The Nation: In the wake of an incursion by U.S. troops into Cambodia, massive antiwar protests break out across the United States. Four students are killed by Ohio National Guardsmen during a protest at Kent State University.

The State: A Minnesotan, Harry Blackmun, is appointed to the Supreme Court by President Nixon. He would later write the majority opinion in the case that legalized abortion. Mary Tyler Moore, aka Mary Richards, throws her hat in the air in downtown Minneapolis and her hit television series begins. The heavily-favored Vikings are defeated by the Kansas City Chiefs, 23–7, in the Super Bowl.

Pop Culture: The Beatles break up, Jimi Hendrix and Janis Joplin die. Best Picture: *Patton*. Best Seller: *Love Story*, by Erich Segal. Top-Rated Television Show: *Marcus Welby, MD*.

The Season: Despite antipathy toward their new manager, Bill Rigney, the Twins win a second A.L. West title, only to be swept for the second successive year by the Baltimore Orioles, who go on to win the World Series, defeating the Cincinnati Reds.

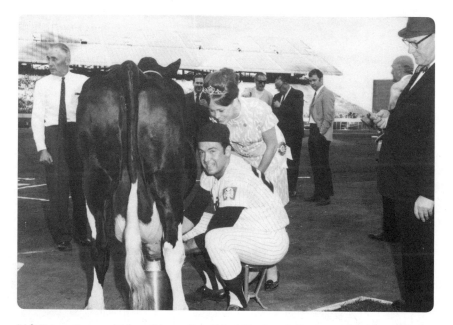

Rich Reese gets an assist from Princess Kay of the Milky Way, Gayle Krogstad of Ada, Minnesota, while milking a cow prior to a 1970 game. The first Princess Kay was crowned in 1954, and these princesses of the American Dairy Association participated in promotions with the Twins into the 1990s. COURTESY OF THE MINNESOTA TWINS.

Most of the Twins had left the tiny clubhouse in Boston's Fenway Park following a 5–3 August loss, the team's eighth successive defeat. The team was still coasting along in first place, 23 games over .500. But Bill Rigney, who had replaced Billy Martin as the manager, was drinking and pacing.

"What are we going to do?" he was asking anyone who would listen. "What are we going to do?"

"He came up to me," recalled Rich Reese, the team's part-time first baseman. "He's asking me, 'What are we going to do?' I say, 'We'll play tomorrow and start over.' He walks away and I think, 'This is my leader?'"

After firing Billy Martin following the tumultuous '69 season, Calvin Griffith surely thought he had hired a manager who would calm the anger of Twins fans, who were driving around the region with "Bring Back Billy" bumper stickers on their cars. Some even had mailed back their season ticket order forms marked "refused."

Rigney had a respectable resume. He'd been a big-league player under the legendary Leo Durocher. He'd managed the San Francisco Giants of Willie Mays fame. He'd managed the California Angels. He even had some Minnesota roots, having managed the Minneapolis Millers to a minor-league title in 1955.

Rigney was beloved by baseball people. He was an affable storyteller, a man who could walk into a restaurant and quickly befriend everyone in the place.

But he wasn't Billy Martin, as noted in a ballad by Minnesotan Ben Lazo following the Martin firing.

So long, Billy, we don't want you to go
The fans are all behind you, as you probably know....
Well, Mister Griffith, when you came to Minnesota you were treated
  cordially
Even though we know the reputation that you had in Washington,
  D.C.
But the feelings of the Minnesota fans could never penetrate your
  dome
So, Calvin, why don't you take your bat and ball and just go home?
Yes, Calvin, why don't you take your bat and ball and just go home?

Rigney, who had been liked by players in San Francisco and California, was not liked by the Twins. Martin believed in accountability. Rigney was a finger pointer. Martin was explosive, but most Twins players saw Rigney as a blowhard, more interested in telling stories about the past than savoring the moment.

"Billy had a heart of gold," said Reese. "Rigney was a phony."

"He was all Hollywood," said Quilici of Rigney. "He definitely was not a fit for this team."

Attendance at Twins games did slip in 1970, from 1.3 million, the second highest in the American League, to 1.2 million, third highest. Given the fans' anger, that small dip had to come as a relief to Griffith.

The Twins of 1970 weren't as aggressive as Martin's Twins had been. Under Martin, they'd stolen 115 bases, fourth highest in the league. Under Rigney, they stole 57 bases, the eighth best in the league. They scored 50 fewer runs under Rigney.

But the simple fact is they won one more game under Rigney and breezed to an American League West title despite the fact that Rod Carew suffered an injury that all but ended his season and his career.

On June 20, the Twins were playing in Milwaukee. Carew, the team's twenty-five-year-old second baseman, was having a phenomenal season, batting .370. But everything came to an end when the Brewers' Mike Hegan

Harmon Killebrew hit 41 homers in 1970, this swing leading to an August 12 blast against his former teammate Jim "Mudcat" Grant. But Frank Howard was the home run king in 1970, hitting 44 for Washington. COURTESY OF THE *ST. PAUL PIONEER PRESS*.

barreled into him when Carew was pivoting and throwing to first on what appeared to be a routine double play. In his autobiography, *Carew*, written with Ira Berkow, Carew described what happened.

"My leg snapped back and it went 'crack!' It felt as if it had broken in half. The pain was excruciating. I rolled over in the dirt. The umpire at second base, Jake O'Donnell, had heard the crack and vomited. Bill Rigney rushed out to me and said, 'C'mon, you gotta get up. You'll be all right.'"

He wasn't all right. That night he was put on a flight to Minneapolis and operated on. Cartilage was removed, torn ligaments repaired. After the surgery, the Twins' physician, Harvey O'Phelan, delivered grim news.

"Rod, your leg looks pretty bad. There is an outside chance you may never

play again. Some athletes have not come back from an injury of this magni-
tude."

Carew did come back, making pinch hit appearances in September and
the playoffs. The Twins got by at second base with a combination of Danny
Thompson and Frank Quilici.

In the meantime, Harmon Killebrew, Tony Oliva, and Jim Perry carried the team into the playoffs. With his 24–12 record, Perry became the first
Twins pitcher to win the American League's Cy Young Award.

And the Twins had found a replacement for Zoilo Versalles at short. In
the fall of 1968, Griffith traded a young pitcher, Jim Merritt, to the Cincinnati
Reds for a Gold Glove–winning shortstop, Leo Cardenas. Cardenas was not
only a wonderful player, he was also delightfully superstitious.

A Cuban by birth, Cardenas was into voodoo. He kept a supply of dolls,
dressed in opponents' uniforms in his locker, along with mysterious potions
he'd mix before games. When in a slump, he'd shower in his uniform to wash
away the evil spirits.

"He didn't flaunt the voodoo stuff, but we all knew it was there," said
Quilici. "He was a good guy, completely different than Zoilo. Zoilo was a ballet
artist. Leo would get to the ball, plant his feet, and fire. He had a great arm.
And he always was smiling, always happy-go-lucky."

But Minnesotans didn't have the passion for this team that they'd had for
teams in the past. For starters, baseball had divided its leagues into divisions
in 1969. The Twins were attached to the less prestigious Western Division,
along with Oakland, California, Kansas City, the Chicago White Sox, and Seattle. That seemed almost minor-league compared to the more powerful Eastern Division. It was assumed by Minnesotans that the Twins should easily win
the division, which they did in both 1969 and '70.

Additionally, though, baseball seemed pretty trivial compared to what
was going on in the country.

In May 1970, Ohio National Guardsmen had killed four students during
protests of U.S. bombings in Cambodia, an expansion of the unending Vietnam War. Closer to home—at the University of Wisconsin—a campus bombing had killed a university physics researcher.

The nation was divided. Nerves were frayed—especially, as it turned out,
the nerves of Bob Casey, longtime public address announcer of the Twins.

On August 25, the Twins were at the Met, playing the Red Sox. There
had been a series of pipe bomb explosions in the metro, and so, when a bomb
threat was called in to Met Stadium, it was taken seriously.

The game was stopped. Police wanted to search the stadium. Casey was asked to announce that the 17,697 people should leave their seats, in a calm and orderly fashion, and move to the playing field or the parking lots.

"Ladies and gentlemen, please do not panic," Casey announced. "But we have been informed by Bloomington police that there will be an *explosion* in fifteen minutes."

Want to understand the mentality of a sportswriter? Here's the *Sporting News* account of that event: "Bomb scare forced 43-minute delay in fourth inning, but only bomb that exploded was the homer by Tony Conigliaro in eighth inning giving the Red Sox 1–0 victory over Twins...."

The Twins were headed to the playoffs for a second successive year against the Baltimore Orioles, a team with great pitching and hitting. Plenty of good seats were still available for the two games played at Metropolitan Stadium. Only 26,847 people showed up for the first game, which matched Perry against one of Baltimore's aces, Mike Cuellar.

"People still hadn't accepted the idea of playoffs in major-league baseball," said Quilici. "In the minds of most fans, the playoffs didn't matter. What mattered was the World Series."

The fans who did show up had little to cheer about. With the game tied, 2–2, in the fourth inning, Cuellar stepped to the plate with the bases loaded. Boom. The Orioles' pitcher homered to right against Perry. Grand slam. Baltimore ended up scoring seven runs in the inning en route to a 10–6 victory.

The suspense lasted a little longer the next day, Game 2 of the best-of-five series. The Orioles led only 4–3 heading into the ninth. But in the ninth, Baltimore pitcher Dave McNally led off with a double and by the time the inning was over, the Orioles had scored seven runs and the stands at the Met were emptying fast. The Twins lost, 11–3, and headed to Baltimore to face Jim Palmer. It was no contest; the Orioles won, 6–1, finishing off the series sweep.

In two seasons, the Twins had gone 0–6 against Baltimore in the playoffs. The Twins looked old and tired and they were about to head into a period of long decline. The rising team in the A.L. West was the Oakland A's, who had a bunch of still unknown players: Catfish Hunter, Blue Moon Odom, Vida Blue, Rollie Fingers, Sal Bando, Bert Campaneris, and Reggie Jackson.

1971
Endings

The World: The People's Republic of China is admitted to the United Nations, and the Republic of China (Taiwan) is expelled.

The Nation: A Harris Poll shows that 60 percent of the American people oppose war in Vietnam; 500,000 protest the war at a rally in Washington, D.C. The Pentagon papers, filled with revelations about U.S. actions in Southeast Asia, are published. Cigarette advertising is banned on U.S. television.

The State: Voyageurs National Park is established. Vikings Alan Page is named defensive player of the year in the NFL.

Pop Culture: Grammy Song of the Year: "You've Got a Friend," by Carole King. Best Picture: *The French Connection*. Best Seller: *Wheels*, by Arthur Hailey. *All in the Family* debuts on CBS.

The Season: Twins attendance falls below one million spectators for the first time since team's arrival in Minnesota. The biggest news in baseball is that Satchel Paige becomes the first Negro League player inducted into the Baseball Hall of Fame.

The end comes quickly for most players. One day they're rising stars, the next, someone is telling them that their careers are finished.

Dick Stigman, for example, was an all-American big-league story. He'd grown up in tiny Nimrod, Minnesota, population of about one hundred when he was a kid. "A Huckleberry Finn" boyhood, he says. He'd been discovered and signed by the Cleveland Indians in 1954 and his fastball carried him to the majors by 1960.

In 1962, he was traded, along with Vic Power, to the Twins and for two seasons, 1962 and 1963, he flourished, winning a total of 27 games in those two years. He struggled in 1964 and by the end of the 1965 season was a seldom-used member of the bullpen. He was not used in the 1965 World Series.

Those years in Minnesota had been so special. He was pitching before friends and relatives. There were laughed-filled hearts games with teammates on flights around the American League. Forty years later, Stigman can still hear Earl Battey's huge laugh when the catcher would stick someone with the queen of spades.

It was when he was with the Twins that he met and married a flight attendant. They bought a home in Burnsville and started a family. The Twins traded him to Boston following the 1965 season, and the Red Sox traded him to Cincinnati a year later. He was just thirty-two years old and still felt young and strong. But the Reds assigned him to their Buffalo farm team prior to spring training in 1967. He was to be paid $9,300.

"I went to one of the personnel people and asked, 'What are your plans for me?'"

The response wasn't what he was prepared to hear.

"Frankly," Stigman was told, "we have no plans for you."

"I hadn't gone to college, I hadn't made any plans," said Stigman. "What could I do? We had one or two kids by then. I needed to have a job. But it was clear it was over. Frankly, it was kind of a sad end."

Stigman was contacted by an old high school friend who had started a business, Continental Loose Leaf, that produced plastic notebook covers. He had a sales job for the pitcher if he wanted it. Stigman took the job and stayed with the company until retiring in 2008.

He is proud of the fact that he never used his status as a former big-leaguer when contacting prospective clients.

"It's not a good idea," he said of falling back on having been a major-league player. "If you're going to walk in the door and say, 'I'm Dick Stigman, I used to pitch for the Twins,' you risk someone saying, 'So what?'"

The "so what?" moment happens to all but a few of the superstars.

The spring of 1971 marked the first time that one of the Twins' original stars, Bob Allison, did not report to spring training. He had announced his retirement from the game following the 1970 season.

Bob Allison was reluctant to make the move from Washington but he became a fixture in the field and in the Twin Cities. Harmon Killebrew (right) presented his friend with a shotgun from his teammates when Allison announced he was retiring from baseball near the end of the 1970 season. COURTESY OF THE ST. PAUL PIONEER PRESS.

Allison was a special case in all ways. An All-America football player at the University of Kansas, Allison had signed with the Washington Senators in 1955, and in 1959 was named the American League's Rookie of the Year when he hit 30 homers and drove in 85 runs. (Harmon Killebrew, who played in his first full season in the majors in 1959, hit 42 homers that year and drove in 105 runs, but didn't qualify as a rookie because he'd played in a total of 113 games in the previous five years with Washington.)

Allison was one of the most disappointed members of the old Senators when Griffith announced that he was moving the team to Minnesota. But he was one of the first players to make Minnesota his full-time home, accepting an off-season job with Coca-Cola shortly after the Twins moved.

He was a powerful athlete. Tony Oliva loved to sit on the bench and watch opposing infielders look nervously toward the 6-foot-4, 220-pound former fullback whenever he was on base. "They would start to sweat," said Oliva, "because they knew he would come at them very, very hard."

Midwest icons Charlie Boone and Roger Erickson share mic time with Calvin Griffith during spring training. COURTESY OF THE MINNESOTA TWINS.

When Allison was hot, he had the ability to carry the Twins for weeks at a time. But no player slumped so totally, so futilely, as Allison.

"Slumps are a funny deal," said Killebrew, who grew up with Allison in the old Senators farm system and roomed with him throughout Allison's big-league career when the Twins were on the road. "The worst is when they start with some line drives. You hit the ball hard but it goes right at somebody."

Killebrew never could figure out what started Allison in one of his tail-spins. But he and the Twins' hitting coach, Jim Lemon, quickly discovered it was impossible to discuss the issue with Allison.

"Most inflexible guy you ever saw," said Killebrew, laughing. "Even if you could see some little thing you thought might help, it was hard to get him to listen. He didn't want to hear it."

So Allison would struggle in silence through 0-for-4 after 0-for-4. Those around him would talk to him about everything, except hitting.

"I was a young guy," said Oliva. "I wasn't going to do any talking to anybody. Besides, in those days, when you were in a slump, nobody would pay much attention because there always was somebody else to pick you up. Killebrew, Battey, Carew, Zoilo, somebody would get it done."

The slumps and the catcalls—"you must be related to Calvin!" fans would shout when Allison was in a deep hitting funk—always ended. Allison finished most seasons with anywhere from 25 to 30 homers and from 75 to 100 RBI.

But Allison, because of injuries and age, had played only a small part in the Twins' division-winning 1970 season. He called it quits and when the Twins reported to spring training in 1971, Killebrew was without his old pal for the first time since 1957. There's not much sentiment among those who keep on playing. A changing roster is a constant for big-leaguers. Even when someone of Allison's caliber disappears, nothing really changes.

"It's something that just happens," Killebrew said. "You don't even really think about it at the time."

The Twins of '71 were slipping fast. They had no speed and shaky defense.

On August 10, 1971, Harmon Killebrew hit the 500th homer of his career at the Met against Baltimore Orioles ace pitcher Miguel Cuellar. After the game, he gave the Hamilton family of Golden Valley an autographed ball in exchange for the ball he hit into the stands. The price for milestone homers has increased dramatically since then. PHOTO BY CRAIG BORCK. *MINNEAPOLIS STAR TRIBUNE NEWS NEGATIVE COLLECTION*, MINNESOTA HISTORICAL SOCIETY.

Even the Twins' trademark—power—was diminishing. The team hit just 116 homers, the second lowest total since their arrival in Minnesota. To make matters worse, they were old, averaging 28.4 years. (For comparison, the average age of the 2008 Twins was 26.2 years.) They finished with just 74 victories. Not since their first season in Minnesota had they won so few games.

Allison was back in the Twin Cities, a solid member of the community, a successful businessman. Even he would quickly come to the "so-what" moment Stigman always feared.

In spring training in 1986, Killebrew and Allison were walking together through the Twins' clubhouse. Killebrew recalled this experience:

"Hi ya, Harmon," said a young outfielder, Billy Beane. "Who's that with you?"

"That's Bob Allison," Killebrew told Beane.

"Who's that?" Beane asked, clearly drawing a blank on the name.

"You better hope that someday you're as good a player as he was," said Killebrew.

Beane never came close to achieving Allison status as a player. Instead, he's made his name as general manager of the Oakland A's.

Allison's legacy may end up being something far more substantial than his career as an athlete. In 1983, the still powerfully built Allison discovered there was something wrong with his health. He had trouble catching a ball during an old-timers' game. Soon after that, he started to stagger when he walked and his speech became slurred. The doctors were perplexed. It took two years to come up with the diagnosis, ataxia, an inherited disorder that destroys cells in the cerebellum, the part of the brain that controls movement. He lost his ability to walk, talk, and write, and died of complications from the disease in 1995 at the age of sixty.

Before his death, he helped to form the Ataxia Research Center at the University of Minnesota, which has become a national leader in searching for a cure for the disease.

1972
Living a Dream

The World: A Palestinian terrorist group, Black September, holds Israeli athletes and coaches hostage during the Olympic Games in Munich, Germany. Ultimately, eleven athletes and coaches, five terrorists, and one police officer are killed in a failed rescue attempt. President Richard Nixon visits China, a huge step toward normalizing relations between the two countries.

The Nation: Five people with connections to the White House are arrested for burglarizing the Democratic Party's headquarters in the Watergate complex in Washington, D.C. President Nixon easily defeats George McGovern in an election in which just 55 percent of the people vote. A flood in the Black Hills of South Dakota kills 238 people.

The State: Record rains—as much as five to eight inches in less than twenty-four hours—cause flooding throughout the state during the summer. After learning where St. Paul is, the elegant Romuald Tecco becomes concertmaster of the St. Paul Chamber Orchestra.

Pop Culture: Billboard's #1 Song: "The First Time Ever I Saw Your Face," by Roberta Flack. Sacheen Littlefeather, an actress pretending to be Native American, accepts the Best-Actor Oscar on behalf of Marlon Brando for his role in *The Godfather*. Brando explains he's upset about exploitation of Native Americans. Best Seller: *Jonathan Livingston Seagull*, by Richard Bach. Top-Rated Television Show: *All in the Family*.

The Season: Like most teams, the Twins play eight games fewer than scheduled because of a strike that brings the season to a halt for ten days in April. This is the first strike in major-league history, and the owners refuse to make up the games because they don't want to pay the players for the missed games. On the last day of the year, baseball mourns. Pittsburgh Pirates star Roberto Clemente is killed in a plane crash while on an aid mission to help hurricane victims in Nicaragua.

The door to the bullpen opened and Dave Goltz, who had grown up listening to Halsey Hall and Herb Carneal broadcast Twins games, walked across the grass of Yankee Stadium.

The Twins were a hurting and aging team. Tony Oliva was injured most of the season. Goltz had been called up because Jim Kaat had broken a wrist

The 1972 season began with Major League Baseball's first strike. Cesar Tovar, Danny Monzon, Rod Carew, Rick Dempsey, and Bobby Darwin survey the empty stadium on April 6, which had been the scheduled opening day. In all, the Twins missed out on eight games in the season. The owners refused to play makeup games because they didn't want players to recover lost salaries, but players did win the right to seek salary arbitration, which would reap huge benefits to future generations of players. PHOTO BY POWELL KRUEGER. *MINNEAPOLIS STAR TRIBUNE* NEWS NEGATIVE COLLECTION, MINNESOTA HISTORICAL SOCIETY.

sliding into second base in a game a few weeks earlier. But Harmon Killebrew was still playing first base and Rod Carew was at second.

The Yankees were in even worse shape. Mickey Mantle had retired four years earlier. Reggie Jackson would not come to the team until 1977. This was a team of catcher Thurman Munson, outfielder Bobby Murcer, and little else.

But Goltz didn't care about any of that. He was living the dream of a million Upper Midwest kids. He was entering a game to pitch for the Minnesota Twins. As he headed out of the bullpen, he could see the three decks of fabled Yankee Stadium above him.

"It looked just like it did on TV," he said. "I don't know if my feet were touching the ground."

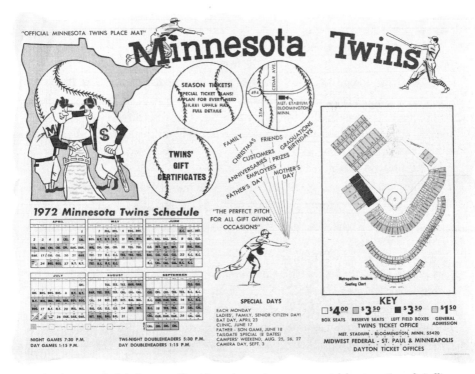

The placemat schedule for 1972 offered low prices and numerous special days to entice a dwindling fan base. It also showed doubleheaders and twi-night doubleheaders. The twi-nighters are believed by many baseball historians to have been an invention of Calvin Griffith, who was seeking a way to get two admissions on one day when attractive opponents were visiting the Met. Except for rescheduling rainouts, doubleheaders of all forms all but disappeared from schedules by the 1990s, in part because the Players' Association opposed twin bills. FROM THE COLLECTION OF CLYDE DOEPNER; PHOTO BY ROBERT FOGT.

By Yankee standards there was a small crowd, just 10,105 people, at the July 18 game. By Goltz standards, that was a whole lot of people. He was from Rothsay, a town of about 500 people on the western Minnesota prairie. He pitched 3 2/3 scoreless innings that day, giving up just one hit. By season's end, he'd compiled a 3-3 record and pitched two complete games as a starter. More than ever, he was the toast of his town.

In 1967, after he graduated from Rothsay High—there were thirty-two kids in the Rothsay senior class—Goltz had signed a contract with the Twins. On the day he left to report to the Twins' rookie farm team in Florida's Gulf Coast League, there was a big send-off for him at the town park.

Goltz, 6 feet 4 inches, 215 pounds, had been a three-sport star at Rothsay. In addition to pitching for the baseball team, he was an end and linebacker on the football team and a forward on a wonderful basketball team that had excited everybody in Rothsay. When tiny Rothsay played nearby archrival Pelican Rapids, the gym was filled by 5:30 in the afternoon for 8 P.M. games.

Goltz had received a number of scholarship offers to play Division II level basketball. But baseball always was his first love.

The first person to discover that Goltz had a special arm was Ken Reitan, Rothsay High's baseball and basketball coach and business teacher. In the summers, Reitan coached kids. Goltz was a ten-year-old catcher when Reitan noticed that the catcher was throwing the ball back to the pitcher harder than the pitcher was throwing to Goltz.

"I think you should try pitching," Reitan said.

There are two basic types of fastballs. The most common is the fastball that has life. It moves as it zips toward home plate and hits the catcher's mitt with a "pop!" that can be heard throughout a stadium. The other type is a "heavy" fastball. Its overspin causes the ball to sink as it heads toward home. It hits the catcher's mitt with a dull "thud."

Hitters hate the heavy ball. On contact, it often feels like they're hitting a chunk of concrete.

Goltz threw a heavy ball. It was not intentional. It was simply the way he pitched. The ball would approach the plate and sink, sometimes so much that even his own teammates thought he was throwing a spitball.

He was a junior in high school the first time a scout, from the Atlanta Braves, showed up in the stands to watch him pitch in a game being played in Battle Lake, Minnesota. That event was the talk of Rothsay.

By the time he was a senior, scouts from several teams, including the Twins, were watching him. In fact, a number of Twins scouts, including Sherry Robertson, who headed the Twins' minor-league operation, had driven to a tournament in Moorhead to watch Goltz and a few other potential prospects play. The only trouble was, Rothsay had been upset in a district tournament and was not playing in Moorhead.

So the scouts stopped by the Goltz home en route back to the Twin Cities and asked Goltz to pitch for them in his backyard.

"The guy I was supposed to pitch to looked old," said Goltz. "I was afraid to throw hard. They told me not to worry."

He pitched. The Twins delegation returned to the Twin Cities and drafted Goltz in the fifth round. He signed immediately.

Goltz had a distinguished career with the Twins, winning 20 games in 1977, and a total of 92 games in eight seasons. "Winning 20 for the home state team is as special as it gets," said Goltz.

Included in a Camper Day promotion, when a section of the Met's parking lot was set aside for campers, was Sunday church service. COURTESY OF THE MINNESOTA TWINS.

Little things stand out in his mind. In 1978, he was pitching well but sustained a number of aggravating injuries, including one in which he burned the fingers on his right hand while moving a barbeque grill on the patio of his Twin Cities condo.

"I was out for eighteen days," he said. "One day, while I was getting over that, I was standing out in the outfield, shagging flies during batting practice. Clark Griffith (Calvin's son) came out on the field carrying this beautifully wrapped package. He said I should open it right there. I open the package and it's asbestos welder's gloves. Clark says, 'Use these the next time you barbeque.'"

The end of his Minnesota dream came following the 1979 season. He was a free agent and frugal Calvin Griffith made no serious offer to resign him. But several other teams, including the Dodgers, Angels, Padres, and Brewers, were all bidding for Goltz. The small-town, Midwest guy was hoping for the Brewers, thinking he'd be most comfortable there.

But then he received a call from his agent. The Dodgers had made an offer—$500,000 a year for three years—that blew everyone else away.

"Congratulations," the agent said on the phone. "You're a Dodger."

"Ah, shit," responded Goltz.

"My agent didn't tell me that it was a conference call," Goltz said. "All of these Dodger executives heard me. It wasn't the best beginning."

Hollywood was a long way from Rothsay. Goltz was never comfortable pitching for the Dodgers. Plus, although known for his durability, he suffered a variety of nagging arm injuries. He won only 10 games in slightly more than two seasons for the Dodgers and had the chance to pitch a few innings in relief in the 1981 World Series, before he was released early in 1982. He was signed by the Angels, compiled an 8–5 record in 1982, and started the 1983 season with California.

"I was throwing the ball just as hard as I ever did," said Goltz, "but it just wasn't getting to the plate as fast. You lose three or four miles an hour off your fastball at that level, it's just devastating."

He was released early in 1983. He was contacted by several teams but said, "It's time for me to stop."

He returned home to Minnesota, opening an insurance business in Fergus Falls, with an office in Rothsay, where twice a week he goes to conduct business, drink coffee with old friends, and talk about the Twins.

"I got to live the dream kids still have," he said.

1973

Old and Slow

The World: On January 27, U.S. Secretary of State Henry Kissinger and North Vietnam's Le Duc Tho sign peace accords in Paris, bringing an end to U.S. involvement in South Vietnam.

The Nation: Months after President Nixon begins his second term in office, the Watergate hearings begin, with a Republican senator, Howard Baker of Tennessee, asking the key question, "What did the President know and when did he know it?"

The State: Governor Wendy Anderson is pictured, holding a fish, on the August 13 cover of *Time* magazine. The headline reads: "Minnesota—A State That Works."

Pop Culture: Billboard's #1 Song: "Tie a Yellow Ribbon 'Round the Ole Oak Tree," by Tony Orlando and Dawn. Best Picture: *The Sting*. Best Seller (again): *Jonathan Livingston Seagull*, by Richard Bach. Top-Rated Television Show: *All in the Family*.

The Season: Rod Carew wins his third batting title and Bert Blyleven is a 20-game winner, but the Twins finish with a .500 record, thirteen games behind the Oakland A's, who win their second successive World Series. A group of investors, headed by George Steinbrenner, purchase the New York Yankees for $10 million.

Frank Quilici was just thirty-three when he took over as manager of the Twins for Bill Rigney midway through the 1972 season. As the players were about to head home at season's end, the young skipper met with Cesar "Pepi" Tovar, the multitalented player who had spent most of his career playing infield positions. Quilici envisioned Tovar as the club's center fielder for the '73 season.

"Pepi, I know you didn't like playing for Rigney," Quilici started. "Here's what I want you to do. Go back home [to Venezuela] and find someone who will keep hitting the ball over your head."

"Okay, Frank," said Tovar.

"Just keep doing that," said Quilici. "You come back next year, you're going to be in the outfield and you're going to be able to run down everything that's hit out there. And you're gonna get 200 hits and you're gonna steal 50 bases and then you're gonna get a great contract."

"Okay, Frank!" said Tovar, pumped by all these positive thoughts.

Now, it was November, 1972. Quilici was in Hawaii for baseball's winter meetings, along with Twins brass, including Calvin Griffith and George Brophy, who headed the team's minor-league system. Quilici got a call to come to Griffith's room.

While fans and Rod Carew watched in wonder, Calvin Griffith served up a hot dog to manager Frank Quilici. COURTESY OF THE MINNESOTA TWINS.

Cesar Tovar, shown here during a Camera Day promotion, was capable of playing any position and was a hit with fans. To the chagrin of many, he was traded following the 1972 season. COURTESY OF THE MINNESOTA TWINS.

"We got a deal going with Philadelphia," Griffith told the manager as he entered the room.

"Who you going to trade?" Quilici asked.

"Cesar," said Griffith.

"Cesar!" exploded Quilici. "This kid is ready to play. He can play. He's popular with the fans. He's the only guy we got who can run, besides Carew."

Long pause.

"Who you getting for him?" Quilici asked, trying to regain his composure.

"We're getting Ken Sanders and Joe Lis," said Griffith. (Sanders was a borderline big-league pitcher. Lis a lumbering minor-league outfielder.)

"Who the fuck is Joe Lis?" asked Quilici.

Brophy entered the conversation.

"He hit 25 homers in Tulsa," Brophy said.

"You ever been to Tulsa?" Quilici asked. "Anybody can hit 25 homers in Tulsa. It's something like 360 feet to right center."

Over Quilici's strong objections, the deal was done.

Throughout the 1960s, Griffith had made masterful trades. Before moving to Minnesota, he'd dealt slugger Roy Sievers to the White Sox for catcher Earl Battey and first baseman Don Mincher. In 1962, he'd traded Pedro Ramos to the Cleveland Indians for first baseman Vic Power and pitcher Dick Stigman. In 1964, he'd traded pitcher Gerry Arrigo to Cincinnati for Tovar. In 1966, he'd sent outfielder Jimmie Hall, Mincher, and pitcher Pete Cimino to California for Dean Chance and infielder Jackie Hernandez. In 1968, he'd sent pitcher Jim Merritt to Cincinnati for Leo Cardenas. Those deals all paid big dividends for the Twins, one of the 1960s most successful teams.

Until 1975, when free agency came along and changed the economics of the game as well as Griffith's ability to judge players, Griffith had been a good judge of baseball talent. But in his early years in Minnesota, he'd also had astute baseball help within the family. His brother, Sherry Robertson, one of the three Robertson vice presidents, and his brother-in-law, Joe Haynes, had been professional ballplayers. Both had a great eye for talent and both also had Griffith's complete trust.

Haynes, who had been an All-Star American League pitcher, was traded by Washington Senators owner Clark Griffith at about the time he was proposing marriage to Clark's adopted daughter, Thelma, who was also Calvin's sister. After his playing days were over, he returned to the Senators organization, first as a pitching coach, and later as a vice president. He died of a heart attack in 1967 at the age of fifty.

The gregarious Sherry Robertson, the Twins' minor-league director, was killed in a car crash while on a pheasant hunting trip in South Dakota in 1970. He was fifty-one. These were huge losses for Griffith and the Twins, on both a personal and professional level. It is not coincidence that the team began to falter following their deaths. The game was simply never again as fun for Calvin, nor were his deals as astute.

So now, in 1973, Quilici had Lis; Harmon Killebrew, with one bad leg and one bad shoulder; and Tony Oliva, with one bad leg. On the plus side, he also had Carew, who batted .350—best in the American League, of course—and stole 40 bases.

And then, there was indestructible pitcher Bert Blyleven. In 1973, not only did Blyleven compile a 20–17 record, he pitched 325 innings and completed 25 games. (For comparison, when Johan Santana won his second Cy Young Award in 2006, he led the league in innings pitched with 233 and had 1 complete game.)

For one glorious day, first round draft choice Eddie Bane filled the Met. COURTESY OF THE MINNESOTA TWINS.

Crusty *Tribune* sportswriter Tom Briere and Quilici would have variations of this conversation after many of the games in which Blyleven pitched.

"You got away with not going by the book again," Briere would say.

"Whaddya mean, 'Not going by the book'?" Quilici would answer.

"Looked to me like Blyleven was starting to get tired out there," Briere would say. "The book says, 'Go to your relief pitchers.'"

"You tell me who I've got in the bullpen that's better than Blyleven?" Quilici would say. "See what your book says about that."

The Twins also had another pitcher in 1973 who was briefly extraordinary. On June 7, the team selected Eddie Bane, a pitcher from Arizona State, in the first round of the draft. Three days later, Bane defeated a University of Minnesota baseball team that included David Winfield in the College World Series. That led to a bit of a Bane buzz in the state.

In that same draft, the Texas Rangers had selected a Texas schoolboy sensation, David Clyde, in the first round. The Rangers had signed him and immediately let him start a game. More than 37,000 people, a sellout at the Rangers ballpark, showed up for the game.

Griffith noticed. If there was money to be made, he wasn't opposed to borrowing an idea.

The Twins signed Bane and, with much fanfare, announced that he would make his debut as a professional ballplayer on July 4 at the Met against the Kansas City Royals. There also would be fireworks after the game. The crowd was so immense—45,890—that the start of the game had to be delayed.

Bane pitched well, giving up 1 run on 3 hits in seven complete innings, before leaving to a huge ovation. The Twins ended up losing the game, but Bane stuck on the roster for much of the rest of the season, ending the year with an 0–5 record. Bane spent the 1974 season in the minors and came back to the Twins briefly in 1975 and 1976 before giving up pitching with a career record of 7–13. But he did stay in the game, as a scout and scouting executive in several organizations, long after his pitching days were over.

Jim Rantz, the team's director of minor-league operations, was a scout for the Twins the year that Bane filled Met Stadium. He looks at Bane's record like this, "Calvin got his bonus money back in one game."

The Twins finished the year at 81–81, a remarkable record given the state of the team. Joe Lis had the most productive year of his major-league career. Because of injuries to Killebrew, he played in 103 games, mostly at first base. He batted .245 with 9 home runs.

"We had a bigger park than Tulsa," said Quilici.

1974

Apathy

The World: Isabel Perón succeeds her late husband, Juan, as president of Argentina. World population reaches four billion.

The Nation: On August 8, President Richard Nixon resigns office; a month later, his successor, Gerald Ford, pardons him of any criminal conduct. Patricia Hearst is kidnapped by the Symbionese Liberation Army and, months later, is shown on tape participating in a bank robbery with the SLA. On April 3, 149 tornadoes hit thirteen U.S. states—not Minnesota—killing 315 people.

The State: The Minneapolis skyline is changed with the opening of the IDS tower. It supplants the Foshay Tower as city's tallest building. Waseca's David Kunst completes his four-year walk around the world.

Pop Culture: Billboard's #1 Song: "The Way We Were," by Barbara Streisand. Best Picture: *The Godfather, Part II.* Best Seller: *Centennial,* by James A. Michener. Top-Rated Television Show: *All in the Family.*

The Season: Rod Carew wins another batting title, but hits only 3 homers. Attendance falls and owner Calvin Griffith grumbles that people don't pay to see a player hit singles. The next season, Carew hits 14 homers.

In the fourth inning of an April 8 game in Atlanta, the Braves' Hank Aaron ripped a pitch from the Los Angeles Dodgers' Al Downing over the left field fence and into the Braves bullpen. It was Aaron's 715th career home run. He had surpassed the legendary Babe Ruth and become the game's greatest home run hitter.

It was the shot heard 'round the baseball world, except perhaps in Minnesota. The night after Aaron's feat, the Twins played their season home opener before 10,409 people. Turned out that would be considered a big crowd in 1974.

Just fourteen years after moving to Minnesota and ten years after playing in the World Series, the honeymoon was over. All those people who had once driven from Sioux Falls and Fargo and Des Moines to see big-league baseball found something else to do. People weren't even driving from Bloomington to see this team. By season's end, the Twins had the poorest attendance in the American League, the first time that had happened, though it wouldn't be the last. They'd drawn 662,401 for the season, which was almost 100,000 people fewer than they'd drawn in 1960, their final season in Washington.

The startling thing about the low attendance figure was that the Twins weren't that bad. They finished two games over .500. Rod Carew won his third consecutive batting title, hitting .364, and Harmon Killebrew and Tony Oliva could still limp to the plate. Between them, they hit 26 homers and drove in 111 runs. But few cared. The stands were usually empty.

Manager Frank Quilici would try to encourage his players to pay no attention to the vast emptiness around them.

"I'd tell them, 'You never know who might be looking at you,'" Quilici said. "I'd tell them some other team might be watching, 'You owe it to yourselves and to your teammates to play as hard as you can.' I even told that to Carew. He dogged it one game and I let him have it. I said, 'Rodney, nobody admires you more when you play hard but nobody gets madder at you than me when you dog it. You're better than that. Besides, you gotta remember, other teams are watching you.'"

Longtime sportswriter Patrick Reusse was in his first year covering the team for the *St. Paul Dispatch* that season.

"There was absolutely no optimism in Minnesota that year," Reusse said. "They had gone something like 5–21 in spring training and that was back in the day when people believed what you did in spring training mattered. I remember the Twins being frantic just trying to win a spring training game so they could build up a little hope in Minnesota."

Fans in the Upper Midwest were coming up with all sorts of reasons not to go to the Met, going so far as to reach back five years when Calvin Griffith had made the decision to fire Billy Martin.

"People were still pissed about that," said Reusse. "Calvin said the reason

A few fans—and their dogs—still arrived at the Met for Camper Day in 1974. COURTESY OF THE MINNESOTA TWINS.

he'd hired Quilici to manage [midway through the 1972 season] was that he was an Italian. Calvin actually thought if he hired another fiery Italian, people would forgive him for firing Billy."

There were other factors that chilled interest as well. There were newspaper articles suggesting that Griffith might, at the urging of the American League, move his team to Seattle to help settle a breach of contract suit that city had filed against Major League Baseball. That suit had been filed in the wake of the one-year history of the underfinanced Seattle Pilots, a team that came into existence in the spring of 1969 and was headed to Milwaukee under the ownership of Bud Selig days before the 1970 season began. So hasty was the move that there was no time for the Milwaukee Brewers to order new uniforms. The word "Seattle" was ripped from the old uniform and replaced with "Milwaukee."

During the period of the suit, the city of Seattle and King County erected the Kingdome, fully expecting that baseball would move back to the region when the stadium was ready, which was why moving the Twins seemed like a possibility. Griffith, it should be noted, did nothing to explicitly suggest that his team was ready to move. But as Carl Pohlad would learn in later years, not even implied threats could help build loyalty to the hometown team. Seattle's suit was finally settled in 1976, when baseball expanded, with Seattle and Toronto gaining franchises.

On what turned out to be his final swing in a Minnesota uniform, Mighty Harmon struck out to close the '74 season. PHOTO BY RICHARD OLSENIUS. *MINNEAPOLIS STAR TRIBUNE* NEWS NEGATIVE COLLECTION, MINNESOTA HISTORICAL SOCIETY.

This was a period of ever-increasing dark clouds for Griffith. Free agency was on the horizon and that would forever change the economic structure of the game.

Curt Flood, in rejecting his 1969 trade from the St. Louis Cardinals to the Philadelphia Phillies, had filed suit against baseball's reserve clause in 1970. That clause essentially bound players to a team for as long as the team wanted them and, of course, kept salaries relatively low. Saying the clause "was a form of slavery," Flood went all the way to the Supreme Court in his battle, ultimately losing.

Still, his legal battle served as a wake-up call for other players, who realized elimination of the reserve clause would give them the freedom to sell their services to the highest bidder. After two pitchers, Andy Messersmith and Dave McNally, played a season without signing a new contract, meaning they played under the "reserve clause" portion of their contract, arbitrator Peter Seitz ruled that they were "free agents," able to sign with any team they chose. Baseball appealed, but a federal court upheld Seitz's decision. The owners knew the handwriting was on the wall and reached a settlement with the Players' Association in 1976. Under terms of that settlement, players could become free agents after six years of major-league experience.

But even before those legal maneuvers were played out, there had been a 1974 case that showed the impact free agency would have on players, owners, and the game. Charlie Finley, the owner of the Oakland A's, had failed to pay $50,000 into an insurance fund for star pitcher Jim "Catfish" Hunter. That amounted to half Hunter's pay at the time. Hunter took the case to arbitration, and Seitz ruled that because of Finley's disregard of the contract, Hunter was no longer bound to the A's.

With Hunter free to pitch wherever he wanted, owners lined up to talk to Catfish. (Griffith was not among them.) But no one could top Yankees owner George Steinbrenner, who came to North Carolina with a contract offering Hunter $3.5 million over five years. It was a jaw-dropping amount, given that during the 1974 season, baseball's highest-paid player was Dick Allen of the Chicago White Sox, who was getting $250,000.

In 1974, Griffith was paying Rod Carew, already a two-time batting champion, $90,000. Changes that Griffith had no chance of keeping up with were coming—and the Met was empty.

1975

Harmon: Going, Going, Gone

The World: Dictator General Francisco Franco dies, ending forty years of rule in Spain. His death paves way for democratic reforms.

The Nation: The last one thousand U.S. citizens flee as communist forces overwhelm Saigon. Jimmy Hoffa disappears. Construction begins on the Alaska pipeline.

The State: The *Edmund Fitzgerald* sinks in the Canadian waters of Lake Superior; all twenty-nine crew members die. A year later, Gordon Lightfoot releases the haunting song that memorialized the event. A final tally shows that 1,053 Minnesotans were killed in the Vietnam war. Vikings defensive end Jim Marshall picks up a fumble and runs the wrong way against the San Francisco 49ers.

Pop Culture: Grammy for Best Male Country Vocal Performance: "Blue Eyes Cryin' in the Rain," by Willie Nelson. Highest-Grossing Movie: *Jaws*. Best Seller: *Ragtime,* by E. L. Doctorow. *Saturday Night Live* debuts on NBC.

The Season: Tom Kelly makes his first appearance in a Twins' uniform. As a first baseman, the team's future manager appears in 49 games and bats .181.

Harmon Killebrew was the perfect hero for Minnesota's introduction to major-league baseball. White, balding, bulky, strong, not given to public displays of either joy or disappointment, modest, nice—and an incredible power hitter.

The 1975 season opened with a big hole in the lineup: no Killebrew. Shown here prior to the game with the Angels are manager Frank Quilici and starters Rod Carew (2b), Lyman Bostock (cf), Larry Hisle (lf), Bobby Darwin (rf), Tony Oliva (dh), Eric Soderholm (hidden, 3b), Steve Braun (1b), Danny Thompson (ss), and Glenn Borgmann (c). Dave Goltz gave up five earned runs in a 7–3 loss watched by 11,909 faithful. PHOTO BY JOHN CROFT. *MINNEAPOLIS STAR TRIBUNE* NEWS NEGATIVE COLLECTION, MINNESOTA HISTORICAL SOCIETY.

Appreciation for Killebrew, the slugger, grows with each decade because the Twins have never come close to finding another player with the power of Number 3. Between 1962 and 1969, Killebrew was the American League's home run champion six times. The Twins haven't had a league leader since. It's not that they haven't tried. Craig Kusick (1973–79), Bob Gorinski (1977), Mark Funderburk (1981), Scott Stahoviak (1995–98) and Michael Restovich (2002–2004) are among the players who have had been damned with the "next Twins slugger" label.

Powerful as he was, the most home runs Kent Hrbek ever hit in a season was 34, in 1987. Killebrew hit 40 or more homers in eight seasons. On 35 occasions, he hit 2 home runs in a game. The next highest Twin on the 2-homer list is Tony Oliva, with 18. So mighty was Harmon Killebrew that in 6,000 major-league at bats he was never asked to lay down a sacrifice bunt and he was never thrown out of a game.

Despite all of this, despite the fact that Killebrew was a good citizen and a perfect match for Minnesota, despite the fact that nobody left a game until Killebrew had batted for the last time, despite the fact that he made millions of dollars for the Griffith clan, Killebrew didn't end his career in Minnesota.

In the single most dunderheaded decision of his baseball life, Griffith got into one last contract quibble with Killebrew. In January of 1975, Griffith asked Killebrew to sign a contract to be a player-coach for $52,000 a year, half what Killebrew had made in his prime. Killebrew, who was struggling with shoulder injuries and knee problems, had had two poor seasons in succession in 1973 and '74. He wanted one last crack at being a full-time designated hitter. Kansas City was offering that chance, plus $70,000 a year. Killebrew asked for his release and Griffith granted it.

"We've been dickering for a month," Griffith said on the day he released Killebrew. "I was surprised when Harmon asked for his release. I'm sorry to see him go."

Harmon Killebrew was known for his monster home runs. The original estimate of the distance he hit this ball against Lew Burdette and the California Angels on June 3, 1967, was 500 feet. But the newspaper photos tracing the flight of the ball included a "?" following the 500 feet. It finally was determined the ball traveled 520 feet, his longest homer at the Met. Killebrew is also credited with the longest home run ever hit in Baltimore's old Memorial Stadium and was one of just four batters ever to hit a baseball over the roof of the second deck of the left field stands in Detroit's old Tiger Stadium. COURTESY OF THE MINNESOTA TWINS.

From a baseball standpoint, Griffith might have been right about Killebrew. The old power was gone. Killebrew homered just 14 times for the Royals in 1975.

"It was the longest season of my life," said Killebrew of his single season in Kansas City. "I thought I was going there to be the full-time DH. But Jack McKeon had other ideas. He platooned me as a DH and he also wanted me to play some first base. That artificial turf destroyed what was left of my knees."

But even if Griffith was right about Killebrew's eroding skills, he was wrong on every other count. Killebrew represented what the Twins had been. Without him, the 1975 season was tedious. The team finished 7 games under .500 and had the lowest attendance in the American League.

The decision not to bend to Killebrew's wishes seemed to be a message to both fans and other Twins players that loyalty was a one-way street with Griffith. That not even Killebrew could finish his career with the Twins was also the fulfillment of a prophecy pitcher Jim Kaat had made in a conversation with the slugger years earlier.

Kaat, as always, was in a contract dispute with Griffith, and Killebrew was trying to calm the pitcher.

"You're just going to make him mad," Killebrew told Kaat.

"Harmon, when you quit hitting them over the wall, they'll forget how to spell your name," Kaat responded.

The Griffiths understood that Killebrew had been money in the bank for the family. Even after he was wearing Royals blue, they tried to milk one more payday out of the old slugger, declaring May 4, 1975, Harmon Killebrew Day at the Met. While he stood at home plate in his Royals uniform, the Twins retired his Twins' number 3. Only 14,000 people showed up to witness this strange event. Killebrew, as always, handled it with quiet dignity.

It had been Calvin's mentor, Clark Griffith, who had stumbled onto Killebrew in 1954. A U.S. senator from Idaho, Herman Welker, kept pestering his friend, Clark, the owner of the always-beleaguered Senators, about a powerful athlete in Payette, Idaho. To shut Welker up, Griffith finally sent his farm director, Ossie Bluege, to see this seventeen-year-old kid Welker was so excited about. In a town game, Killebrew sent a ball flying more than 400 feet. Bluege was impressed and hustled back to Washington saying, "Sign the kid!"

Because of his blocky build, there are some who still believe that Killebrew was a one-dimensional player. In fact, he was a skilled, multisport athlete, with extremely quick hands. The Senators weren't alone in wanting Killebrew on their side. The University of Oregon also wanted the all-state quarterback. Killebrew had signed a letter of intent to play football and baseball for the Ducks.

Never one for bragging, Killebrew often tells the story about what might have been had he played football.

"Oregon wanted me to take over at quarterback for George Shaw [who ended up in the NFL]," Killebrew says. "I didn't go to Oregon, but four years later Oregon went to the Rose Bowl. I've always wondered, 'If I had been there, would they have gotten to the Rose Bowl?'"

There are a couple of other stories Killebrew frequently repeats in interviews.

How'd you get so strong?

"My father [Clayton] was a very strong man and my great-grandfather, during the Civil War, was supposed to have been the strongest man in the Union Army." [There are news briefs showing that Killebrew's great-grandfather was a Union Army wrestling champion.]

Another favorite story of Killebrew's is of a dispute his parents, Clayton and Kate, once had when the Killebrew boys were growing up.

Kate: "Clay, the boys are digging holes in the yard and tearing up the grass."

Clay: "Kate, we're not raising grass here, we're raising boys."

On June 19, 1954, Bluege returned to Payette, carrying with him a contract package worth $30,000. Killebrew said goodbye to the Oregon Ducks and cast his fate with baseball.

Baseball rules at the time required teams to carry "bonus babies" on their major-league roster for two years before they could be sent to the minors. So Killebrew, the country boy, went straight from Payette to Washington and Griffith Stadium.

"When I got there, it was huge," Killebrew recalled. "I think it was something like 405 feet down the left field line. Later, they shortened the distance a lot. But when I got there they hadn't done that yet, but it didn't really make an impression on me. I just figured that's what all major-league parks must be like. There was a guy named Johnny Schmitz throwing batting practice and I started hitting them into the seats. Everybody stopped what they were doing to watch. I was too naïve to really pay any attention. I just figured I was supposed to be doing that."

For those two bonus-baby seasons, Killebrew didn't do much but sit on the bench. After the two years had passed, he was quickly sent to the minors to get much-needed playing time. He spent most of three years in the minors, returning to Washington with a bang in 1959, when he hit 42 home runs.

Killebrew didn't merely hit home runs. His homers traveled such great distances that even fellow big-leaguers were amazed. "The homers he hit against us would have been homers in any park, including Yellowstone," former Baltimore Orioles manager Paul Richards once said of Killebrew.

But those grandiose homers were the opposite of his personality. In the clubhouse, Killebrew was unassuming. He never expected star treatment. Managerial changes rolled off his back. There were times when his teammates had grievances with management that they wished he would speak up. But it wasn't his style.

He did have a dry sense of humor that occasionally lightened difficult times. With the Twins trailing the Dodgers, 2–0, in the seventh game of the 1965 World Series and Sandy Koufax on the mound for Los Angeles, Killebrew singled in the ninth inning. Bob Allison stepped to the plate, carrying the Twins' last hopes. But he was no match for Koufax. He struck out and pounded the ground with his bat so hard the bat broke. Killebrew approached Allison.

"If you had swung at the ball as hard as you swung at the ground, we might have won the game," Killebrew told his friend.

Both laughed.

In a bizarre moment in Twins history, the club held a Harmon Killebrew Day when he returned to Minnesota wearing a Kansas City Royals uniform. PHOTO BY POWELL KRUEGER. *MINNEAPOLIS STAR TRIBUNE* NEWS NEGATIVE COLLECTION, MINNESOTA HISTORICAL SOCIETY.

Through it all, Killebrew remained unflappable. Even when difficult parts of his private life became fodder for newspaper stories, Killebrew did not outwardly waver. For example, one of his sons, Ken, went through hard times as an adolescent, at one point getting in trouble with the law. The Killer stuck by his son and said, "It'll be okay." Killebrew was right. It did turn out okay. Ken Killebrew is the one member of the family who stayed in Minnesota, where he manufactures "Killebrew Root Beer."

A divorce and business woes also have been part of Killebrew's biography, proof that even superstars have real lives, filled with painful times. Killebrew never stopped signing autographs, a pleasant smile on his face.

Gaining a spot in the Hall of Fame tested Killebrew's calm, public persona. After he was out of the game for five seasons—baseball's requirement before a player is eligible for Hall of Fame consideration—he waited for the word that he'd been selected. He didn't get the required votes. The baseball writers, who select those who are to be enshrined, felt that Killebrew was a one-dimensional player, overlooking the fact that few in the game's history ever had such power, and apparently forgetting he could play left field, third, and first base.

He waited a second year and a third. Each time he was passed over. Each time he accepted the verdict with silence.

In 1984, the fourth year of his Hall of Fame eligibility, Killebrew stayed at his Ontario, Oregon, home, not far from Payette, on the day selections were announced. His wife, Elaine, kept up a steady line of chatter, trying to take her husband's mind off the telephone.

"Harmon," she said, "I had an éclair for lunch today. It was wonderful. Chocolate and filled with Bavarian cream."

Killebrew nodded and smiled. Usually his wife ate only healthy foods.

"I had a taco salad," he said.

"That's very good for you," she said. "Did you just have beans on it? No sour cream?"

"Just beans," he said.

She patted him on the back approvingly and continued chatting, trying to keep him distracted.

Finally, the telephone rang. Killebrew picked it up. A smile crossed his face and he gave his wife the thumbs-up sign. He'd made it to Cooperstown.

"Boy, boy," he said.

From Killebrew, that was an exclamation of sheer joy.

In 1997, Jeff Arundel, a Minnesota musician and writer, released an album, *Ride the Ride,* which included the song "Harmon Killebrew." At least in Minnesota, many believe it is one of the best baseball songs ever written. Certainly, it touches the sentiment of old Twins fans.

> *Harmon Killebrew, did you ever get my letter?*
> *Ten pages of clear blue sky*
> *Green diamond days gone by*
> *Wonder why*

Those days are going, going, gone, gone.

1976

Bye-Bye Bertie

The World: Mao Tse-tung dies after ruling China for twenty-five years. North and South Vietnam unite, forming the Socialist Republic of Vietnam.

The Nation: Bicentennial celebrations are held across the country. Jimmy Carter, with Minnesota's Walter Mondale as his running mate, defeats Gerald Ford in the presidential election. Apple Computer, Inc., is formed by Steve Jobs and Steve Wozniak.

The State: Walter Mondale's move from the Senate to the vice president's office sets off a flurry of political activity in Minnesota. Governor Wendy Anderson steps down so that he can be appointed to the Senate by the new governor, Rudy Perpich. Both pay a price for this gamesmanship two years later when they are defeated in their elections.

Pop Culture: Billboard's #1 Song: "Silly Love Songs," by Wings. Best Picture: *Rocky*. Best Seller: *Trinity*, by Leon Uris. Top-Rated Television Show: *All in the Family*.

The Season: Gene Mauch becomes the Twins' manager, and a rookie catcher, Butch Wynegar, is compared to Johnny Bench, a comparison that haunts the rest of his solid career. Rod Carew and Wynegar both are named to the American League All-Star team.

From a fan's perspective, major-league baseball is all about loving, loathing, or indifference. By 1976, the Twins were falling toward the indifference the team had known in most of its years in Washington.

Tony Oliva, the last of the old stars, was limping through what would be his final season. Metropolitan Stadium was a sea of empty seats. For the third season in a row, the team was headed toward the worst attendance in the American League.

On May 31, Twins pitcher Bert Blyleven, who was locked in public and acrimonious contract negotiations with Calvin Griffith, walked off the mound after pitching nine strong innings against the California Angels. But he hadn't been strong enough, and the Twins were losing, 3–1, as Blyleven walked toward the dugout.

There had been 8,379 fans rattling around in the stadium at the start of the game, but by the ninth, only a few remained, including a group of about a dozen young men, who appeared to be drunk.

"Bye-bye Bertie!" they yelled at Blyleven as he left the mound.

Normally, Blyleven didn't look into the stands on nights he worked. But with so few in attendance, the pitcher, who had been the subject of trade

Halsey Hall, by this time a goodwill ambassador for the Twins, releases some pigeons prior to a game in which the Detroit Tigers' hugely popular Mark "The Bird" Fidrych was pitching. Scout Angelo Giuliani holds the microphone. PHOTO BY JIM MCTAGGART. *MINNEAPOLIS STAR TRIBUNE NEWS NEGATIVE COLLECTION*, MINNESOTA HISTORICAL SOCIETY.

rumors throughout the spring, looked up angrily and flashed the hecklers his middle finger.

That turned out to be his farewell wave to Minnesota. Shortly after the game, Blyleven, one of the few bright spots on a dismal team, was traded, along with shortstop Danny Thompson, to the Texas Rangers for third baseman Mike Cubbage, shortstop Roy Smalley, and pitchers Bill Singer and Jim Gideon.

The trade of Blyleven and Thompson underscored the harshest sides of Griffith's personality. A decade later, the deal also would show how fans are able to forgive and forget.

Thompson had been an up-and-comer for the Twins. Hard-nosed, fun, filled with potential, he was a country boy who'd been drafted by the team after an All-America career at Oklahoma State.

In 1974, Thompson was diagnosed with leukemia. He refused to yield to the disease, batting .275 in 1975, the top batting average among all American League shortstops. But he struggled at the start of the 1976 season.

Griffith uttered one of his graceless lines, which echoed throughout the region: "I can't understand what's wrong with him. There must be something on his mind besides baseball."

Surely Griffith, who could cry just watching a syrupy television show, didn't mean the words to come out as they did. But there they were, in black and white, in newspapers throughout the region. When Thompson was made a throw-in in the Blyleven deal, it was a sign to Minnesotans that Griffith was not only cheap, but also coldhearted.

Getting rid of Blyleven had been Griffith's priority in the deal. The pitcher and the owner had battled over contracts for years.

Blyleven was just nineteen years old in 1970 when he pitched in his first game for the Twins. His was a wonderful story. Born in the Netherlands, his family had moved to California when he was a child. His father, Johannes, was a big, powerful man who worked in a factory as a welder.

Johannes Blyleven fell in love with baseball listening to Vin Scully broadcasts of Los Angeles Dodger games. Soon, he was playing catch with Bert, then attending little league games to watch his son pitch. Johannes did not win sportsmanship awards.

"I'd throw a pitch, the umpire would call a ball and I'd hear, 'Gut damnit! You sons of a bitch! Can't you see?' He got thrown out of a few games. Sometimes, it was a little embarrassing, but I never had any doubt who he was pulling for."

His passion for his kid's pitching and his contempt of umpires followed Bert to the big leagues.

"Even when there were a lot of people in the stands I could still hear my dad yell at the umps. 'You son of a bitch!' My mom didn't understand baseball, but she knew my dad was different than everybody else. She'd be so embarrassed she'd sit on the other side of the field."

After just 21 minor-league starts, Blyleven was called up by the Twins, making his first start, in Washington, on June 5, 1970. The first batter he faced, Lee Maye, homered. The Twins' manager, Bill Rigney, rushed to the mound.

"I'm thinking, 'My God, this is going to be it, he's taking me out, my ERA is going to be infinity for the rest of my life,'" said Blyleven.

But Rigney came to the mound only to offer encouragement. Blyleven stayed in the game for seven innings. The only run he allowed was that homer to Maye and he was the winning pitcher in a 2–1 Twins victory. By season's end, he became the thirteenth teenager ever to win 10 or more games, and soon he found himself in Griffith's office negotiating a contract. This was the pre-agent era of baseball. The kid faced Griffith one-on-one.

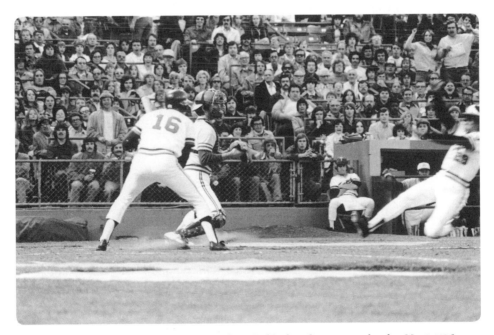

Rod Carew turned stealing home into an art form. In this photo from a game played on May 1, 1976, he successfully steals home against the Oakland A's. Twins catcher Butch Wynegar looks on from the batter's box. Carew stole home seventeen times in his career. PHOTO BY JIM MCTAGGART. *MINNEAPOLIS STAR TRIBUNE* NEWS NEGATIVE COLLECTION, MINNESOTA HISTORICAL SOCIETY.

Griffith invited Blyleven to sit on a soft couch.

"I just kept sinking and he was behind his desk in this big chair," Blyleven said. "It was like I was looking up at God."

The conversation went something like this, Blyleven recalled:

Blyleven: "How are you?"

Griffith: "I'm fine, son. Whaddya think?"

Blyleven: "I think I should get a raise, sir."

Griffith: "How much?"

Blyleven: "Well, I'd like to buy a place to live here."

Griffith: "You can rent."

Blyleven: "Well, umm, I want $15,000."

Griffith: "$15,000! You think you should double your salary? You only got $7,800 last year."

"By that time I was thinking, 'By God, I am asking for a lot,'" Blyleven said.

In the end, Griffith offered to pay Blyleven $12,000 and would throw in a $2,000 bonus if he won 15 or more games in 1971. He won 16. Griffith couldn't remember the bonus arrangement, but Blyleven had held on to a slip of paper with Griffith's signature, promising the bonus. He got the money, but Griffith was not happy.

Each year, negotiations between Blyleven and Griffith became more rancorous. By the start of the 1976 season, Griffith had offered Blyleven, who'd had a decent season in 1975, a cut in salary from $65,000 to $52,000. Blyleven, not surprisingly, was furious. The Twins organization portrayed him as greedy.

Thus, the "bye-bye Bertie," chants.

Immediately after he was traded to Texas, Blyleven received a call from the owner of the Rangers, Brad Corbett.

"He said, 'We'd like to give you a three-year contract,'" Blyleven recalled. "'We'll start you at $150,000, then go $175,000, $200,000.' And then they threw in a Mercedes. I'm thinking, 'Geez, the grass is greener on the other side.'"

Over the next ten years, Blyleven pitched for the Rangers; the Pittsburgh Pirates, where he won a World Series ring in 1979; and the Cleveland Indians before returning to the Twins. He would become a star pitcher on the 1987 World Series championship team before becoming a beloved television broadcast figure.

How beloved? On September 3, 2006, Blyleven thought he was taping a pregame show. He stumbled over something and muttered, "We're going to do this fucking thing over again, cuz I just fucked up."

He was told the show was being done live.

"Oh, we're live?" he said. "I didn't know that."

During the broadcast of the game, Blyleven apologized profusely for his slips. But the next day he was suspended as Twins and television executives pondered his future in the booth.

While Blyleven was under suspension, Twins fans, who had once taunted him with calls of "bye-bye Bertie," showed their affection. "Free Bert!" they chanted.

He quickly was reinstated.

1977
Rod's Lumber Company

The World: French is adopted as the official language of Quebec. An earthquake in Bucharest, Romania, kills 1,500 and a cyclone in India kills 20,000.

The Nation: The World Trade Center opens in New York City. President Carter pardons draft resistors from the Vietnam War era. The United States turns over control of the Panama Canal to the Panamanians. The average income in the United States is $15,000 and the average house costs $49,000.

The State: Rosalie Wahl becomes Minnesota's first female justice on the state's Supreme Court. The Vikings lose 32–14 to Oakland in the Super Bowl.

Pop Culture: The King, Elvis Presley, dies. Highest-Grossing Movie: *Star Wars*. Best Seller: *The Silmarillion*, by J. R. R. Tolkien. The miniseries *Roots* is shown on ABC.

The Season: Rod Carew, in his pursuit of .400, is a cover story in *Time, Sports Illustrated,* and *Ebony* magazines. The other major baseball story of the season is Reggie Jackson, who becomes Mr. October in leading the Yankees to a World Series title over the Los Angeles Dodgers. This would be Billy Martin's only World Series championship as a manager.

The Twins opened the season in Oakland with a 7–4 loss before a sparse crowd. Rod Carew went 1-for-4. He was 3-for-5 in the second game of the series, a 9–6 loss. In the third game of the season he was 0-for-5 in a 7–1 Twins win over the A's. The Twins headed out of Oakland for Seattle with a

The joys of outdoor baseball include sunshine, starry nights—and sometimes frozen fields. Here, groundskeepers use a massive weed burner to dry the field prior to installing new sod at the start of the 1977 season. PHOTO BY DARLENE WOYT. COPYRIGHT 2009 *STAR TRIBUNE*/MINNEAPOLIS-ST. PAUL.

1–2 record. Carew was batting .280. In four games in Seattle, Carew had 3 hits in 15 at bats as the Twins split the series with the Mariners.

It was time to go back to Minnesota for the home opener. The team, managed by Gene Mauch, had a 3–4 record, Carew was batting in the .240s and Minnesotans were disinterested. Only 14,788 people showed up to watch the Twins lose, 4–2, to Oakland. Carew was 2-for-4. The crowd was even more sparse (6,946) for the second home game of the season, a 3–1 victory in which Carew was 1-for-4. And there were even fewer at Met Stadium (5,921) for a Sunday afternoon game in which Carew went 3-for-5 in a 10–2 Twins victory.

The team was back on the road again, headed for Kansas City with a 5–5 record. Carew, who had won four successive batting championships from 1972 to 1975, was batting .304 after 10 games and showing no indication that this would be the year the Twins would be followed by national television networks and reporters from national publications.

The Twins, a team that had generated only yawns in recent seasons, were suddenly the game's best-hitting team, earning the unoriginal nickname "The Lumber Company." Larry Hisle, picked up in a ho-hum trade with the Cardinals following the 1971 season, was fulfilling the promise he'd always shown. In 1977, he led the American League with 119 RBI. Lyman Bostock was proving to be one of the league's best hitters. He finished the season with 199 hits, 90 RBI, and a .336 average.

But it was Carew who brought everything together and drew all the attention to the Twins. In late June and early July he was batting above .400. Could he be baseball's next .400 hitter?

Sports Illustrated lured Ted Williams from salmon fishing on New Brunswick's Miramichi River to pose for a cover with the thirty-one-year-old Carew and analyze his chances of hitting .400, a mark that hadn't been achieved since Williams accomplished it in 1941.

Said Williams, "Carew is the best hitter-for-average in the big leagues today, but because of his lack of power, he has never seemed that impressive. I didn't even know he was hitting .400 until somebody called me. News moves slowly on the Miramichi. But Carew is like that—his ability kind of sneaks up on you. I remember when I was managing (in Washington) and we'd go into Minnesota and Carew would dribble one, and bunt one, then drill one through the middle, and you didn't realize until you read the boxes the next day that he had had three hits."

In the same week, *Time* magazine hit the newsstands with its massive cover story on Carew.

> Whatever the outcome in October, Carew's quest for the elusive .400 is a welcome and joyous event for baseball, helping to turn the sport away from its fractious present and back to its roots. After a generation of musical franchises, a decade of labor unrest in the locker room, a time of free agents and frostbitten World Series in mid-October, baseball sorely needs to get down to basics. Carew is the right man at the right time, a modern Wee Willie ('Hit 'em where they ain't') Keeler pushing the ball past grasping gloves, a Paul Waner incarnate lashing out hits to every field. Rod Carew—stirring the statisticians, enthralling the fans, enlivening the game, making memories.

And *Time* had this to say about Carew's home office: "Despite a long career at the top of his sport, Rod Carew is the least-known star in baseball's galaxy. He works his wonders in Bloomington, a suburb of Minneapolis–St. Paul, cities owned—in the national mind, if not in reality—by Fran Tarkenton, Mary Tyler Moore and blizzards."

The national accounts of Carew's pursuit of .400 were filled not only with

Rod Carew's picture showed up everywhere, including on Holiday Inn cocktail coasters, in the season in which he flirted with a .400 batting average. FROM THE COLLECTION OF CLYDE DOEPNER; PHOTO BY ROBERT FOGT.

glowing accounts of what a great hitter he was, but what a wonderful guy as well. A team leader. A great man in the community. A diligent worker, who played through injuries. A simple man who lived a simple life in the suburbs. A man who cooperated with the media.

Said Mauch of Carew, "As impressed as I am with Rod Carew the hitter, I am more impressed with Rod Carew the man."

This praise didn't square with the feelings most Twin Cities sportswriters had about the team's star. Local writers found him aloof and moody. Not only didn't they like him, they said his teammates didn't much care for him, either.

So which was he? Good guy, or as one former *Minneapolis Tribune* sportswriter, M. Howard Gelfand, described him, "a temperamental jerk."

In a 2008 interview, Carew said that he did often distance himself from reporters. He had to, he said, to give himself time to focus on the game.

"Gene [Mauch] worked with me on that," Carew said. "He said that I had to set limits. He said that from this time to this time, I could be open but after that, I needed to have my time. He helped me. He'd tell reporters who wanted to talk to me, 'Not now.' I appreciated that. He understood what I needed."

In his book, *Carew*, written in 1979 with Ira Berkow, Carew wrote of always being a loner, presumably because of a childhood in Panama made miserable by his abusive father, Eric.

He used a knotted cord from a pressing cord to whip me and sometimes the welts he raised were bad. In gym class at school, we'd have to take our shirts off. This was mortifying to me because of the way my back might look. Mr. French, the gym teacher, understood this and often allowed me to keep my shirt on. I was the only boy who did. That was nearly as embarrassing as having the shirt off. When you're a kid, you want to be like everyone else.

Carew's mother, Olga, was the balance in his life. "She was everything to

Everybody in baseball, including Boston's Ted Williams, was talking about Rod Carew as he made a bid to hit .400. Williams was the last player in major-league baseball to bat over .400 when he hit .406 in 1941 at the age of twenty-three. COURTESY OF THE MINNESOTA TWINS.

me," says Carew. She finally left her husband and moved the family to New York when Carew was fifteen. The family was poor, but she gave what she could to her children.

"She would buy a pair of shoes or a shirt and she'd say, 'Take care of this. We don't know when we'll be able to get another one.' So I cleaned my shoes every night, and I ironed my shirts and pants."

On and off the field, Carew was always perfectly dressed. If he got his uniform dirty sliding into second, he'd change it between innings. Say what you want about Carew's persona, nobody ever looked better in a baseball uniform. And as the hits kept piling up in 1977, Minnesotans warmed up to him as never before.

The height of the excitement came on June 26. The Twins were giving away Rod Carew T-shirts. Carew was batting .396 as the fans started pouring into the Met. By game time, there were 46,463 people in the stadium and the Twins and White Sox put on a show.

The White Sox starting pitcher, Steve Stone, didn't make it through the second inning. The Twins' starter, Bill Butler, didn't make it to the third. The Twins' Glenn Adams hit a grand slam and finished the game with 8 RBI as Minnesota won 19–12. But it was Carew who left the Twins fans who attended the game with a lifetime of memories.

He had 4 hits in 5 at bats, drove in 6 runs, and scored 5 times.

In his first at bat, he doubled and in the second he singled.

This message flashed on the Twins-o-Gram at the Met: "ROD CAREW IS BATTING .400!!!"

The place went wild. Carew tipped his cap.

He grounded out in the third, his average again falling below .400. But he singled in the fourth. Back over .400. Again, huge roars from the crowd. Again, he tipped his cap.

He walked in his next at bat, but then homered in the eighth inning, his average going to .403. The roars of the crowd grew louder, louder, louder.

That day, says Carew, was his most memorable in baseball.

Carew, who batted .486 in the month of June, "cooled off" in July, batting .309. But he roared through the final five weeks of the season, finishing the year at .388, a handful of hits shy of .400. The Twins, with little pitching, did manage to finish 7 games over .500 but ended the year in fourth place in the division, far behind the Kansas City Royals.

And following the season, the Lumber Company was splintered, with Bostock and Hisle both signing free agent contracts elsewhere. Carew had a long, painful parting from the Twins, and was finally traded after the 1978 season.

Carew played seven seasons with the California Angels, then signed on as a hitting coach with the club. Life was good in Southern California until April 17, 1996, when the Carew's youngest daughter, Michelle, died. She was seventeen and had a seven-month battle with leukemia. It was during her struggles that Carew, a private man, turned public, seeking a bone marrow match for Michelle.

The match was made more difficult because of the backgrounds of her parents: Rod, black and Panamanian; Marilynn, white, of Russian-Jewish roots. Minority marrow donors, the Carews discovered, are especially rare. Carew continues his volunteer work with the Minneapolis-based National Marrow Donor Program.

Carew, who was inducted into the Baseball Hall of Fame in 1991, returns frequently to Minnesota because Michelle is buried in the Twin Cities, the place of her birth.

He also comes back because he has a personal services contract with the Twins to do community work. In the summer of 2008 he was in the Twin Cities working with kids at a Twins baseball clinic.

"Tough age," he said, trying to get the kids, who appeared to range in age from eight to twelve years, to pay attention. Laughing, he added, "None of these kids know I used to play. It's their parents who get excited."

But he was patient, correcting batting stances, offering encouragement. He was also impeccable in his perfectly fitted Twins baseball uniform.

"It's something I learned as a kid and never forgot," he said. "When you don't have much, you take care of what you have."

1978
The Speech

The World: Egyptian President Anwar el-Sadat and Israeli Prime Minister Menachem Begin, with the aid of President Carter, sign the Camp David Accords, a major moment of hope in the Middle East. The two are awarded the Nobel Peace Prize. After thirty years in production, Volkswagen stops making the Beetle, a favorite car all over the world.

The Nation: Cult leader Jim Jones instructs 900 of his followers to commit suicide in Guyana. San Francisco mayor George Moscone and city supervisor Harvey Milk are killed by former supervisor George White. The cellular mobile phone system is invented.

The State: Senator Hubert Humphrey, the former vice president and former mayor of Minneapolis, dies on January 13. Following an antigay campaign by Anita Bryant, St. Paul becomes the second U.S. city to repeal its gay rights amendment.

Pop Culture: Billboard's #1 Song: "Shadow Dancing," by Andy Gibb. Best Picture: *The Deer Hunter.* Best Seller: *Chesapeake,* by James A. Michener. Top-Rated Television Show: *Laverne and Shirley.*

The Season: Rod Carew wins his seventh and final batting title in his final season with the Twins. Fourteen games out of first place in July, the New York Yankees overcome turmoil in the clubhouse and everybody else in baseball, winning their second successive World Series.

TRADE CAL GRIFFITH

Anger over Griffith's ownership of the team reached new heights following his infamous speech in Waseca late in the 1978 season. FROM THE COLLECTION OF CLYDE DOEPNER; PHOTO BY ROBERT FOGT.

Fairly or not, "the speech" in Waseca, on September 29, 1978, defined Calvin Griffith for the rest of his life. Speaking to the Lions Club, while braced with a couple of cocktails, Griffith lambasted modern ballplayers and made bigoted comments. He didn't know that a reporter, the *Minneapolis Tribune*'s Nick Coleman, was in the audience, a guest of his then father-in-law.

A day later, Griffith learned of Coleman's presence. The story of Griffith's speech appeared on the front page of the *Tribune*. The first paragraph read: "Rod Carew is a 'damn fool' for playing for as little as he pays him; ballplayers should take advantage of free love rather than get married and have their performance suffer like Butch Wynegar; Billy Martin 'never punched anyone his own size;' the stadium commission 'can go to hell,' and the Minnesota Twins decided to come to Minnesota 'when I found out you only had 15,000 blacks here.'"

There was something to offend everyone. Reaction to the speech was immediate.

Carew, locked in a bitter contract dispute with Griffith, said his days with the Twins were over. "I'm not going to be another nigger playing on his plantation," Carew said.

The *Minneapolis Star* ran an editorial, under the headline: Calvin Must Go. "After Griffith's appalling performance in Waseca the other day, a complete change in ownership might be necessary to save major-league baseball in this state," was the opening sentence in the blistering editorial. "... Nothing he has done before—not his firing of Billy Martin as manager, not his failure to keep Larry Hisle and the late Lyman Bostock on the roster, not the likelihood (now the virtual certainty) that Carew will sign with another team, not even his inability over the past decade to field a consistently entertaining club—has given so many fans so many reasons to stay away from the ballpark."

Griffith tried to say he was misquoted or taken out of context. (Some members of the Lions Club agreed with that.) He tried to explain what had happened. He tried to apologize.

"Look, I'm no bigot," he said at one point. "When we sign a prospect, I don't ask what color he is. I only ask, 'Can he run? Hit? Throw?' After this season, I'm going to ask one more question, 'Can he field?'"

What was going through his mind when he spoke to the Lions?

"I had a couple of drinks and in answering questions from the group I was trying to be funny. But I honestly did not intend to hurt anyone."

But he couldn't shake the most brutal of the comments. They hang on Griffith's legacy to this day. "I'll tell you why we came to Minnesota," Coleman quoted Griffith as saying. "It was when I found out you had 15,000 blacks here. Black people don't go to ball games, but they'll fill up a rassling ring and put up such a chant it'll scare you to death. It's unbelievable. We came here because you've got good, hard-working white people here."

Griffith was far more complex than that Waseca speech. He was born December 1, 1911, one of seven children of Jimmy and Jane Robertson. Calvin's father tried to support his huge family by delivering newspapers and ice on a horse-drawn wagon in Montreal. It was a futile struggle.

Craig Kusick has manager Gene Mauch happy and Twins fans dancing when he hits a game-tying, pinch-hit homer in the ninth inning of a May 24 game against the Texas Rangers. Alas, the Twins lost in eleven innings, 3–2. PHOTO BY STEVE SCHLUTER. *MINNEAPOLIS STAR TRIBUNE* NEWS NEGATIVE COLLECTION, MINNESOTA HISTORICAL SOCIETY.

Calvin's father was the brother of Addie Anne Robertson, the wife of Clark Griffith, owner of the Washington Senators. The Griffiths were childless and to help Jimmy they "adopted" two of the Robertson children, Calvin and Thelma, when Calvin was eleven years old. Questions remain as to whether they were ever formally adopted, but the Griffiths did take the children into their hearts and home and gave them their last name. They taught the kids lessons in life, baseball, and, most of all, family.

Clark Griffith, known as "The Old Fox," also taught Calvin the importance of frugality. In 1933, for example, the Senators won the pennant behind manager Joe Cronin, who was also the team's star shortstop. Beyond being a star player and manager, Cronin was married to Clark's niece, Mildred Robertson. But none of that mattered to Clark Griffith when the Boston Red Sox offered $250,000 to Griffith for Cronin in 1934. "No ballplayer is worth that much money," the Old Fox said, and he made the deal.

But Clark Griffith was also generous. Every year, he would let an old, black minister use Griffith Stadium for a revival at no cost. In the height of the Depression, he would see a story in the newspaper about some poor family being evicted from their home and send money. And when Calvin's father died in an accident in Montreal, he brought Calvin's five siblings to Washington to care for them, though only Calvin and Thelma were named Griffith and stayed in the Griffith home.

Clark often told Calvin and Thelma that they had been "the lucky" ones. That it was just kind fate that had brought them to Washington first; that they had a fundamental obligation to always care for their siblings. Calvin and Thelma Haynes, who together owned 52 percent of the Twins after the Old Fox died, took those lessons on family to heart. The Twins organization was jammed with family. Sherry Robertson ran the team's farm system. Billy and Jimmy Robertson were vice presidents. Calvin's son, Clark, and Thelma's son, Bruce Haynes, were executive vice presidents.

Calvin took care of family and he understood the game and old-school economics. After all, he'd been brought up in both. He was the batboy for the Senators. One of his lasting memories came when the Senators, behind the pitching of legendary Walter Johnson, won the World Series in 1924. In the joy and celebration that came with the victory, young Calvin fell and somebody ran off with the baseballs Calvin was charged with overseeing. While others celebrated, little Calvin cried.

He also understood harsh criticism. In a 1982 interview with the *Minneapolis Star Tribune*, he talked of being a manager in the Senators farm system.

"People would say, 'If it wasn't for your goddamned uncle, you wouldn't be out there on the field managing that ball club,'" Griffith recalled. "I didn't worry about that. Hell, I had people cutting at me like nobody's business. You get used to it."

The Old Fox taught Calvin that acts of kindness were to be done quietly. "He [Clark] was a hell of a good Christian," recalled Griffith in that 1982 interview. "He believed in patience and tolerance. People in the black community in Washington thought he was Jesus Christ because he was always doing things for them. But my uncle told me, 'Don't worry about praise. You get praise and you get conceited.'"

So Calvin Griffith's acts of generosity typically were done behind the scenes. He helped such players as Earl Battey and Zoilo Versalles when they had financial problems. He often made sure that veteran players, on the verge of qualifying for baseball's pension, were on the roster long enough to be pension eligible. He contributed to Little League Baseball organizations throughout the Upper Midwest. When the team prospered, Twins front office personnel also prospered, receiving substantial bonuses at Griffith's annual Christmas party.

But what Calvin couldn't cope with was the revolution in baseball's economic system that came in 1976 and, for the first time in the game's history, allowed players freedom on the open market. The Twins were hit hard. Two stars of the hard-hitting 1977 team, Lyman Bostock and Larry Hisle, signed free agent deals and were gone in 1978.

Bostock, by all accounts a good man as well as a potential superstar, signed a five-year contract with the California Angels for what at the time was considered a staggering $2.5 million. When Bostock got off to a slow start with the Angels, he felt so guilty he tried to turn his April salary back to the team. Owner Gene Autry refused to take the money, so Bostock donated that portion of his salary to charities.

By the end of the 1978 season, Bostock was batting .296. On September 23, the Angels were playing a series against the White Sox and, as was his custom when in Chicago, Bostock went to visit his uncle in Gary, Indiana. During that visit, Bostock was shot and killed by a man who was trying to kill a woman who was a passenger in Bostock's car. Bostock was twenty-seven years old.

Hisle signed a six-year, $3 million contract with the Brewers following the 1977 season. In 1978, he starred, hitting 34 homers and driving in 115 runs. "He is the kind of player kids should look up to," said Brewers manager George Bamberger.

The Twins were left punchless and uninteresting, finishing 16 games under .500. Fans were apathetic.

When there is little of interest happening on the field, sportswriters are challenged to find stories elsewhere. In 1978, M. Howard Gelfand, a young sportswriter at the often-stodgy *Tribune*, took up the cause of Moe Hill, a minor-league lifer. In August, Gelfand started a campaign to have Hill called up to the Twins, so he'd have just one chance to breathe big-league air. Hill was a wonderful story. He'd spent fourteen seasons in the minors, a big-hearted, slow-footed slugger.

"Moe Hill is a symbol of the hopes of a million kids whose dreams of playing in the big leagues died with reluctant adulthood," Gelfand wrote. "Give Moe back his dream and all of us can hope again."

Gelfand even wrote a ballad about Hill:

For fourteen years now I've played the game
in Appleton, Batavia, the Rapids—
it's all the same.
Started out slow, couldn't get a break;
by the time I got hot, they said it was too late....

Fans took up the cause, pleading with Griffith to hold a Moe Hill day at the Met. The story gained national attention. Griffith spoke kindly of Hill.

"He's a beautiful person," Griffith said, adding that the reason the Twins had kept him in Wisconsin Rapids so long was because he was a positive influence on young players.

But in the end, the Twins didn't bring Hill to the Met, not even for a day. He's remained in the minors ever since, a beloved coach in the minor-league system of the Baltimore Orioles.

Hisle, Bostock, and Moe Hill were the baseball stories in Minnesota in the summer of 1978. But they all were forgotten on September 29, the day Griffith delivered his Waseca speech. That speech was recalled in every obituary written about Griffith when he died on October 20, 1999.

But it's a far too simplistic summary of a complex man. Carew, for example, didn't dwell on the speech or his contentious contract negotiations with Griffith after he left the Twins. What he remembered about Griffith was that Griffith, in 1967, insisted that Carew play second base for the Twins rather than be sent to the minor leagues.

"This is something most people don't know," Carew said in a 2008 interview. "The first person I called when I was elected to the Hall of Fame was Calvin Griffith. I woke him up at 3 A.M. and told him. He said, 'Rod, I've got tears in my eyes.' And I told him, 'Thank you for believing in me.'"

1979
Mauch's (Almost) Miracle Team

The World: Led by Ayatollah Khomeini, Iranians overthrow the Shah, Moham-mad Reza Pahlavi, and Islamic law becomes the law of the land in a previously secular country. Margaret Thatcher becomes prime minister of Great Brit-ain, the first woman to reach such high office in Europe. Soviet Union forces invade Afghanistan.

The Nation: Islamist "students" take over the U.S. Embassy in Tehran in sup-port of the Iranian revolution and hold fifty-two U.S. citizens hostage. Jerry Falwell establishes the "Moral Majority" as a force in American politics. A partial meltdown at the Three Mile Island power plant in Pennsylvania raises safety concerns about nuclear power.

The State: While patrolling in Marshall County near the North Dakota bor-der, deputy sheriff Val Johnson's car is struck and damaged, and Johnson left unconscious for thirty-nine minutes. The cause? Never determined. Many believe this is clear sign of UFOS.

Pop Culture: The first commercial rap hit, "Rapper's Delight," by the Sugar Hill Gang, is released. Best Movie: *Kramer vs. Kramer.* Best Seller: *The Mata-rese Circle,* by Robert Ludlum. ESPN—all sports all the time—goes on the air.

The Season: Roy Smalley, enjoying the half-season of a lifetime, is named the American League's starting shortstop in the All-Star Game. More than one million fans come back to the Met as the unlikely team contends for most of the season.

The inevitable happened a few weeks before spring training was to begin. Rod Carew, winner of seven batting titles in twelve seasons, was traded to the California Angels for outfielders Ken Landreaux and Dave Engle, and pitchers Paul Hartzell and Brad Havens.

There was little outrage left in the Twin Cities, where baseball fans had become shockproof.

On his return to the Met as a member of the California Angels, Carew slides home safely under the tag of Butch Wynegar in an April game. COURTESY OF THE *ST. PAUL PIONEER PRESS*.

The deal ended months of sparring between Calvin Griffith and Carew, who said he would play out the final year of his contract and become a free agent if he wasn't dealt. Both seemed relieved when it was over.

"I love the Minnesota fans and like living here," Carew told reporters when the deal was done. "But it was no longer fun playing for Mr. Griffith. I'm convinced he will never have a winning team here. You have to pay the good ballplayers and he doesn't want to pay them."

Said Griffith, "We wouldn't have made the deal with the Angels unless we thought it would help us."

The biggest furor over the trade centered around the New York Yankees and their owner, George Steinbrenner. The media had been pushing for a trade that would have sent Carew to New York in exchange for pitcher Chris Welsh, first baseman Chris Chambliss, outfielder Juan Beniquez, and second baseman Brian Doyle, a player Griffith didn't want. In the end, however, the Yankees pulled out because of Carew's reluctance to go to New York and Griffith's inability to pull the trigger on that trade.

"We have great respect for Rod Carew as a player," Steinbrenner said days before the trade with the Angels was done. "But if a man doesn't understand the privilege of playing for the New York Yankees, in the greatest baseball city in the world, and has stated that New York would not be his first choice and that he'd be more comfortable someplace else, then I don't think it would be fair to our fans in New York or to our other ball players to pursue the Carew matter any further.

"When a man [Carew] is asking for $4 million over five years and says he feels like he's being tossed around like a grocery item, it's a little humorous."

So Carew was gone, in return for players Twins fans never had heard of. On paper, the 1979 Twins team that assembled in Orlando for spring training looked awful.

But baseball is all about hope—and surprise. And, until the 2008 Twins came along, the 1979 team may have been the most surprising in the organization's history.

The team had no power and few recognizable names, but it did have Gene Mauch as manager. It also had two veteran starting pitchers with Minnesota roots, Dave Goltz from Rothsay and Jerry Koosman, an Appleton native who had requested to be traded away from the fading Mets to Minnesota. The Twins also had Roy Smalley, who had the season of his life in '79, and relief pitcher Mike Marshall, a quirky closer with a rubber arm and a leftist philosophy.

That Marshall was in a Twins uniform was ironic. He was the game's

One of the more painful moments for Griffith in his tenure as the team's owner came when he signed Mike Marshall, clad in his trademark leisure suit, to a four-year contract. Griffith and Marshall were polar opposites on labor issues, but Twins manager Gene Mauch wanted Marshall and Griffith was desperate to build credibility with Twins fans. COURTESY OF THE *ST. PAUL PIONEER PRESS*.

most passionate union man and starting in 1978 he was being paid by the game's most passionately antiunion owner. How did the relief pitcher with a doctorate in exercise kinesiology, a Cy Young Award (1974 with the Los Angeles Dodgers), and a reputation for union activity end up with the Twins?

"Gene Mauch," says Marshall.

Mauch had learned to appreciate Marshall's talent—and radical pitching concept—when both were in Montreal. But it was Carew who put Griffith in a position where he had no choice but to sign Marshall.

Marshall was a free agent in May of 1978, when he tried out with the Twins while the team was in Chicago. Mauch liked what he saw, but Griffith wanted nothing to do with him.

"Rod got involved and said we can't let this guy get away," recalled Marshall.

In fact, Carew took the Marshall case to the public, saying that if Griffith didn't sign him, it would be further proof that the Twins weren't really interested in winning. Griffith relented and sat down to negotiate with Marshall.

"Calvin said, 'I'll pay you $40,000,'" Marshall said. "I said, 'Calvin, I was making $150,000. But I tell you what. You pay me $100,000 if I do a good job.' He said, 'What's a good job?' And I said, 'Don't you worry about it. If you let me pitch, you and I will both agree that I did a good job.'"

Marshall did a good job in 1978, saving 32 games in the last two-thirds of the season. Griffith's hand was forced. He signed Marshall to a four-year contract.

In 1979, that looked like a great deal. Marshall was extraordinary. "Iron Mike" appeared in 84 games, pitched 142 innings (as many innings as some starters pitch now), won 10, and saved 32. Typically, Mauch brought Marshall into games in the eighth inning when the Twins were either leading or tied.

"Our team may not have looked like much," said Marshall, "but it was a great group of guys. In my fourteen years in major-league baseball, no team was so much fun to be around as that team. There was no me-me-me on that team."

For half a season, there was one player who carried the offensive load of the team, Mauch's nephew, Smalley.

The two key players, Smalley and Marshall, couldn't have been more dissimilar. Marshall, stout, balding, may have been the worst dresser in major-league baseball. He favored leisure suits and clip-on ties. (The Twins required that players wear coats and ties on the road.)

"My wife at the time was into sewing," said Marshall. "She made my suits. Was I supposed to tell her I wouldn't wear them?"

Smalley was young and, like his uncle, a sharp dresser. And for half a season he batted nearly .350 and always seemed to be coming up with crucial hits.

The left field bleachers became a popular—and rowdy—spot for young Minnesotans, shown here ducking for cover as a home run ball approaches. PHOTO BY PETE HOHN. *MINNEAPOLIS STAR TRIBUNE* NEWS NEGATIVE COLLECTION, MINNESOTA HISTORICAL SOCIETY.

"It's like golf," said Smalley of his tremendous half-season. "You get on a streak and you say, 'Aha, I've figured it out.' I'd finished the 1977 season strong. Remember, I was the MVP on a team with Rod Carew, who hit .338 that year. It just continued the next spring. Everything was falling into place. You either always seem to be facing a pitcher you can handle, or you're facing a pitcher who is not going well. You always seem to have a 2–0 count. I can't explain it.

"I remember one game. We were playing Oakland on a Saturday. They had a lefthander, John Henry Johnson, going. He threw hard. Somebody got on, I come up. I say to myself, 'I've got to see his fastball.' He throws a fastball for a ball. I tell myself, 'I want to see it again.' He throws another fastball, low. So now I've seen it twice. It's 2 and 0. He throws another fastball and I hit it into the seats. It went like that until the All-Star Game."

It wasn't just at the plate where things were going well. Smalley was solid at short, too.

"All of us were having a ball," recalled Smalley. "I think we led everyone in double plays. We just clicked. We'd get some sort of goofy double play and Wilfong [second baseman Rob Wilfong] and I would go to the bench and start laughing."

Mauch was at his best, patching together a powerless lineup. On flights, he played bridge with his veteran players. He arrived at the park early, sometimes standing in the dugout in his underwear looking out over the field, smoking a cigarette, a dreamy look in his eye. He loved the game.

"I think I can honestly say he was the most inventive, thoughtful manager I ever played for," said Smalley. "It wasn't always easy playing for my uncle. Sometimes, you couldn't help but wonder if other guys weren't careful about what they were saying around me. But I wouldn't have given up that experience for anything. There was nothing that was going to happen in a game that he hadn't thought of."

Pete Redfern, a starting pitcher that 1979 season, remembers something else about Mauch. He was a hard-core realist.

"Writers would ask Mauch about the sensational year Roy was having," said Redfern. "And Mauch would say, 'Everything levels out in baseball. .260 hitters end up being .260 hitters.' Roy would say, 'I wish Gene would stop saying that.'"

By season's end Smalley's average had dropped to .271 and the Twins faded into fourth place, six games behind the first place California Angels, where Rod Carew batted .318.

1980

Collapse

The World: Massive labor strikes in Poland show cracks in the Soviet system. The United States boycotts the summer Olympic Games in Moscow because of the Soviet Union's ever-increasing military operations in Afghanistan.

The Nation: Eight U.S. servicemen are killed in a failed attempt to rescue the hostages in the U.S. embassy in Tehran. Ronald Reagan overwhelms incumbent Jimmy Carter in the presidential election. Former Beatle John Lennon is shot and killed in New York City.

The State: Minnesota company 3M introduces Post-It notes. Last iron ore shipment leaves the Cuyuna Iron Range.

Pop Culture: Grammy Song of the Year: "Sailing," by Christopher Cross. Best Picture: *Ordinary People*. Pulitzer Prize for Fiction: *The Executioner's Song*, by Norman Mailer. Top-Rated Television Show: *Dallas*.

The Season: Gene Mauch, weary of the second-guessing from some of Calvin Griffith's minions, resigns as manager in August. Kenny Landreaux is the team's lone member of the All-Star team. Kansas City's George Brett is the story of the season, batting .390.

The closeness that defined the 1979 Twins was undone before the 1980 season began. After months of negotiations, players and owners failed to reach agreement on a contract. The Players' Association called on its members to strike the final eight days of spring training.

Twins manager Gene Mauch was horrified. Players were putting a union ahead of the game? In Mauch's mind, nothing was more important than the game.

Mauch thought he'd had an agreement with reliever and longtime union activist Mike Marshall when Marshall had been signed by the Twins in 1978.

"Don't be the player's representative," Mauch had told Marshall.

"I don't plan to be," Marshall had responded.

Things changed, however, in spring training when the Twins' representative to the union stepped down and the players asked Marshall to take the job. So now it was Marshall, the political leftist, dealing directly with Mauch, the ultimate authoritarian, in matters regarding the second strike in big-league history.

As the strike was about to begin, the two had a brief confrontation.

"Gene wanted to call a team meeting and tell the players they shouldn't strike," Marshall said. "I told him, 'Gene, you can't do that. It's a violation of the National Labor Relations Board rules.'"

With each word Marshall said, Mauch kept getting redder.

"He told me, 'This is *my* team. I say what goes on.' I told him, 'Gene, normally that would be right. But this is a different situation. You can't have that meeting.' That was it. He was furious with me."

The strike ended and the season began, but Marshall knew his days with the Twins were numbered. He and the manager who'd spent so much time talking baseball were not talking at all.

Even in hard times, baseball fans find players to celebrate. The Mike Cubbage fan club was never big but it was passionate—and had plenty of room to spread out at the Met. COURTESY OF THE MINNESOTA TWINS.

The 1980 Princess Kay of the Milky Way, Jean Lidig, pours milk for Roy Smalley during the pregame at the Met. Since 1954, a Princess Kay has been named on the eve of the Minnesota State Fair as a promotion for the American Dairy Association. The relationship with the Twins began with the arrival of the team in 1961, but fizzled out in the 1990s. COURTESY OF THE MINNESOTA TWINS.

"As we were headed north, I heard that he told somebody, 'Pretty soon this is going to be *my* team again,'" Marshall said. "Sure enough, two weeks later, he released me."

It would be years before Marshall and Mauch spoke again.

There was a reunion in 1988 of an old Expos team. Mauch was in the hotel lobby as Marshall checked in.

"He sees me and says, 'Come over here,'" recalled Marshall.

Marshall walked over, wondering what was going to happen.

"He apologized and that was it," said Marshall. The two men who loved studying baseball started talking about the game again, just like old times.

But in 1980, the Twins needed Marshall—and a whole lot more.

In the off-season, they'd lost Dave Goltz, a durable starter, who had won 10 or more games in six successive years and had been a 20-game winner in 1977. But Goltz, the first Minnesotan drafted by the Twins to make it to the Twins roster, signed a six-year, $3 million free agent contract with the Los Angeles Dodgers. (Goltz was a bust with the Dodgers and was released early in the 1982 season. He pitched well again, after being picked up by the California Angels, but his career was ended by a torn rotator cuff in 1983.)

There were other problems, too. The team was powerless—slick-fielding John Castino led the team in homers with 13. And it was colorless. Not surprisingly, it was also last in the league in attendance.

The most noteworthy events were negatives. A young pitcher, Terry Felton, lost three games without a win. That was the foundation of what would become a major-league record. After spending the 1981 season in the minors, Felton came back to the Twins in 1982 and compiled a 0–13 record. He left baseball with a 0–16 record. No pitcher ever has lost so many without ever winning.

On August 24, following a 3–2 loss to the Detroit Tigers, the Twins' record fell to 54–71 and Mauch could take it no more. He resigned.

"I'm not contributing anything," he said as he headed out the door. "I hate the word quit and I want to avoid using it. I don't think that I'm quitting. I just think it might be better for the players to hear different words from a different manager in a less intense atmosphere than I represent."

Some players wept openly at Mauch's departure. Tough as he could be, he also was tremendously loyal to his players. They felt they had let him down.

"This club is messed up," said second baseman Rob Wilfong. "If he can't motivate this club, nobody can."

Rick Sofield, a young outfielder whom Mauch had shown great faith in, expressed the feeling of many of the team's younger players.

"I'm disappointed that he didn't stay," Sofield said. "He helped a kid tryin' to make it in the majors. I owe a lot to that man."

Some were angry. Mauch's nephew, Roy Smalley, the last star on the team, bit his tongue.

"I've got nothing to say now," Smalley told reporters in the downcast Twins' locker room. "What I would have to say would be more than your editors could handle."

The general assumption was that Mauch wasn't upset with his players. He was tired of the financial decisions of the front office. Larry Hisle, Lyman Bostock, Rod Carew, and Dave Goltz could have been the nucleus of a contending team. All had left for better contracts elsewhere. As Mauch looked ahead, he saw that nothing would change; that competing would be nearly impossible.

Griffith hired John Goryl to finish up the season as manager. The team responded with an improbable 12-game winning streak in the final two weeks of the season that stood as a team record until the 1991 Twins won 15 games in a row.

That streak seemed to justify Griffith's belief that he'd been right all along and that Mauch had been wrong. Low budget baseball could be successful.

But most of baseball recognized that Mauch's departure was another low for the Twins. Despite the fact that Mauch is known by many fans as the manager who never won a pennant—he is the winningest manager in baseball history never to have made it to the World Series—he was hugely respected by his peers.

"His record may not show it," said Sparky Anderson, "but he may be the best manager who ever managed."

He loved the game to the day he died in 2005 after a long battle with cancer. Smalley went to visit his uncle in his final days.

There was a baseball game on TV in Mauch's room. An outfielder for the Tampa Bay Devil Rays made a nice catch and Mauch smiled.

"I asked him if he'd seen Torii Hunter injured [July 29, 2005] in the game in Fenway Park," Smalley said.

Mauch winced at the memory of Hunter leaping against the wall in Fenway and being carted off the field with a broken ankle and torn ligaments for his effort.

"I told him, 'You would have loved that kid. He plays hard, he's fearless, and he's a good guy in the clubhouse.' Mauch just smiled," Smalley recalled.

1981

Last Rites for the Met

The World: Pope John Paul II is shot and critically wounded by Turk Mehmet Ali Agca. The Polish government cracks down on the Solidarity movement.

The Nation: President Ronald Reagan is inaugurated on the same day that 52 Americans who were held hostage in Iran for 444 days are released. President Reagan fires striking air traffic controllers, a moment many regard as the beginning of the downward spiral of the union movement in the country. Sandra Day O'Connor becomes the first woman on the U.S. Supreme Court. The first reports of gay men dying from Acquired Immune Deficiency Syndrome (AIDS) surface.

The State: The Minnesota Kicks, a soccer team briefly adopted by tailgaters, goes out of business. The last Vikings game is played at the Met on December 20.

Pop Culture: Grammy Song of the Year: "Bette Davis Eyes," by Kim Carnes. Best Picture: *Chariots of Fire*. Best Seller: *Noble House*, by James Clavell. Top-Rated Television Show: *Dallas*.

The Season: In the last year at the Met, a strike causes a split season. The Twins are not particularly interesting in either half, but Kent Hrbek, Tim Laudner, and Gary Gaetti each make their first big-league appearances, each homering in their first game.

From a national perspective, this was one of baseball's truly ugly seasons. A mid-season strike, starting on June 12 and lasting until July 31, wiped out 713 games; 38 percent of the season.

In Minnesota, there was another reason to mark this season with gloom. On September 30, the Twins played their final game in Metropolitan Stadium. Tom Bartsch, a member of a battered group called Save the Met, wore a cassock to the last game and, surrounded by other Save the Met members, performed last rites for the old ballpark.

Despite all the romantic stories you hear of old Metropolitan Stadium, only 15,900 people showed up to say farewell to the place. So indifferent were most Minnesotans to the demise of the Met that the Twins averaged just 7,951 fans per game, the lowest in team history. They had the worst attendance in baseball, 460,090, for the second straight year despite the fact that they sort of contended for a half-season title.

To try to bring back some semblance of fan enthusiasm following the strike, owners had created a split-season format. Pre-strike division leaders were to meet post-strike division winners in a best-of-five playoff series. The Twins had been a hopeless pre-strike team under Johnny Goryl, finishing with

Bat Day is one of baseball's oldest and most popular promotions. Bats are the most expensive item teams give away; the current price for a giveaway bat is around $4. COURTESY OF THE MINNESOTA TWINS.

a 17–39 record. They surged to mediocre under Billy "Slick" Gardner, who replaced Goryl, compiling a 24–29 record following the strike.

As the Twins prepared for their final game at the Met, they were still mathematically alive for a second-half title. The fans obviously didn't care about this so-called race. Even the Twins didn't act as if they really believed they were in it.

"This may not be the Last Supper, but they're setting the table," Gardner told *Minneapolis Tribune* reporter Jay Weiner prior the Twins playing the Kansas City Royals in the Met's last game. The Royals finished setting the table and served the Twins a 5–2 loss, which seemed an appropriate way to end the season, if not the era.

"Sad and gloomy," is how Julian Empson Loscalzo, a longtime beer vendor, Save the Met founder, and later an activist in trying to turn the Twins into a public entity, described that last game. "Not many cared."

It hadn't always been so grim. In 21 seasons at the Met, 20,175,287 people passed through the turnstiles. In two seasons, 1963 and 1965, the Twins drew more people than any other team in the American League.

Kent Hrbek (wearing uniform number 26 as a rookie) grew up blocks from the Met and made his big-league debut there in 1981. On September 13, Hrbek's pinch-hit double drove in two runs, giving the Twins a 7–6 victory over the White Sox. Rob Wilfong (*left*), Gary Ward, and Hosken Powell rush to greet the kid after his big hit. PHOTO BY MIKE ZERBY. *MINNEAPOLIS STAR TRIBUNE* NEWS NEGATIVE COLLECTION, MINNESOTA HISTORICAL SOCIETY.

Over the years, fans saw Jack Kralick (1962) and Dean Chance (1967) throw no-hitters for the Twins. No opposing pitcher ever threw a no-hitter against the Twins at the Met. On June 3, 1967, they saw Harmon Killebrew hit the longest home run ever hit in the stadium, a blast into the second deck of the left field pavilion, and on August 10, 1971, they saw him hit career homer number 500. They saw Zoilo Versalles become MVP in 1965 and Tony Oliva and Rod Carew win a total of ten batting titles. They saw a World Series and an All-Star Game, and Mickey Mantle and Frank Robinson. And, briefly, there was Bombo.

Bombo Rivera played, sparingly, in parts of three seasons, 1978, '79, and '80, after being acquired by the Twins from the Montreal Expos. His name,

Not even the players really believed they were in a pennant race in the strike-split 1981 season. But mathematically, the team was in contention deep into the second half of the season that was to have first- and second-half champions. The organization had to prepare for a World Series just in case of a miracle. The Twins posted a paltry 17–39 record in the first half (last in the A.L. West), 24–29 in the second half (fourth), and 41–68 for the season. FROM THE COLLECTION OF CLYDE DOEPNER.

not his skills, made the Puerto Rican outfielder a cult hero. Garrison Keillor even wrote a ballad about him.

> It takes two to tango and two to mambo
> But you can do it all with just one Bombo
> Bombo Rivera will carry us to victory.

But by the end of the 1981 season that all seemed like a long time ago.

There was a ray of light peeking through the clouds over the Met, though only the most astute fans could see it. This was the season that a brighter Twins future started arriving in Minnesota.

Kent Hrbek played his first major-league game on August 24 and hit a twelfth-inning, game-winning home run against George Frazier in Yankee Stadium.

Tim Laudner played in his first major-league game on August 28 and he hit a homer at the Met against Detroit's Dave Rozema.

Gary Gaetti played in his first major-league game on September 20 and homered in his first at bat against Texas Ranger pitcher Charlie Hough.

There's one other thing Twins fans should think about when they consider 1981. June 12 of that season might have been one of the greatest days in the team's history.

Yes, this was the start of the strike. Owners desperately wanted to rewrite the basic agreement with the players so that teams losing a free agent would receive compensation for the lost player. The players understood that that would greatly diminish the value of free agency.

The strike was costly on all sides. Players lost about $4 million a week in wages. Owners lost $72 million in total revenue. Fans were contemptuous of both sides.

But in the heat of the strike, Calvin Griffith allowed members of his front office staff to take a rare summertime break.

"Everyone was pulling their scouts off the road to try to save some money," said Jim Rantz, who was an assistant to the director of minor-league operations at the time.

With the unexpected opportunity for a summer vacation, Rantz and his wife, Pearl, loaded up the family car and drove to Peoria, Illinois, to watch their son, Mike, play in the Illinois College League.

"There were about twenty people in the stands and we were watching Peoria play a Quincy team," said Rantz. "Quincy had this short, bald guy playing for them. He was always smiling."

The Quincy player with the big smile hit a home run and a couple of doubles in the game Rantz saw. Heart pounding, Rantz made a call back to the Twins offices. He'd seen this wonderful kid. He's talented and he loves the game. He's got a funny name, Rantz continued: Kirby Puckett.

In January, 1982, the Toronto Blue Jays had the first pick in the draft and used it to select Kash Beauchamp, a nineteen-year-old outfielder from Bacone College in Oklahoma. He never made it to the big leagues.

With the second pick in the first round, the Chicago Cubs selected an eighteen-year-old catcher from Palomar College in California, Troy Afenir. From 1987 to 1992, Afenier played in 45 big-league games for the Houston Astros, Oakland Athletics, and Cincinnati Reds.

Then it was the Twins turn to pick. They selected the twenty-one-year-old outfielder Rantz had seen. He was signed to a contract, by Twins scout Ellsworth Brown, for a bonus of about $20,000. The strike hurt the game. But it may have saved the Twins

For years after, Rantz laughingly grumbled about how the Twins owed him money for his trip to Illinois. The vacation, he explained, had turned into a working trip.

"Finally, at a Christmas party in the late 1990s, I got this check for the mileage to Illinois," Rantz said. "Everybody said they hoped that would shut me up. But I said, 'What about my hotel room?'"

Two Bloomington fans, Gary Franson and Gary Jacobson, displayed their sad sign at the final baseball game played at the Met. For all the romantic recollections of the old ballpark, the turnout for this historic game was small: just 15,900 people passed through the turnstiles. COURTESY OF THE *ST. PAUL PIONEER PRESS*.

1982

Moving Indoors

The World: Argentina invades the United Kingdom's Falkland Islands. Princess Grace of Monaco dies in a car crash.

The Nation: The Vietnam Veterans Memorial is dedicated in Washington, D.C. The first issue of *USA Today* is published, ultimately changing the look of newspapers across the country. The nation is hit with a severe recession. Average yearly income is $21,050. The Dow Jones Industrial Average closes the year at 1046.

The State: Four years after losing the race to Al Quie, Rudy Perpich makes a political comeback and is elected governor. A dramatic Thanksgiving Day fire destroys the vacant Donaldson's department store building in the heart of downtown Minneapolis.

Pop Culture: Michael Jackson's album, *Thriller,* sets a sales record of more than twenty-five million. Highest-Grossing Movie: *E.T. The Extra-Terrestrial.* Best Seller: *Space,* by James A. Michener. Top-Rated Television Show: *Dallas.*

The Season: In their first season in the Dome, the Twins lose more than 100 games (102) for first time in their Minnesota history. Kent Hrbek leads the team in hitting (.301) and RBI (92). Gary Ward hits a team-leading 28 homers. The top pitcher is Bobby Castillo, 13–11.

David Kessler and Missy Abrams of St. Paul at the old Met, tailgating in their favorite spot, prior to heading to the Metrodome for the Twins' season opener. COURTESY OF THE *ST. PAUL PIONEER PRESS*.

None of us had ever seen anything quite like it. Was it good? Bad? Ugly? Certainly, the Hubert H. Humphrey Metrodome was an unusual marvel, its lumpy roof framing the south edge of downtown Minneapolis.

The Dome opened on April 3, with an exhibition game against the Philadelphia Phillies. More than 25,000 people attended the game, won by the Twins, 5–0. But few watched the contest. Instead, most gazed at the ten acres of roof and absorbed the 70-degree temperature inside, a pleasant contrast from the early spring sloppy combination of snow and slush outside. Could that massive roof really be held up by air? (In fact, the roof had collapsed once during the construction process, on November 19, 1981, under the weight of the snow.) There was so much blue, so much gray, so much artificial turf. Was baseball really meant to be played this way?

Donald Poss, the executive director of the Metropolitan Sports Facilities Commission and the Dome's project manager, saw only functional beauty when he looked at the stadium.

"This is the world's best stadium for the money that was spent on it," Poss said in an interview with a *Minneapolis Star* reporter the day before the weekend opener. "It's a classier building than I expected it to be and it was built well within budget, as I always thought it would be."

The term "classy" didn't quite fit the thoughts of most. But the Dome clearly seemed to define Midwest practicality. It had been built relatively quickly (construction began on December 20, 1979). It had been built relatively cheaply, for $68 million. But time would show its big functional weaknesses. There was no easy public access to the playing field level, so the Dome wasn't a good fit for such things as trade shows. And the long rows of seats between aisles meant that the view of a baseball game—or a football game or a Billy Graham revival—was constantly interrupted by someone from the middle of a section trying to get to the concession stands or restrooms.

The most oft-heard refrains at a Dome event:

"Excuse me, excuse me, excuse me...."

"I can't see. What just happened?"

But from their first day in Minnesota, the Twins had counted on support from fans traveling great distances for a ballgame. Nothing was as discouraging to a baseball fan from South Dakota, for example, as getting to Met Stadium in time to learn that the game had been postponed because of rain—or snow.

To long-distance fans, the Dome was, from the beginning, a guaranteed night at the ballgame.

Calvin Griffith was always of many minds about the stadium.

There was the pragmatist.

"Baseball is the only game played with a rain check," he said. "The threat of postponement is our single largest problem attracting fans. We estimate that with a dome, our attendance would be increased by 500,000 a year and we would consistently surpass 1.3 million. We would approach two million when we were in a pennant fight."

But there also was the traditionalist.

"Baseball was developed to play in the afternoon and the true game of baseball is played on natural turf and in the daylight where everybody can see the ball very plainly. The hitters can see the ball better. It's more realistic to them, the perspiration and everything else in the afternoon."

And there was the practical man with an artistic flair.

"Well, maybe they could paint a moon and some stars on the roof."

The regular season opener came on April 6, against the Seattle Mariners. The Twins did it up big. Pearl Bailey was brought in to sing the National Anthem. Muriel Humphrey threw out the first pitch. Musical groups greeted the 52,279 fans as they poured into this new stadium.

In the meantime, at the Met, a group of outdoor baseball purists gathered and played baseball on the old stadium's deteriorating parking lot.

What those at the Dome saw was a team of mystery players.

"We got a no-name offense," said Twins manager Billy Gardner. "We should just put 'player' on the backs of their uniforms."

There were players with names like Hrbek and Gaetti. And there was Jim Eisenreich, a special story.

He'd won the center field job in spring training. Great speed, a perfect stroke at the plate. He was a classic case of a kid who'd come out of nowhere, in this case, St. Cloud.

He'd been the 402nd player selected in the amateur draft in 1980 and now, at twenty-two, he was getting ready to play his first big-league game in this new stadium.

His teammates, the manager, physicians, and sportswriters all misunderstood this young player in the hours before his first big-league game. We saw shyness, nervous tics, and found them quaint.

As the Twins were about to open the season, Mickey Hatcher joked about the kid center fielder.

"Look at him, just look at him," Hatcher said as Eisenreich went through a series of seemingly nervous movements as he suited up for his first major-league game.

Eisenreich took a long swig of orange soda.

"He sure can pound that orange pop," said Hatcher, watching in wonderment.

He also sure could hit. Line drives flew off his bat. And he sure could cover ground in center field. He was a natural, except for those tics. They turned out to be something more than first night jitters. By the end of April, Eisenreich was batting over .300 but he was caught in a vicious cycle. He was increasingly embarrassed about the tics, which made them worse. In Boston's Fenway Park, Eisenreich had to pull himself from the game on three successive nights.

Gardner loved the kid, but was mystified by the problem, which he assumed was extreme nervousness. Gardner, known as Slick, was a good-hearted man from baseball's old school. He prescribed an old baseball remedy for Eisenreich.

"I keep telling him to go out and get drunk and get laid," Gardner said. "But he won't listen to me."

Following the series in Boston, Eisenreich left the team. It would be years before physicians could identify the problem—Tourette's syndrome—and medicate it in a way that would allow Eisenreich to play the game he loved. As physicians experimented, Eisenreich played town ball in St. Cloud, pounding out line drives across central Minnesota.

In the fall of 1986, the Twins waived their rights to Eisenreich and he

Ron Davis sits alone with his thoughts after giving up a grand-slam homer to Don Baylor in an August 11 game against the California Angels. PHOTO BY STEVE SCHLUTER. *MINNEAPOLIS STAR TRIBUNE* NEWS NEGATIVE COLLECTION, MINNESOTA HISTORICAL SOCIETY.

was picked up by the Kansas City Royals. That turned out to be the start of a distinguished big-league career that ended in 1998 with Eisenreich winning a World Series ring with the Florida Marlins. His playing days over, the "nervous" player now heads the Jim Eisenreich Foundation For Children with Tourette's Syndrome.

In 1982, Eisenreich was only part of the Twins soap opera.

It became immediately clear to Griffith that the Metrodome wasn't going to be the answer to all of his economic woes. After drawing the massive crowd for opening night—a night in which the Twins were hideous in an 11–7 loss to the Mariners—the team attracted only 5,000 fans for its second game.

Griffith unloaded salaries. First to go was shortstop Roy Smalley, to the Yankees on April 10 for pitcher Ron Davis and a minor-league shortstop, Greg Gagne. The Twins players were stunned. Smalley was disgusted but not particularly surprised. He had signed a four-year, $2.2 million contract.

"It was a death warrant," said Smalley. "But it turned out to be a great trade."

A month later, the team's closer, Doug Corbett, and second baseman Rob Wilfong were dealt, to California, for an unknown named Tom Brunansky.

A day after that May 11 deal, catcher Butch Wynegar and pitcher Roger Erickson were sent to the Yankees in a trade that yielded little, except to Griffith's bottom line. The Twins locker room had been swept clean of high salaries for more unknowns.

Pete Redfern, a veteran pitcher, recalled standing on the mound, taking a deep breath and looking around the field. Everywhere he looked there were young players, just weeks away from the minor leagues: Tim Laudner catching, Hrbek at first base, Ron Washington at second, Lenny Faedo at short, Gaetti at third, Gary Ward, Bobby Mitchell, and Dave Engle in the outfield.

"I had six years in the big leagues and when I looked around it dawned on me: They were almost all rookies! They'd cleaned house. Why not me?"

Redfern, who once had been a highly touted prospect, did make it through most of the 1982 season, before an arm injury forced him to undergo surgery. The Twins released him during spring training in 1983 and he signed a minor-league deal with the Los Angeles Dodgers. He felt positive about some late season minor-league performances and went home to Southern California feeling as if he had a chance to make the Dodger roster in 1984.

But in October 1983, Redfern, a lifelong swimmer, went to the ocean with friends.

"I thought I was over about three and a half feet of water," said Redfern. "I did a racing dive—but the water was only a foot deep."

He has spent the rest of his life in a wheelchair. After emotionally rocky early years, he says he's come to feel good about life. He coaches kids, working especially hard on the mental aspects of pitching.

"I'm blessed," he says. "Major League Baseball has a great benefits package that's taken care of me. I've got a wonderful son. I've come to believe that everything happens for a reason in God's world."

But back in 1982, Redfern recalls looking around a brand-new field and barely recognizing his teammates. Griffith had unloaded, or, depending on your point of view, he'd reloaded.

There was no honeymoon season for the Twins in the Dome. They lost 102 games, finishing thirty-three games behind California in the West Division. They weren't just last in the standings. Fans showed their indifference to the team and the Dome by staying away in droves. The Twins drew 921,186 people, the worst attendance in baseball.

1983

A New Foundation

The World: Truck-driving suicide bombers strike the barracks of U.S. Marines and French paratroopers in Beirut, Lebanon, killing 241 Marines, fifty-eight French personnel, and six civilians. Music is first available on compact disc.

The Nation: The United States incurs worldwide denunciation by invading tiny Grenada. It hands out more medals for this attack than were given out during the entire Vietnam War. Sally Ride becomes the first woman in space, and Vanessa Lynn Williams becomes the first African-American Miss America.

The State: The State court of appeals is established. Members of the Starbuck Lions Club bake the world's largest lefse—70 pounds, 9 feet 8 inches in diameter.

Pop Culture: Billboard's #1 Song: "Every Breath You Take," by the Police. Best Picture: *Terms of Endearment*. Pulitzer Prize for Fiction: *The Color Purple*, by Alice Walker. The final episode of M*A*S*H is aired on CBS.

The Season: The Twins (70–92) don't finish last in the Western Division—that spot belongs to Seattle Mariners—but still are twenty-nine games behind the division-winning Chicago White Sox. Mickey Hatcher has highest batting average (.317), Tom Brunansky leads in homers (28), and Gary Ward in RBI (88). Ken Schrom's 15–8 record tops the pitching staff.

In the early years, the roof of the Dome collapsed with nerve-jangling frequency, typically because of the weight of the snow, as was the case of this collapse in April 1983. PHOTO BY CHUCK BJORGEN. *MINNEAPOLIS STAR TRIBUNE* NEWS NEGATIVE COLLECTION, MINNESOTA HISTORICAL SOCIETY.

You could tell when it was game time, Gary Gaetti said. "The smoke would come rolling out of the tunnel by the dugout. You could almost hear people say, 'Twins are getting ready for a ballgame.' That's how we got ready. A cup of coffee, a Marlboro red, touch your toes a couple of times, and play ball."

The group of players known as "The Class of '81" was maturing, so to speak. Gaetti, Kent Hrbek, Tom Brunansky, Tim Laudner, Randy Bush, and Frank Viola were special because they loved to play hard on and off the field, and they seemed indifferent to individual statistics.

"Sometimes I think we were the last generation before everything got to be about numbers," said Gaetti. "We were that last generation before the huge salaries and the commercialization, before everything got so serious."

The Twins of '83 weren't yet ready to win. There still were huge holes in the Twins lineup. Kirby Puckett wouldn't come along to solve the center field problem until 1984. Greg Gagne didn't become the team's starting shortstop until 1986. Tom Kelly didn't take over as manager until late in the '86 season.

But the foundation was being built and Gaetti symbolized what the Twins would become. He was a talented player, but more importantly he was a team guy. He never let stardom go to his head. He treated everybody in the clubhouse the same. He threw his body in front of line drives and never took a game for granted.

"When I was a kid, I never thought about someday playing in the big leagues," he said. "All I cared about was winning the game we were playing that day. Same thing in the minor leagues. I didn't play to make it to the majors, all I thought about was winning the game that day. That's just the way I was."

In retrospect, Gaetti thinks the best thing that ever happened to the Class of '81 was that Calvin Griffith, in a move to save money, had cleared out the clubhouse of veteran players in 1982.

"We didn't have any veterans around to turn to," said Gaetti. "We couldn't say, 'He's a veteran, he's our leader.' It was all on us to figure it out. It was trial by fire. So, we'd get knocked down and have to get back up again."

There was much that was unique about Gaetti, who was a first round draft choice of the Twins in 1979. For starters, there was his looks. His teammates said he looked like a rat, and that became his official nickname. "The Rat."

There were other special features. No pitcher could slip a fastball past Gaetti. In the 1980s, players were calling a fastball "cheese," as in "that pitcher's throwing cheese today." Often as not, when a pitcher tried to throw a fastball to Gaetti, he'd hit it a long way.

"Don't ever try to sneak cheese past the Rat," Hrbek would say.

"I didn't care if somebody was throwing it 105," said Gaetti. "I was gonna get it. You got to know your strengths."

The other thing that was unusual about Gaetti was his thoughtfulness. He was, in his own Marlboro-smoking, beer-drinking, hell-raising way, the team philosopher, a title he still renounces.

"Naw," he says, "I was the dumb-ass of the team."

Unlike so many professional athletes, Gaetti had the good grace to be amazed—and often puzzled—by his good fortune.

"I keep thinking about all my old buddies back in Centralia," he said one summer evening in a pub in Milwaukee. "Here I am, playing baseball and having a beer. They're back home working as prison guards. If things had been just a little different, that's where I'd be."

There was almost a high school attitude about these players. They were so happy to be in the big leagues.

On those occasions, when the players were a little too loose, Carl Kuehl, the team's third base coach would have a little chat with them.

"You have to have the red ass to play this game," he said over and over again. "It's okay to screw around but ninety minutes before the game, get down to business. No interviews. No screwing around. Think about the game."

Kuehl wasn't alone in trying to keep these exuberant kids focused.

After a 4–1 loss in Boston on May 19, left fielder Gary Ward summoned a number of players to his room, telling Hrbek, Gaetti, Brunansky, and a handful of others that they were thinking too much at the plate.

The opening-day lineup in 1983 featured the core group of players—Kent Hrbek, Tom Brunansky, Gary Gaetti, Randy Bush, and Tim Laudner—that would create excitement, victories, and, eventually, a World Series title. On this night, however, Jack Morris and the Detroit Tigers snuffed out opening-day excitement with an 11–3 victory. PHOTO BY REGENE RADNIECKI. *MINNEAPOLIS STAR TRIBUNE* NEWS NEGATIVE COLLECTION, MINNESOTA HISTORICAL SOCIETY.

"Tomorrow it's simple," he said. "You go out there thinking, 'See the ball, hit the damned ball.'"

On May 20, every time the Twins came to bat, they were yelling at each other, "See the ball, hit the ball."

Gaetti and Brunansky each hit a three-run homer and the no-name Twins pounded a star-laden Boston team, which featured players such as Jim Rice, Wade Boggs, and Dwight Evans, 10–4. A few days later, they traveled to Baltimore and swept the Orioles in three straight games, outscoring them 25–9.

Pitcher Bobby Castillo was so excited following that third victory, he jumped out of the dugout with a broom. In front of Cal Ripken Jr., Eddie Murray, and Orioles fans, he made giant sweeping motions on the Oriole infield.

"Ummm, probably not the best idea he's ever had," said Twins manager, Billy "Slick" Gardner.

A few weeks later, Baltimore came to the Dome and beat the Twins two out of three. And in August, when the Twins returned to Baltimore, the Orioles swept the Twins three straight, outscoring them 25–7. The two teams matched up again in Minnesota in September and again the Orioles swept three straight, outscoring the Twins, 23–6.

There was a lesson about showing up your opponent in there somewhere.

There were other lessons, too. Ward, who in many ways was the team leader, was hit in the face by a fastball thrown by Detroit's Dan Petry on August 30.

"I've been hit in the head," said Gaetti, "but I'd never seen anything like that. His face was broken."

Six days later, his face still puffy and bruised, Ward returned to the lineup and went four-for-four.

But at the end of the season, the Twins were in fifth place in the American League West Division, 18 games under .500, twenty-nine games behind the first-place Chicago White Sox.

Calvin Griffith decided something had to be done to build up a pitching staff that had been one of the worst in baseball. He traded Ward to the Texas Rangers for two pitchers, Mike Smithson and John Butcher.

"Gary was as good a teammate as you could ever have," said Gaetti. "When we won the World Series, the one thing I kept thinking was 'Gary should be here to share this with us.'"

1984

Carl, Kirby, and Quirk

The World: India's Prime Minister, Indira Gandhi, is assassinated by two Sikh bodyguards; rioting breaks out in New Delhi and 2,000 Sikhs are killed. A gas leak at the Union Carbide plant in Bhopal, India, kills 2,000 and injures 150,000. Famine in Ethiopia kills more than a million people.

The Nation: Walter Mondale names Geraldine Ferraro as his running mate, the first woman nominated by a major party in the United States for such high office. The Mondale–Ferraro ticket loses to Reagan–Bush in a landslide. The Soviet Union and most Soviet bloc nations boycott the Los Angeles Summer Olympic Games. Unemployment in the United States hits 7.5 percent.

The State: Governor Rudy Perpich travels to seventeen countries in an effort to raise Minnesota's profile in the global marketplace. The last iron ore shipment leaves the Mesabi Range, deepening the recession on the Iron Range.

Pop Culture: Billboard's #1 Song: "When Doves Cry," by Prince & The Revolution. Best Picture: *Amadeus*. Best Seller: *The Talisman*, by Stephen King and Peter Straub. *The Cosby Show* begins its successful run on NBC.

The Season: The Twins attract 1,598,692, the highest attendance so far in franchise history. They stay in the Western Division race up to the final days of the season despite an 81–81 final record. Kent Hrbek leads the team in hitting (.311) and RBI (107), and Tom Brunansky in homers (32). Frank Viola's 18–12 record tops a thin pitching staff.

Speedy young outfielder Kirby Puckett is tagged out by Toronto Blue Jays infielder Alfredo Griffin as he tries to steal second during his May 15 Metrodome debut. Puckett had joined the Twins on May 7, and baseball in Minnesota would never be the same. COURTESY OF THE *ST. PAUL PIONEER PRESS*.

Late in the 1970s, Calvin Griffith was grousing to M. Howard Gelfand, baseball writer for the *Minneapolis Tribune*, about what a sorry business baseball had become. "Every year, we're losing money." He started running off a litany of complaints about what the game had become. Free agency, arbitration, declining fan interest. "How can you make any money?"

"Ummm, Calvin?" Gelfand asked. "Why don't you sell the team?"

A startled look came over Griffith's face.

"If I did that, how would I make a living?"

Griffith couldn't live with baseball and he couldn't live without it. But by 1984, the end was near. His right-hand man, Howard Fox, and all of Griffith's family members, other than his son Clark, were looking to either relocate the team or sell it to out-of-town interests. Tampa was the most appealing spot to Fox, Calvin's sister, Thelma Haynes, her son Bruce, and Calvin's two brothers, Billy and Jimmy Robertson. The team would never have more value than it had, Bruce Haynes would say in meetings. The others would nod their heads in agreement. Only Clark, who was not in good graces with the clan, would object.

Still, Calvin was torn. He felt an obligation to his family name; Griffiths had been in baseball since the 1890s. Besides, there were aspects of the game that still delighted him. He loved the young team that was coming together with Hrbek, Gaetti, Viola, Brunansky, and Laudner.

And on May 7, this young group was joined by a the hottest prospect in the Twins system, Kirby Puckett. Calvin and George Brophy, who headed the Twins minor-league system, believed Puckett would develop into a special player.

"He hasn't shown power yet," Brophy said. "But we look at him and see a guy who could become a power hitter like Jimmy Wynn. He's got that sort of body and that sort of power."

Wynn, known as the Toy Cannon, had spent fifteen seasons in the majors, mostly with Houston. He didn't hit for a high average, but he could be relied on for 28 homers a year. That's what the Twins hoped they had in Puckett.

The Twins, desperate for a center fielder and a leadoff hitter, decided to push Puckett along faster than they'd intended. He was playing for the team's top farm team, the Toledo Mudhens, when he got the call that he was being promoted. The Mudhens were playing a series in Portland, Maine.

Puckett was up at 5:30 in the morning to fly across the country to join the Twins, who were playing the Angels in Anaheim. He got to Atlanta, but his flight to Los Angeles was delayed for four hours because a windshield in the cockpit had to be changed.

He finally made it to Los Angeles and grabbed a cab for the long ride to the Angels' ballpark in Anaheim. En route, the young player began to understand he would not have nearly enough money to cover the cab fare.

He arrived at the ballpark as his teammates were finishing batting practice for game that night. Puckett's first words as a member of the Twins were spoken to the team's traveling secretary.

"I got to get some money, man," he said. "I got to pay the cab. It was $83!"

His new teammates laughed as they heard the story about the phenom. Billy Gardner, who had intended to start Puckett in that first game, decided the kid needed to relax. Downtown Darrell Brown was placed in center for what would be just about the last time. With Puckett watching, the Twins won, 11–1.

The next night, May 8, Puckett got his first big-league start. He had 4 hits in 5 at bats, stole a base, and scored a run in the Twins, 5–0, victory. The Twins' center field problems were solved.

Back in the Twin Cities, Griffith and Brophy were elated. This was what made baseball so damned much fun.

Calvin Griffith laughed—and cried—on the day he signed a letter of intent to turn over ownership of his ball club to Carl Pohlad during a ceremony at home plate prior to a Twins–White Sox game. COURTESY OF THE *ST. PAUL PIONEER PRESS*.

But the decision to sell was all but finalized. That one dissenting voice was barely heard. Clark Griffith, now a Minneapolis attorney, said that even though he was one of the team's vice presidents, he'd lost clout shortly after his father's speech in Waseca. Ironically, Clark was damned by being praised.

After that speech, Minneapolis Chamber of Commerce leader Jerry Moore, a longtime friend of Griffith's, came to Calvin's office, telling Griffith that he had no choice but to step down as the team's president and turn the position over to his son Clark. At the time, Clark Griffith was a fair-haired young man in major-league circles. Handsome and well-spoken, he headed a number of major-league committees and was often a key spokesman for the game.

Calvin seemed to understand. He told Moore to have the conversation with his sister, Thelma Haynes, who technically shared power with Calvin.

"I was told years later that Jerry went to Thelma and started telling her what needed to be done," Clark Griffith said. "He told her how well I was doing."

Thelma, mother of Bruce, who was also a team vice president, was not impressed. In her mind, her son should be the rising star.

"From the moment Jerry had that conversation with Thelma, I was seen as the enemy," said Clark.

By 1984, Fox and Bruce Haynes were pushing Calvin hard to sell the team. As June approached, Clark had a conversation with his father.

"We're done," Calvin told Clark.

"Want to talk about it?" Clark asked.

"Nothing to talk about," responded his father. "We're gonna do it."

The team was sold for roughly $36 million to Carl Pohlad, who was little known in the Twin Cities outside big business circles. Prior to a June 22 game with the White Sox at the Dome, Pohlad and Griffith signed the sale agreement. Pohlad immediately was hailed in the Twin Cities as the local guy who'd saved the Twins.

There were tears in Griffith's eyes as he told reporters, "This was the toughest day of my life. I never thought it would happen. I planned to die owning the team."

Within the sale agreements, there were vague stipulations that the Griffith organization would stay in charge of managing the ball club. In fact, Fox was temporarily put in charge of running the club.

"I kept telling Calvin, 'If you could manage the team, you wouldn't be selling it, they're going to make changes,'" Clark said. "But he really believed he had a unique ability to manage a baseball team and Bruce thought that, too.

Right after the sale, I was in New York for a baseball meeting. I got two calls. The first was that my brother-in-law had died, and a few minutes later I got a call from Peter Dorsey. He told me I was being fired by Howard Fox. I said, 'You mean he won't even call me to tell me he's firing me?' Dorsey said, 'You're being fired.'" Calvin himself quickly discovered that his "consulting" role was not going to be needed.

In the meantime, the first months of ownership were sheer pleasure for Pohlad. The Twins were involved in a delightfully wacky pennant race.

The Western Division was weak. The young Twins, much to everyone's surprise, were strong enough to compete for the title. From September 20 to 24, they went on a five-game winning streak and found themselves tied with the Kansas City Royals for first place. Then came two straight losses in Chicago, but as they headed into Cleveland for the final series of the season they were still alive, trailing the Royals by one and a half games, with four left to play.

The Indians were playing in huge, dumpy Memorial Stadium on the shores of Lake Erie. Rats frequently scurried through the dugouts. A lone fan with a drum sat out in far right field, his drumbeats echoing through the empty park.

"This place is eerie," said Gaetti as the Twins prepared to play their 159th game of the season before 3,752 fans. He laughed at his wordplay. "The fans here don't do the wave, they do the undertow."

The Twins took a 2–0 lead in the seventh inning of the first game of the series with Laudner hitting a two-run homer. They built it to 3–0 in the eighth when Ron Washington hit a home run. But Cleveland came back in the bottom of the eighth against Twins starter Mike Smithson, who gave up two runs before manager Billy Gardner turned to the bullpen and Ron Davis. Davis walked a couple of batters and gave up a run. The game was tied 3–3.

The Twins failed to score in the ninth, Davis struck out the first two batters he faced and Jamie Quirk stepped to the plate. Boom. Quirk hit his only homer of the season. The Indians had a 4–3 victory and the Twins were in shock.

"When I talked to Quirk a few years later, he told me he was as shocked as we were when that ball went out of the park," said Gaetti.

The Twins were now two games behind the Royals, with each team having three games to play. The good news for the Twins was that they had their ace, 18-game winner Frank Viola, on the mound for game 160. The better news was that they had a 10–0 lead after just three innings. By the sixth inning, the Twins still had a 10–2 lead.

And everything fell apart. Gaetti made a throwing error that led to two unearned runs, Viola gave up a homer, and by the time the inning was over, Cleveland had scored seven runs and trailed 10–9.

In the eighth, Gardner turned to Davis. Joe Carter crushed a homer. It was 10–10 heading to the ninth and Davis walked a couple of batters, the winning run eventually scoring. Coupled with a Kansas City win that same night, the Twins were done. They ended up losing their final two games in Cleveland, finishing the year in second place with an 81–81 record.

But the season that brought Minnesota Puckett and Pohlad, also brought one of baseball's most memorable lines.

Said Gaetti of his error that helped set the stage for losing a 10–0 lead: "It's hard to throw with both hands around your neck."

1985

Boy Wonder

The World: Mikhail Gorbachev becomes the leader of the Soviet Union, quickly ushering in a broad range of freeing reforms.

The Nation: Leaded gasoline is banned in the United States. Coca-Cola changes its formula, introducing New Coke to the marketplace. The new formula is a flop and Coca-Cola Classic is back on the market in less than three months.

The State: Minnesota's Robert Bly publishes the highly acclaimed book of poetry, *Loving a Woman in Two Worlds.* Lou Holtz resigns as Gophers football coach and heads to Notre Dame.

Pop Culture: Dozens of musicians perform together in Live Aid Concerts in London and Philadelphia to raise money to help famine relief efforts in Africa. Movie star Rock Hudson dies of AIDS at age 59. Best Seller: *The Mammoth Hunters,* by Jean M. Auel. Top-Rated Television Show: *The Cosby Show.*

The Season: Billy "Slick" Gardner, who resided at a Roseville Super 8 while managing the Twins, checks out in mid season and is replaced by Ray Miller, as the Twins drop back below .500 (77–85). "It's got a bed, a TV, and an ice machine and it's ten minutes to the ballpark, what more do I need?" Gardner said of his humble home.

The Pohlads were in charge and they were looking to make changes. Howard Fox, who owed his career to Calvin Griffith, was running the Twins as "interim" president of the team. But he wanted help and the Pohlads wanted new blood in the organization.

Fox received permission from the Houston Astros organization to have the Pohlads talk with Andy MacPhail, who only a year earlier had become an assistant general manager with Houston. MacPhail, a little bewildered, sat down for an interview with Carl and Jim Pohlad in January 1985.

MacPhail has a long baseball lineage. He is the son of Lee MacPhail and the grandson of Larry MacPhail, the only father-son combination in the Baseball Hall of Fame.

Lee MacPhail was a baseball executive for forty-five years. He was player personnel director of the New York Yankees during the 1949–58 period when they won the World Series seven times. He then became president and general manager of the Baltimore Orioles, turning that franchise from an also-ran to a powerhouse, and then became president of the American League.

Grandpa Larry, a colorful character, was chief executive of the Cincinnati

General Manager Andy MacPhail, the Boy Wonder, arrives in Minnesota's front office in 1985.
COURTESY OF THE MINNESOTA TWINS.

Reds, the Brooklyn Dodgers, and the Yankees. He generally is credited with bringing night games to baseball and getting games on television, and he was the first in baseball to transport his teams by plane.

Andy?

"I'd never managed anything," he said. "I was flattered they wanted to talk to me. I came in, I met with Carl and Jim, answered a series of questions, and went back to Houston."

Later, MacPhail learned that following that first interview, Carl Pohlad thought MacPhail looked more like a Boy Scout than a baseball executive.

For months, MacPhail heard nothing from either Fox or the Pohlads. But in June, he received a call out of the blue. The Pohlads wanted to meet with him again. This time, there was more urgency in their voices. They had seen the old Griffith operation up close and personal and they weren't impressed. MacPhail was offered a job, though the title was vague.

As it happened, the All-Star Game was being played in the Metrodome on July 16. It was a dreadful game with the National League posting a 6–1 win. The only excitement came when Nolan Ryan was on the mound for the National League. Ryan seemed to be in a foul mood as he buzzed a handful of A.L. hitters.

There is one bit of baseball history tied to the game. The Minnesota All-Star Game was the start of baseball's popular Home Run Derby. Tom Brunansky, the Twins' only representative on the A.L. team, finished second to Cincinnati's Dave Parker in the Derby.

MacPhail was at the game, but as a representative of the Houston Astros. However, after consulting his fiancé in Chicago, he had decided to accept the Pohlad offer. On August 5, the Pohlads introduced MacPhail to the media as the vice president of player personnel.

It didn't seem that anyone really was prepared for his arrival. Fox was out of town. Whether he understood it or not, his days were numbered with the team. He didn't fit the Pohlad mode for running a modern business. In the meantime, other Twins employees didn't know what to make of the new guy. Why, he looked like a Boy Scout.

MacPhail went to see Jim Rantz, an assistant to George Brophy, who ran the Twins' minor-league operation. He asked Rantz to show him the team's scouting reports.

"Rantz didn't know if I had the authority to look at them," MacPhail recalled.

A call or two was made and it was determined that MacPhail could check out the reports and when he saw them he was horrified.

"They had their scouting reports on little 3 x 5 cards," MacPhail said. "And I don't mean a 3 x 5 card for each player. Each card was for a whole team. It was just incredible. I don't mean to put them down. That organization came up with great players over the years. But things were changing in baseball. I think the median age for their scouts was about seventy-three. They had two scouts living in North Dakota, which is not exactly rich in baseball talent. But they didn't have anybody in Texas."

Everything was swirling around him. Within days of his arrival, the Major League Baseball Players' Association called for a strike, the sixth such action since 1972. This strike lasted just two days, but MacPhail found himself being interviewed by the local media about the meaning of it all.

Much to MacPhail's relief, Fox did make two major moves that paid off hugely for the Twins.

In August 1985, Fox traded promising infielder Jay Bell and three minor-league pitchers to Cleveland to bring Bert Blyleven back to Minnesota. Bell would go on to a productive career in the National League, but without Blyleven there would have been no World Series for the Twins in 1987.

In September 1986, Fox fired manager Ray Miller, replacing him on an "interim" basis with the Twins' third base coach, Tom Kelly.

What the Twins were doing on the field in the summer of 1985 was not of the greatest significance to MacPhail, which was a good thing because the Twins weren't doing much. The pennant race of the 1984 season had proved to be a fluke. The 1985 Twins didn't have enough defense, their starting pitching was unreliable, and the bullpen was explosive. The decision that Fox had made early in the 1985 season to fire Billy Gardner, always a joy to be around, and replace him with Ray Miller, a joyless fellow, seemed only to weigh the team down more.

But MacPhail's big concern in his first months on the job was to

On a return visit to Minnesota, Rod Carew uses Herb Carneal's back to sign an autograph reported to be for Carneal's daughter. COURTESY OF AP IMAGES.

modernize the scouting operation. His first major hire was Terry Ryan, who was named scouting director in January 1986. Ryan had once been a late-round draft choice of the Twins. He'd pitched four seasons in their system when an arm injury ended that doorway to a life in baseball. He went to college, graduated with a physical education degree and then turned right back to the game he loved, becoming the Midwest scouting supervisor for the New York Mets.

MacPhail showed Ryan the scouting department's index cards and had two words of advice for his new employee.

"Good luck."

1986
TK

The World: Corazon Aquino ends the corrupt, twenty-year regime of Ferdinand Marcos in the Philippines. While walking with his wife after a night at the movies in Stockholm, Sweden's prime minister Olof Palme is shot and killed. The murder remains unresolved.

The Nation: The space shuttle Challenger explodes seventy-three seconds after launch. Millions of schoolchildren are watching the event because a schoolteacher, Christa McAuliffe, was among the crew of seven astronauts. All perished. Attorney General Edwin Meese reveals that profits of secret sales of weapons to Iran were diverted to assist anti-communist Contras in Nicaragua. President Reagan denies any knowledge of the Iran-Contra scandal.

The State: Greg LeMond becomes the first American to win the Tour de France, the first of the three titles the Minnesotan would win. The Summit Brewery opens. Three University of Minnesota basketball players are arrested in Madison, Wisconsin, on rape charges. They forfeit a game and coach Jim Dutcher resigns in protest. Eventually all three players are acquitted. *St. Paul Pioneer Press* reporter John Camp receives a Pulitzer Prize for feature writing.

Pop Culture: Billboard's #1 Song: "That's What Friends Are For," by Dionne Warwick and Friends. Best Picture: *Platoon.* Best Seller: *It,* by Stephen King. Top-Rated Television Show: *The Cosby Show.*

The Season: Twins continue a two-year fall from their 1984 highs, despite 34 homers and 108 RBI from Gary Gaetti. Tom Kelly replaces Ray Miller as "interim manager" for the closing weeks of a 71–91 season. The story of the baseball season was poor Bill Buckner, first baseman for the Boston Red Sox. A ground ball rolled between his legs in the bottom of the tenth inning of Game 6 of the World Series, giving the New York Mets a victory and a chance to play a Game 7, which they also won. One play wiped out twenty years of distinguished play for Buckner.

Late in the season, Andy MacPhail, the Twins' new assistant to everything, had been made "the quarterback" for finding a new manager for the Twins. The Twins had been lethargic all season and Howard Fox, still the "interim" president, made the decision to fire Ray Miller.

Finding a suitable manager for the 1987 team was a job MacPhail took seriously. He started with a list of about eighty candidates, cut it quickly to thirty, and finally ended up with two main candidates, Jim Frey and Tom Kelly, who had finished out the season as the team's interim manager.

Frey, fifty-five years old, was a safe-hire candidate. Though he'd never reached the major leagues as a player, he'd built a solid reputation as a coach with the Baltimore Orioles and then as manager of the Kansas City Royals, a team that had gone to the World Series in 1980 with Frey as manager.

Kelly, thirty-seven, was not so safe. Though he'd been a minor-league manager in the Twins system before he became the team's excitable third base coach, he was young and he definitely was not smooth.

But MacPhail was impressed by the fact that in the last month of the 1986 season, the Twins had shown more energy under Kelly than they'd ever shown under Miller. The young executive was also impressed by the sincerity of the calls he'd received from such Twins players as Gary Gaetti, urging MacPhail to make Kelly the team's full-time manager. There was one other thing MacPhail liked about Kelly. Unlike Miller, who'd always been knocking on front office doors begging for better players, Kelly's mantra was, "You give us the players, we'll take care of the rest."

Kelly's interview with the Pohlads, Fox, and MacPhail was Kelly-like, meaning it wasn't impressive. Kelly mumbled. He didn't even try to inspire. "He was just Tom," said MacPhail.

But Frey ended up taking himself out of the running, with Pohlad pointing the way to the exit.

Given that MacPhail had not yet been named general manager, Frey had come to the Twin Cities expecting that he'd have the opportunity to be both the general manager and field manager. Pohlad quickly made it clear to him that's not what he had in mind. He was going to promote MacPhail to general manager, which was news to MacPhail. Frey was being interviewed *only* for the manager's job, Pohlad said.

Frey's response went something like this, according to MacPhail: "I don't

Tom Kelly, a light-hitting first baseman, made little impact on the Twins when he arrived from the minors in 1975. COURTESY OF THE MINNESOTA TWINS.

have interest if MacPhail is going to be the general manager. It's nothing personal, but he's just a kid."

Pohlad's response was sharp.

"See you later," he said.

And that was the end of Frey's days in Minnesota.

Still, the Pohlads were nervous about Kelly, who had become MacPhail's top choice. MacPhail sought a one-on-one meeting with Pohlad.

"I'm struggling with the managing thing," he told Pohlad. "You asked me to be the quarterback of this thing. I've done that. What are your issues with Kelly?"

"Andy, I just spent $45 million for this team," Pohlad said. "I want you to be the general manager. But at thirty-four, you're untested, and now you want me to hire a thirty-seven-year-old manager. I'm looking for some balance here."

Balance was found in the person of Ralph "The Major" Houk, who at age 68, was living comfortably in retirement, after having built a reputation in baseball as manager of pennant-winning Yankee teams in the early 1960s and later as a manager with Detroit and Boston. MacPhail urged Houk to accept a newly created job, vice president of personnel. He was to be a consultant to MacPhail and Kelly.

"Essentially, it was his job to bring comfort to the Pohlads so that they just didn't have a couple of rookies running their baseball team," said MacPhail.

Bert Blyleven, a man of many talents, chases down a rat in Cleveland Stadium. Unfortunately, it was a swing and a miss. COURTESY OF AP IMAGES.

"I think he prevented us from making some rookie mistakes. He just stayed a year or two. We couldn't even get him to come for the postseason in 1987. He did his thing here and rode into the sunset. He didn't care about getting credit for anything he'd done."

With Houk, the Pohlads were at least not totally uncomfortable having Kelly manage the 1987 team. In short order, they became Kelly's greatest admirers.

The stamp Kelly put on the team—play hard, don't get too up, don't get too down, play defense, respect the game, take care of your teammates, and have fun—remained with the team long after Kelly left following the 2001 season.

From his first spring training as manager until his last, Kelly emphasized defense. No player was excused from simple, boring, repetitive defensive drills.

There was one other special quality about Kelly: As much as he appreciated hard work and hustle, he also admired talent.

As a player, he managed to make it briefly to the big leagues with the Twins in 1975, getting 127 at bats. He hit just .181 and that was it. He'd made it that far on hard work alone. But his talent was short. He appreciated that which he didn't have. He loved guys like Hrbek, Gaetti, and Puckett because they got their uniforms dirty—and because they had talent.

He also respected the fact that no amount of managing was enough to win games.

"It's the players who hit the ball, catch the ball, pitch the ball, not me," he once said.

His most dramatic way of expressing his admiration for his players came following the last out of the 1987 World Series. They all raced onto the field, leaping on each other. Typically, managers join in this celebration. Kelly stayed on the bench. The players had made the plays. It was their time to celebrate.

But he never did get the public relations part of the job down. He never really tried. His weekly Sunday morning show on WCCO Radio with Sid Hartman may have been the crabbiest program in radio.

Earnest fans would call with a question for TK. If there was even a hint of second-guessing in the question—"why didn't you bunt in the third inning?"—Hartman would get angry and Kelly sarcastic. It was a devastating one-two punch for hapless callers who would try so hard not to insult, but always failed.

"That's a stupid question!" Hartman would say.

"Oh, I'm sure this guy used to coach in little league," Kelly would chime in.

It was brutal to listen to.

"I'd be listening on Sunday mornings," said Jerry Bell, "and I'd turn to my wife and say, 'Between Sid and TK, why does anyone call?'"

"We actually had people who would come in and work with TK on his radio, ummm, style," said MacPhail. "But it didn't do much good. He always was who he was."

Bell thinks that the mentor, Houk, was partially responsible for Kelly's often abrupt behavior with the media and fans. Bell, who'd replaced Fox as the team's president in January 1987, was visiting the team at spring training one day when a sports writer wandered into the dressing room shared by Kelly and Houk and asked a question.

"Usually, Houk just sat in the corner and kept his mouth shut," said Bell. "But for some reason, there was something about this question that set him off. He got up and really lit into the writer. 'You dumb son of a bitch. Why are you asking a question like that?' He just kept going and TK sat there listening. I think TK was thinking, 'Hmmm, this is good.'"

In 1986, the Twins had finished 20 games under .500. But good things had begun to happen. They had played better under Kelly, winning 12 and losing 11 in the last month of the season. Greg Gagne had established himself as the starting shortstop.

And on August 13, one of the most important symbolic changes came. Ron Davis was traded to the Chicago Cubs for two pitchers of little consequence, George Frazier and Ray Fontenot, with minor-leaguer Julius McDougal thrown into the deal.

Davis simply did not have the makeup to be an effective closer. He became legend for the games he blew, not the games he saved. There was much that was good about the pitcher known as RD. He could throw hard. He'd been an effective seventh and eighth inning pitcher when he was a member of the New York Yankees. He was the first player the Twins called on if there was a sick kid in a hospital who wanted a visit from a Twins player.

But as a closer, he was a flop. It got to the point where fans, his teammates, perhaps even RD himself, dreaded that moment when the manager— be it Gardner or Miller—went to the mound and called for RD. A Jamie Quirk moment always seemed imminent.

"RD was sort of the embodiment of the past," said MacPhail. "We thought we needed to make that change."

But that also meant that the Twins also had to find somebody to close out games. In early February 1987, MacPhail worked a deal with Montreal. The Twins would give up pitcher Neal Heaton, catcher Jeff Reed, and a couple of minor-leaguers to the Expos for closer Jeff Reardon and catcher Tom Nieto.

Before pulling the trigger on his first big deal, the Boy Wonder general manager turned to the team's new president, Bell.

"I'd been on the job for about two weeks," said Bell. "I honestly didn't know a thing about the National League or Jeff Reardon, but I did know that Heaton was a pretty good pitcher. I asked the most embarrassing question I ever asked Andy. I said, 'Ummm, did you talk to your dad about this?'"

MacPhail was not insulted by the question.

"As a matter of fact, I did," he said.

1987
Laughing to the Title

The World: In history's largest peacetime sea disaster, the passenger ferry *MV Doña Paz* collides with an oil tanker in the Tablas Strait in the Philippines and as many as 4,000 people are killed.

The Nation: President Ronald Reagan nominates Robert Bork to the Supreme Court in July and after contentious debates between the left and right, Bork is rejected by the Senate in October. In January, the Dow Jones Industrial Average hits 2,000 for the first time. It rises to 2,500 by July. And then it crashes by 23 percent on October 19, the new black Monday. Prozac gets FDA approval for use in the United States.

The State: A Carleton College political science professor, Paul Wellstone, becomes the state's campaign manager for Jesse Jackson's bid for the presidential nomination. Though he was born in Pittsburgh, August Wilson was at his most prolific in St. Paul, and receives the first of his two Pulitzer Prizes for his play, *Fences*.

Pop Culture: Billboard's #1 Song: "Walk like an Egyptian," by the Bangles. Best Picture: *The Last Emperor*. Best Seller: *The Tommyknockers*, by Stephen King. Top-Rated Television Show: *The Cosby Show*.

The Season: Kirby Puckett (28 homers, 99 RBI, .332 batting average) is sensational in leading the Twins to the postseason. Homer Hankies are introduced by the *Star Tribune* at the American League playoffs.

Over the course of a 162-game season, each team participates in around 8,700 plays, at bat and in the field, that result in outs. Good hitting teams score 800 runs, good pitching teams allow 700 runs. Teams will get 1,500 hits and give up about the same total. They'll walk 500 times and give up roughly the same number of bases on balls. Each team's staff will throw as many as 20,000 pitches. Players come and players go in a regular season that lasts about 180 days.

Amid all of those numbers, Bert Blyleven thinks the 1987 season might have come down to one play in the first inning of the 156th game.

The Twins, despite a woeful road record, were leading the weak Western Division of the American League. The final home stand of the season had started on a promising note, with the Twins winning six straight over Cleveland and Texas. Then the Kansas City Royals came to town, trailing the Twins by seven games with only nine games left in the season.

But the Royals won the first game of the series, cutting the Twins' lead to six. They won the second game, cutting the lead to five. And then, in the first inning of the Twins' final home game of the season, the Royals had Kevin Seitzer on first and Willie Wilson on third with nobody out and George Brett stepped to the plate.

"I've always wondered what would have happened if they got that run home and taken the lead in that game," said Blyleven, the starting pitcher that day.

But they never got that run. Brett hit a grounder to Gary Gaetti at third. Gaetti fielded the ball and threw to Al Newman, who was covering second. So far, so good.

The by-the-book play would have been for Newman to throw to first to complete a double play and allow Wilson to score the run. Newman, though, played it differently.

"I'm watching Newmie take the throw at second and thinking, 'Okay, Newmie take your time,'" recalled Blyleven, "and all of a sudden the baseball's coming right at my head. I mean it's going to hit me right between the eyes. I'm thinking, 'What the hell!' I'm ducking and it dawns on me, 'He's trying to get Wilson at home.'"

Newman fired to catcher Tim Laudner who put the tag on the sliding—and very surprised—Wilson.

"That play right there relaxed us," said Blyleven. "We went on, won the game and clinched the division a day later in Texas. I still think about it. I see that ball coming at my head and Newmie making the damndest play I've ever saw."

After taking a throw from Gary Gaetti, Kent Hrbek stepped on first base, then leaped in the air—
and the celebration of the Twins World Series triumph over the St. Louis Cardinals had begun.
COURTESY OF THE *ST. PAUL PIONEER PRESS*.

Blyleven got out of the inning without giving up a run, Kirby Puckett hit a two-run homer in the bottom of the first and the Twins, before 53,106 screaming fans, rolled to an 8–1 victory.

They headed to Texas with a six-game lead with six games to go. Second baseman Steve Lombardozzi was the hero of the division-clinching night, hitting a three-run, game-tying homer in the fourth inning and driving in the go-ahead run in the eighth as the Twins won, 5–3.

Oh, how the division winners partied that night. They didn't care that they'd just won the weakest division in baseball. In 1986, they'd lost 91 games. Now, they were number one.

After the party, they went back to work—and promptly lost their last five games of the season, two in Texas and three in Kansas City, finishing the season with an 85–77 record. They had only nine road victories after the All-Star Game. They finished the season with a woeful 29–53 road record. They ended up just two games ahead of the Royals. What if Newman hadn't made that throw....

A million little things—some planned, some, like Newman's throw, that seem to come from out of the mists—go into a winning season.

Entering the '87 season, there was no real sense in the Twins organization that this was a championship level team. General manager Andy MacPhail has always said that in many ways the 1991 championship season was more gratifying than 1987. The second title was "planned." 1987 was a scramble.

Entering the season, MacPhail did make a number of small deals that turned out to be huge. The first was the deal with Montreal that brought backup catcher Tom Nieto and closer Jeff Reardon to the Twins.

Later that month, he traded two more young pitchers, Mike Shade and Jose Dominguez, to Montreal for Newman, an invaluable utility infielder.

In the final days of training camp, pitchers Bryan Hickerson and Ray Velasquez were traded to San Francisco for an outfielder, Dan Gladden. Gladden was supposed to give the Twins a leadoff hitter and some fire. He did both, though when he showed up, he was almost silent.

"The only guys I knew were Newman and Reardon, cuz I'd played against 'em," he said. "When you're the new guy, you keep your mouth shut [he laughed] for awhile. What I did like was that when I got there they were passing out the new uniforms. They'd gotten rid of those old baby blues and we're going to those classy uniforms with pinstripes."

Gladden immediately liked the feel of his new home. The Twins locker room was filled with laughter. On the day the new uniforms were being distributed, the players proudly strutted about in their new classic look.

Spontaneous celebrations broke out across downtown Minneapolis—and in family rooms across the region—on the night that the Twins defeated the St. Louis Cardinals and became World Series champs. COURTESY OF THE *ST. PAUL PIONEER PRESS.*

In the midst of the festivities, Roy Smalley, who had returned to the Twins prior to the '85 season, stood in the middle of the dressing room, acting outraged.

"Hey!" he yelled.

His teammates all looked toward him.

"This isn't right! Hrbek's got more stripes on his uniform than I've got on mine!"

The players roared.

The Twins could laugh. They could drink remarkable amounts of beer. They could hit for power. They could field. But they had no starting pitching, beyond Blyleven and Viola.

MacPhail spent the entire season trying to find at least one more reliable starter to fit into the mix. Joe Niekro arrived in June. He'd been a star, but after twenty years in the majors, he was at the end of the line. His biggest con-

Kirby Puckett shares his joy with the thousands of fans at the state capitol on October 27, a day that found Minnesota closed for business to celebrate a championship. COURTESY OF THE *ST. PAUL PIONEER PRESS*.

tribution to the '87 Twins was that on August 3, he was caught with a fingernail file in his pocket while on the mound.

Niekro always insisted that he had the file because, between innings, he filed his nails so he'd have a better grip on his knuckleball. He'd simply forgotten to leave the file on the bench, he said.

He was suspended for ten games and made the best of the situation by appearing on the David Letterman show during the suspension. For that appearance, he wore a carpenter's apron and carried a power sander.

On July 31, pitching legend Steve Carlton came to the Twins from Cleveland for a player to be named later. Like Niekro, there was nothing left in Carlton's once mighty arm.

In the end, the Twins never did find a third starting pitcher of substance. In fact, pitching was always a problem during the season.

So, back to those little things that make a big difference. On June 3, in Boston, the Twins had lost for a second night in a row when the Red Sox scored in the bottom of the ninth.

"I was walking out of the clubhouse with Gaetti and Gladden," Smalley recalled. "Everybody was pissed about the pitching. It was really tense. You could just feel the tension. TK gets on the bus and he obviously could tell what was going on. He gets up and says, 'I don't want to hear any shit about pitchers. We're rowing this boat together.'"

For Kelly it was a long speech. But it seemed to work.

The players spent the rest of the season rowing the boat. Before every game, Gaetti recalls, players would say things like, "Did you bring your oar today?" They'd mimic rowing the boat and laugh, and they advanced to the playoffs, the first team ever to do so that allowed more runs than they scored.

Once they hit the postseason, Blyleven and Viola and a remarkably resilient bullpen were enough. In the playoffs and the World Series, Viola and Blyleven combined for a 6–2 record. In ten postseason victories, the Twins won only one game not started by their Big Two, that was the sixth game of the World Series when Les Straker started and Dan Schatzeder, in relief, was credited with the victory.

Ultimately, this was a team too loose to lose. They went into the postseason with a perfect, hell-raising attitude.

After beating heavily-favored Detroit in just five games, after their huge small-town welcome back at the Dome, the Twins were determined to have even more fun in the World Series against a battered St. Louis team. The Cardinals' most powerful hitter, Jack Clark, was out with an injury. Their Gold Glove third baseman, Terry Pendleton, couldn't play in the field because of a rib injury.

Still, the Cards had the magnificent back-flipping Ozzie Smith at short and Vince Coleman, who stole 109 bases, at the top of the order. The Cardinals also had manager Whitey Herzog and experience. This was their third trip to the World Series in six years.

Herzog was comfortable in the environment and enjoyed the bull sessions with reporters, often using them to attempt to gain competitive advantage. For example, after the second game of the series, he complained that Blyleven wasn't pausing long enough in his delivery when the Cardinals had runners on base. Obviously, Herzog wanted both Blyleven and umpires to see the story.

Blyleven did see it and he laughed.

"Tell Whitey not to bother if he's tying to mess with my mind," Blyleven told writers. "I have no mind."

When reporters delivered the message to Herzog, he chuckled.

"I know," he said.

But the Cardinals were not prepared to step into the first World Series ever played in a Dome. The place was bursting with noise and it kept getting louder and louder.

Cardinal players bought earplugs. Twins fans bought earplugs. Noise became the event's story line.

Networks brought in devices to check the sound level. They reported that it was 110 decibels, as loud as standing next to a jet airplane at takeoff. And the noise grew louder.

Many were offended. There was this from *New York Times* television sports columnist Michael Goodman: "For baseball, that level of noise is exciting occasionally and distracting mostly. Let's hope spectators across the country don't get the idea that their team will win it if they make jet-proportion noises."

The Twins were lifted by it. They blew open the first game when Gladden hit a grand slam and Lombardozzi hit a two-run homer in a 7-run fourth inning en route to a 10–1 victory. There was more of the same in the second game. This time, the Twins scored 6 runs in the fourth inning and won easily, 8–4.

As both teams headed to St. Louis, the World Series stopped being so important in most of the country. Monday, October 19, an off-day in the Series, became grimly known as "Black Monday." The stock market plunged 508.32 points, or 22 percent of value. It was the biggest dive since 1939. Patrick Reusse, a sports columnist with the *St. Paul Pioneer Press* at the time, figured he understood the reason for the crash.

"The Twins lead the World Series, 2–0. Something's not right with the world."

The players barely noticed. Professional athletes live in an isolated place, far from war, peace, and stock market crashes.

"Citizens of the world we're not," said Smalley. "In general, players are self-absorbed first, team absorbed second."

In truth, most Minnesotans likely were more absorbed with their suddenly-beloved baseball team than the market for these few days in October. That's because, in St. Louis, the Twins plunged, too, losing three straight to the Cardinals. To make matters worse, their two aces, Viola and Blyleven, were the losing pitchers.

That meant the Twins were on the brink of elimination with the nervous rookie, Straker, headed to the mound. The Twins' solution to the problem: Good timing.

Don Baylor, a mighty hitter in his day, had been picked up by the Twins on August 31. But during the final month of the regular season, the playoff series with Detroit, and the first five games of the World Series, Baylor had not hit a home run. That all changed with one swing in the fifth inning of Game 6. With the Twins trailing, 4–2, Baylor crushed a two-run homer to left, tying the game.

Then, in the sixth, Hrbek, who'd been struggling throughout the playoffs, stepped to the plate with the bases loaded and two outs. Herzog brought in a lefty, Ken Dayley, to face Hrbek.

In his book, *Tales from the Dugout*, Hrbek said he looked to the bench and saw Kelly making an "S" sign across his chest, which meant, "Don't try to be Superman. Just get the bat on the ball."

He did. On the first pitch he saw from Dayley, Hrbek swung and the ball didn't land until it had traveled 439 feet, over the fence in center. The grand slam led the Twins to an 11–5 victory and Game 7.

They approached it laughing. Hrbek started the day by going duck hunting. Others looked for practical jokes. Trailing 2–1 in the fifth, the Twins noticed that public address announcer Bob Casey had left his little booth located behind home plate to use the bathroom, located just off the Twins' dugout.

Tom Brunansky held the bathroom door shut. Casey couldn't get out. In the meantime, other players went to his booth and put shaving cream on the telephone and in a towel Casey kept handy. The Twins released Casey, who was screaming in anger, from the bathroom just in time for him to do his announcing chores for the bottom of the fifth inning. When he got back to the booth, a player made a call from the dugout to Casey. He picked up the phone

The parade through Minneapolis and St. Paul sometimes came to a complete stop, as it did here on Wabasha Street, as fans mobbed their team. COURTESY OF THE *ST. PAUL PIONEER PRESS*.

and his ear was covered with shaving cream. He grabbed the towel to clean his ear and ended up with shaving cream all over his face.

The Twins, laughing, scored a run in the bottom of the fifth to tie the game, scored another in the sixth to go ahead and Viola and Reardon put down the Cards.

It was celebration time in Minnesota. No longer was this the state of runners-up—of the Twins losing the '65 World Series, the Vikings losing four Super Bowls, of Hubert Humphrey and Walter Mondale losing presidential bids.

"When it counted," said Gaetti, "we were the best team in baseball."

There was dancing inside the Dome and outside. There was a huge parade. ("We felt like we were astronauts," said Gaetti.) But the sweetest scene of all may have been in the crowded corridors of the Dome. Following the Twins' triumph and their victory lap around the field, Calvin Griffith stepped out from his suite and into the corridor. He was immediately recognized by hundreds of fans.

They cheered Griffith and patted him on the back and shook his hand. They understood that this was the team he had built. Tears came to the old man's eyes.

1988

God's Squad?

The World: After eight years, the Soviet Union begins withdrawing its troops from Afghanistan. Benazir Bhutto becomes prime minister of Pakistan, the first woman to lead an Islamic state.

The Nation: George H. W. Bush defeats Michael Dukakis in the presidential election. The Evangelical Lutheran Church in America is formed, becoming the largest Lutheran denomination in the country.

The State: Zebra mussels are discovered in the Great Lakes. The Indian Gaming Regulatory Act is passed in the state legislature, creating a casino boom on tribal lands. Record drought scours the state. *St. Paul Pioneer Press* reporter Jacqui Banaszynski receives a Pulitzer Prize for feature writing.

Pop Culture: Grammy Song of the Year: "Don't Worry, Be Happy," by Bobby McFerrin. Best Picture: *Rain Man.* Pulitzer Prize for Fiction: *Beloved,* by Toni Morrison. Top-Rated Television Show: *The Cosby Show.*

The Season: The Twins win six more games than they won in 1987, but finish second, to Oakland, in the American League West. Kirby Puckett hits .356, which would be the highest of his career, but finishes behind Wade Boggs who wins the A.L. batting title by hitting .366.

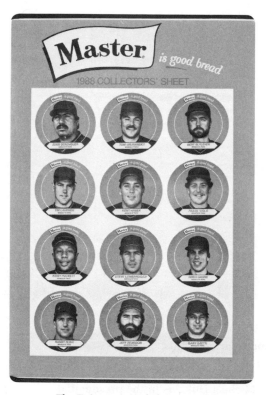

The Twins remained the toast of the towns entering the 1988 season. FROM THE COLLECTION OF CLYDE DOEPNER; PHOTO BY ROBERT FOGT.

Twins players were shocked. Tommy Herr arrived in Minnesota with a Bible in his hands, a tear in his eye, and a broken heart. Who was this guy?

Just thirteen games into a new season after winning the World Series, Twins general manager Andy MacPhail, the Boy Wonder who could do no wrong, decided that a change was needed in the Twins clubhouse and in the lineup. The Twins were off to a 4–9 start and MacPhail, with the advice and consent of manager Tom Kelly, sent Tom Brunansky to the St. Louis Cardinals for second baseman Tom Herr.

At first, sports scribes praised the April 22 deal. Wrote *Star Tribune* sports columnist Dan Barreiro: "This is a trade that will make the Twins a better team." MacPhail, Kelly, and the writers thought the deal made sense because they believed the Twins were getting a hard-nosed, clutch-hitting second baseman. As a switch hitter, he would be ideal at the top of the order. At thirty-two, Herr had been an over-achieving All-Star in St. Louis, where he was beloved by the game's most knowledgeable fans. Why wouldn't he be the same sort of player in Minnesota?

The Cardinals were willing to part with Herr because they feared they would lose him to free agency at the end of the season, plus they needed power. The Twins were willing to part with Brunansky because he was a streak hitter of the Bob Allison mold. Brunansky was hitting just .184 with one home run when the deal was made. But he was part of the team's inner circle, a close friend to core players on a close-knit team.

"It's like a cold shower with a slap in the face thrown in," Gaetti told *St. Paul Pioneer Press* sportswriter Mike Augustin on the night of the deal. "I'll remain good friends with Tom Brunansky whether he's on the same field with me or not."

As it turned out, Herr was even more shocked and hurt than the Twins players. "It's really hard to say goodbye," he said as he packed up his gear in St. Louis. "I wanted to play my whole career here and that dream is out the window."

The deal seemed to break his spirit. He arrived in Minnesota and moped. On a team filled with players who liked everybody, Herr quickly became disliked by many of his teammates.

"This was one of those deals that within eight days you knew it was a big mistake," said MacPhail years later.

Herr did accomplish one extraordinary thing. He turned sportswriters into students of religion. They believed Herr didn't just play poorly—when he played at all—but that he undermined the chemistry of the clubhouse by turning Gaetti on to Jesus.

There were high hopes for Tommy Herr when he stepped to the plate for the first time as a member of the Twins. The trade of Tom Brunansky for Herr drew positive reviews from sports writers—for a few days. But Herr was unhappy with the deal and, within a few days, Twins management was, too. COURTESY OF THE *ST. PAUL PIONEER PRESS*.

Tom Brunansky was a big part of the team—both in the lineup and in the clubhouse—and tears were shed when he was traded to St. Louis for Herr. Former Twins executive Andy MacPhail said it likely was the worst deal in team history. COURTESY OF THE *ST. PAUL PIONEER PRESS.*

Wrote *Star Tribune* sports columnist Sid Hartman in his book *Sid!:* "Herr spent the whole season in the trainer's room. Even worse, he was pushing religion in the clubhouse. He gave Gary Gaetti a pamphlet about the world coming to an end. Gaetti jumped in with both feet, so much so that he went downhill as a player for a couple of years."

Gaetti did undergo a conversion in 1988 and shortstop Greg Gagne also was a born-again Christian. That gave the Twins the prayingest infield in major-league baseball. All the prayers and Bibles caused Kelly to raise his eyebrows. This was not the clubhouse he had known.

Hrbek was saddened because when Gaetti found the Lord, Herbie lost his best friend. Not only did Gaetti stop smoking, chugging beer, and raising hell, he told Hrbek that it was time for the big first baseman to repent, too. Hrbek told Gaetti to keep his religion to himself.

Watching Gaetti, affectionately known as the Rat, change before their eyes did nothing to endear Herr to his new teammates. In the eyes of Twins players, Herr had to be the one responsible for converting Gaetti. What else could explain such a huge transformation? But Gaetti scoffs at the notion that Herr was responsible for his conversion or that his lifestyle change changed him in any way as a ballplayer.

"My conversion was the result of a series of events," said Gaetti in a 2009 interview. "There were personal things going on with me that got me to reflecting on my life. 'Who am I becoming? What am I doing with my life?' I wasn't happy with the answers I was getting to those questions. There wasn't one moment. I did some reading. I had conversations with Gagne and a special call from my brother-in-law that touched me."

Gaetti was saddened by "the public beating I took" over something that was so deeply important to him. People were reacting negatively to something that he felt he needed. Prayer wasn't the Twins' problem in 1988, he said.

"The Oakland A's had some extremely strong guys," he said, a reference to the beginning of baseball's steroid era. "They were incredible."

With or without religion, the Twins of 1988 were better than the World Series team. They won more games (91 victories as opposed to 85 wins in 1987). They scored nearly as many runs, while their pitchers allowed a staggering 134 fewer runs. They also were a huge hit at the gate, becoming the first team in American League history to attract more than three million fans.

Though relationships changed in the club, there were still fires burning in the bellies of the Twins. Dan Gladden, for example, exhibited that fire all over the face of Steve Lombardozzi outside Gladden's Twin Cities apartment on Thursday, July 21.

Gladden never had been a big Lombardozzi fan, thinking he too often put himself ahead of the team.

On Wednesday, July 20, the Twins were playing in Boston and, late in the game, Kelly called on Kelvin Torve, a seldom used rookie, to bat for Lombo. Lombardozzi was furious. He stalked off the field, through the dugout and into the clubhouse. Torve made an out and Gladden was ready to explode. He wasn't angry at Torve, but at Lombardozzi.

After the game, he approached the second baseman and said that Lombardozzi was putting himself in front of the team; that Lombardozzi should have stayed in the dugout after he was lifted, and pulled for his teammate. Lombo didn't want to hear it. He told Gladden to back off and mind his own business. Gladden had more strong words for Lombardozzi. The tension was still at the breaking point as the team left the clubhouse and headed for the airport. As the players were boarding the plane, Kelly was heard to say to Gladden, "Whatever you're gonna do, don't do it on the plane. The boss [MacPhail] is on the plane."

The team had an off day on Thursday. Gladden was at home, playing with his daughters, when Lombo knocked on the door. More words were exchanged. The two stepped outside and fists flew. Lombo showed up at the Dome for the game Friday with bruises on his face.

"Two men had a disagreement and they settled it like men," Kelly told reporters. "It's done. It's over with. My understanding is that everything's hunky dory. It's probably better it happened."

To this day, players such as Gaetti and Hrbek praise Gladden and Lombardozzi for "settling their differences" away from the clubhouse.

In an indirect way, it is possible to even blame that brawl on Herr. No Twins player was more hurt by the arrival of Herr than Lombardozzi. In 1987, he'd been a key player down the stretch—coming through with big hit after big hit in the final games of the regular season and through the playoffs and World Series—and suddenly it was clear the Twins weren't satisfied with him. At the end of the '88 season, Lombardozzi was traded to Houston and was out of baseball by 1990.

Through it all, the prayers and fights and wins, and huge crowds at the Dome, the Twins simply couldn't keep pace with an Oakland team that won 104 games. The A's had come up with a new form of team chemistry. In 1988, huge, muscular Jose Canseco hit 42 homers, stole 40 bases and was the American League's Most Valuable Player, and Mark McGwire also hit for power, with 32 homers.

Some of the secrets of the A's success may have come out in a book Canseco wrote in 2005, *Juiced: Wild Times, Rampant 'Roids, Smash Hits and How Baseball Got Big*. In it, Canseco wrote that he, McGwire and other members of the A's had discovered the wonders of steroids in 1988.

Canseco's revelations, which at first were denied by everybody in baseball, enlightened and angered Gagne. He recalled that when he first saw McGwire and Canseco in 1988 he was amazed at how big they were.

"I remember thinking, 'Geez, those guys must really lift weights,'" Gagne said. "Then all the other stuff [about steroids] started coming out and all I can think is that they stole a couple of more division titles from us. They took money out of our pockets. Without that, maybe we could have been in a couple more World Series."

At the end of the season, MacPhail sent Tommy Herr to the Philadelphia Phillies and said that he'd never again make a deal for a player "without knowing more about the man." Brunansky had a very nice season in St. Louis, where he hit 22 homers, drove in 79 runs and was lauded for being a great team player.

Years after the deal, MacPhail was asked, "Which was the bigger blunder, MacPhail's trade for Tommy Herr or Terry Ryan's decision in 2003 to simply release David Ortiz?"

"At least Terry didn't give up Tom Brunansky in his deal," MacPhail said. "I guess that makes my deal the worst."

1989

Sweet Music Sours

The World: The Berlin Wall comes tumbling down on November 9, twenty-eight years after construction began on the huge symbol of repression. Students protest on Tiananmen Square in Beijing, and the Chinese Army opens fire on the protesters, killing between 3,000 and 7,000 people.

The Nation: The oil tanker *Exxon Valdez* runs aground and spills 10.8 million gallons of crude oil on Alaska shorelines. U.S. forces invade Panama, eventually arresting former strongman Manuel Noriega.

The State: Jacob Wetterling, eleven years old, is kidnapped from his home near St. Joseph on October 22.

Pop Culture: Milli Vanilli receives a Grammy Award; it's later learned that the duo was lip-synching. Best Picture: *Driving Miss Daisy*. Salman Rushdie writes *Satanic Verses* and faces a fatwa issued by Ayatollah Khomeini. Top-Rated Television Show: *Roseanne*.

The Season: Kirby Puckett wins his only batting title (.339) but Twins slip below .500, 80–82. Baseball's story of the year: Pete Rose is banned for betting on games while he was the manager of the Cincinnati Reds.

Frankie "Sweet Music" Viola loved to talk, but sometimes the words sped ahead of his thoughts. That's what happened in the spring of '89, he says. He was talking faster than he was thinking. The Twins had made him what he saw as an inferior contract offer in spring training and he was upset.

"I made a stupid comment. I said something like, 'If the Twins don't want to give me a contract, then I'll play out the season and check out free agency.' That's the last thing Midwest fans wanted to hear."

Viola, the Most Valuable Player of the 1987 World Series, the 1988 Cy Young Award winner after compiling a 24–7 record, was suddenly seen by many Twins fans as just another greedy ballplayer.

"We came north that spring and I took my kids, my son and my two daughters, to the circus," Viola said. "We get to the circus and they introduce me and I get booed! It didn't bother me, though you don't expect to get booed when you take your kids to the circus. But it bothered the hell out of my kids. The next week, there's a little ceremony on the field where I get the Cy Young Award. The fans were just sort of quiet. It got to the point that I knew I was gone."

Viola became the second member of the Class of '82 to leave the Twins. (Tom Brunansky had been the first to go in the disastrous Tommy Herr deal.) He was traded to the New York Mets on July 31, for four unknowns, Rick Aguilera, Tim Drummond, Kevin Tapani, and David West.

"What's funny about that deal is that West was supposed to be the key guy the Twins were getting," said Viola.

It didn't turn out that way. Aguilera and Tapani would become key components of the 1991 World Series championship team. West was one of those players always on the verge of fulfilling expectations.

The trade of the twenty-nine-year-old Viola was greeted with a huge sigh of relief by virtually everyone in the Twins' organization, including the players. The team was struggling and Viola had become a distraction and, to make matters worse, he was pitching poorly. He had an 8–12 record at the time of the deal. Viola, in retrospect, thinks his poor pitching was a result of his contract status.

"I was a lousy contract year player," he said, referring to the fact that he was in the final year of a contract. "Some players are great contract-year players. Manny Ramirez, Carlos Beltran, those guys. But I'm the sort of guy who puts more pressure on myself."

Tom Kelly and pitching coach Dick Such did everything they could to get inside Viola's head. They called him into Kelly's office for meetings.

"TK would ask, 'What's going on in your head,'" Viola said. "He'd say, 'Just relax, you're a great pitcher. Just relax.'"

But Viola couldn't relax. His teammates started seeing him as a "me-first" guy, which was not a fit in a Twins clubhouse filled with "team-first" players.

Andy MacPhail, who still was a young general manager, looks back with regret on how he handled the Twins' negotiations with Viola.

Frank Viola, a hero of the 1987 Twins, ended up in a New York Mets uniform by 1989. COURTESY OF AP IMAGES.

"When you get into those circumstances, it's generally never one-sided," MacPhail said in a 2009 interview. "Looking back, I would have done a lot of things differently. We should have made a contract offer quicker and we should not have let things go public. Everything just went sour. I remember seeing a cartoon somebody put up in the clubhouse of Hagar. It showed a bunch of guys in a Viking ship rowing, masculine guys in helmets. There was one guy, a boy, standing in the boat, saying, 'I can't row, I have a blister.' It just got to the point where there had to be a change and, in retrospect, I feel I was responsible for that."

When he was dealt, Viola felt bitter toward the Twins and MacPhail. It wasn't until fifteen years after the trade, when he was working as an analyst with ESPN in 2004 that Viola said he sat down with Andy MacPhail, who by then was president of the Chicago Cubs, and learned the Twins' side of the story of his trade.

"I'd always liked Andy when I was with the Twins," said Viola. "I'd thought he was a good person, but after the trade I'd carried around a lot of dislike for him. Then we sat down and he talked to me about their side of the story. He told me he knew I'd be gone during spring training [of 1989]. He told me I was to go to the Yankees. But then Dwight Gooden [of the Mets] got hurt. He explained the whole thing. He said, 'We knew we needed to refurbish our pitching. But how could I trade Hrbek, Puckett, or Gaetti?' So they decided to trade their best pitcher. That helped me understand. I got over my bitterness."

Stepping into the Mets clubhouse for the first time was a jolt for Viola. In Minnesota, going to the clubhouse had been a daily joy. Card games, laughter, music, friends, and baseball, who could ask for anything more? In New York, it was so different. There was a coolness about the place and bickering everywhere. In Minnesota, the star players were also the best guys to be around. In New York, the star, Darryl Strawberry, was always mad at somebody.

Viola got a multimillion-dollar contract from the Mets. He was a 20-game winner for the team in 1990, but the game was never as much fun as it had been with the Twins.

"What's that people say?" Viola said. "'You don't know what you got 'til it's gone.' That's what it was like for me."

Following the 1991 season, Viola, a free agent again, signed a three-year, multimillion-dollar deal with the Boston Red Sox. In his first two years, he was reasonably effective but was injured in most of the third season. He faded out of the big leagues, with stops at Cincinnati and Toronto, and retired following the 1996 season.

His son, Frankie Jr., was a professional ballplayer, a pitcher. But arm injuries stopped him from ever making it to the majors. One of his daughters, Brittany, is a national collegiate diving champion with Olympic aspirations.

Viola, meantime, has been a high school baseball coach, and in 2009 went to work with the Cleveland Indians as a spring training pitching instructor. And, in his heart, corny as it sounds, he's a Minnesota Twin with genuine appreciation of Twins fans.

For starters, he said, how could he not love Minnesota? He met the love of his life, Kathy Daltas, at a Twins game. She was a graduate student who had a part-time job selling tickets at the Dome. After the ticket booths were closed, she'd find a seat in the stands, study, and watch baseball. In the meantime, on the field, Viola watched her.

"I had good eyes then," he said.

The two met and married and have lived happily ever after.

There is something else that's special about his old workplace, Viola said.

"You talk forgiveness," he said. "People in the Midwest are the best. I go back now and it's like none of the bad stuff ever happened. They like to think about the good stuff that happened. I love that about the Midwest. It would be a great thing for people in other parts of the country to learn."

1990

An Angel Booed

The World: Iraq invades Kuwait, ignoring warnings from President George H. W. Bush and the United Nations to retreat. After twenty-seven years, Nelson Mandela is released from a South African prison.

The Nation: Washington, D.C., Mayor Marion Barry is arrested on a crack cocaine charge.

The State: Soviet President Mikhail Gorbachev, recipient of the 1990 Nobel Peace Prize, visits Minnesota. *Star Tribune* reporters Chris Ison and Lou Kilzer receive a Pulitzer Prize for Investigative Reporting. Arne Carlson, a last-moment replacement for scandal-plagued Jon Grunseth on the ballot, defeats two-time incumbent and three-time Governor Rudy Perpich in the November election. Paul Wellstone defeats incumbent Rudy Boschwitz in a stunning U.S. Senate race and takes his famous green bus to D.C.

Pop Culture: The Three Tenors—Luciano Pavarotti, Placido Domingo, and Jose Carreras—sing together for the first time. Highest-Grossing Movie: *Ghost.* Best Seller: *The Plains of Passage,* by Jean M. Auel. Top-Rated Television Show: *Cheers.*

The Season: With virtually no reliable starting pitching, the Twins fulfill the "last" portion of their last-to-first turnaround, compiling a 74–88 record. Shane Mack is the one bright spot. Acquired from San Diego, the former collegiate All-America bats .326.

Andy MacPhail likes to say that in 1987, "We won the World Series while we were trying to get organized." As an executive, he feels much better about the World Series title that came in 1991, because the team that won that championship was "planned."

If there was a master plan, it looked pretty shaky following a 1990 season in which the Twins crashed to dead last in the American League West, twenty-nine games behind the division-winning Oakland A's. The Twins were the awful blend of no offense (they ranked twelfth in runs scored and thirteenth in home runs) and no pitching (they ranked tenth in runs allowed). Kent Hrbek was their top home run hitter and he had only 22. The "big four" of their pitching rotation had a combined record of 31–45.

To make matters worse, Gary Gaetti signed a contract with the California Angels following the 1990 season. Gaetti was sad about leaving, but felt he had no choice.

"I had gone in to meet with Carl Pohlad," Gaetti said. "We talked for a long time. He said, 'What's it gonna take.' I said I wanted the same thing Hrbek's getting. We shook hands, I left and I never heard anything. In the end, they finally made an offer, a one-year deal, but it was nothing close to what the Angels were offering."

Gaetti signed a three-year, $8.4 million contract with California and was startled in 1991 at the reception he received the first time he showed up at the Dome wearing an Angels uniform.

"I got booed out of the ballpark," he said. "I couldn't believe it. It was hard, really hard."

What few in Minnesota ever realized about Gaetti was that he was probably the most softhearted guy on the team. Sure he was called the Rat. And sure he was a tough-as-nails player. But nobody cried harder than Gaetti when the team was greeted by that thunderous ovation at the Dome after winning the American League pennant in 1987. Nobody loved his team or the Twin Cities more than Gaetti in his early years in the big leagues.

So it was hard for him when people seemed to turn away from him when he was "born again" in 1988, and it was downright painful when he was booed by the Twins crowd in 1991.

Long after his career was over—after productive years in Kansas City and St. Louis—Gaetti came back to the Dome in 2007 to be inducted into the Twins Hall of Fame. He received a huge ovation. He was thrilled. All was forgiven on all sides.

"I bawled like a baby," said Gaetti. "It was the greatest thing that ever happened to me as a ballplayer."

First it was religion that put some distance between close friends Kent Hrbek and Gary Gaetti. Then it was business that separated them. Following the 1990 season, Gaetti signed with the California Angels. COURTESY OF THE *ST. PAUL PIONEER PRESS*.

But back in 1990, Gaetti's departure meant that the Twins had another huge hole to fill. He'd had a mediocre season, batting just .229 in the '90 season. But he had hit 16 homers and driven in a team-leading 85 runs and he had been a four-time Gold Glove award winner at third base. His departure also meant that the Twins had lost a fourth member of the vaunted Class of 1982. Tom Brunansky was traded in 1988, Frank Viola in 1989 (he was a 20-game winner for the Mets in 1990), and Tim Laudner reluctantly retired after the 1989 season.

There had been a couple of bright spots in the 1990 season. Rick Aguilera had been converted from a starting pitcher to a closer and had saved 32 games. Additionally, Scott Erickson had been remarkable. In just his second year of professional ball, the Twins called him up to the majors and on June 25 he started his first game. He was twenty-two, handsome, and it turned out he could pitch, going six innings in a 9–1 victory over the Texas Rangers. By season's end he had an 8–4 record and hot rumors about his dating life circulated throughout the Minneapolis Warehouse District.

Generally, though, the MacPhail "plan" was full of holes.

MacPhail started plugging them on January 7, 1991, signing Mike Pagliarulo, a free agent third baseman who'd been with the New York Yankees and the San Diego Padres in his steady career. This deal was made only after MacPhail stepped into a debate between the team's scouting department and manager Tom Kelly. The scouting people wanted MacPhail to go after Jim Presley, a free agent who had hit 19 home runs and driven in 72 runs for the Atlanta Braves in 1990. But Kelly kept insisting on Pagliarulo, who'd had a very quiet, 7-home run, 38 RBI year in San Diego.

"They kept going back and forth," MacPhail said. "Our scouting reports on Presley were good. TK kept saying 'Pags.' The scouts would say, 'He's got no range.' He said he liked the way Pagliarulo played. I finally said, 'Why am I ramming someone down his throat he doesn't want? Let's give him the guy he believes in.'"

Three weeks after Pagliarulo was signed, the Twins announced that they had signed free agent Chili Davis, who had long been a feared hitter for the California Angels and the San Francisco Giants. He was, however, a danger to himself with a glove on his hand. Davis was hired—for $1.7 million—because the Twins had become punchless. But it turned out that the Twins got much more than they bargained for in Davis.

"We'd had some reservations about Chili, but he seemed like the best option available," said MacPhail. "We had no idea what a good guy he turned out to be. He had the most wonderful, positive way about him. It was just little things. In spring training he walked past Chuck Knoblauch one day and said, 'You're the best rookie I've ever played with. Keep working, you're going to be special.' You don't know how much that means to a rookie. Chili was constantly doing things like that."

A week after Davis was signed, St. Paul's own, Jack Morris, signed a one-year, $3.7 million contract after winning 198 games over 19 seasons in Detroit. The plan suddenly looked a whole lot better.

1991
Greatest Show on Earth

The World: Led by U.S. troops and air power, UN forces invade Iraq and liberate Kuwait. The war begins on January 16 and a ceasefire is declared on February 27. With the Baltic states declaring their independence, the Soviet Union crumbles. Boris Yeltsin replaces Gorbachev as the leader of the Russian Republic.

The Nation: In spite of sexual harassment charges, Clarence Thomas wins Senate confirmation and a seat on the U.S. Supreme Court. The Los Angeles Lakers' Earvin "Magic" Johnson announces that he is HIV positive.

The State: A Halloween snowstorm dumps 28.4 inches of snow on the Twin Cities, while Duluth receives 36.9 inches, the largest snowfall ever recorded in the state in a single storm event. The University of Minnesota's "Gopher" becomes the first user-friendly Internet interface.

Pop Culture: Billboard's #1 Song: "(Everything I Do) I Do It for You," by Bryan Adams. Best Picture: *The Silence of the Lambs.* Pulitzer Prize for Fiction: *Rabbit at Rest,* by John Updike. Top-Rated Television Show: *60 Minutes.*

The Season: Only two players—Chili Davis and Kent Hrbek—have 20 or more homers and no member of the team has 100 RBI, but Twins finish eight games ahead of the White Sox to win the Western Division. The Pittsburgh Pirates have the best record in baseball, 98–64, but lose in the playoffs to the Atlanta Braves.

The greatest World Series ever. That's what *Sports Illustrated* and ESPN both called it. Twins versus Braves, seven games. Homer Hanky redux. Kirby Puckett's magnificence. ("Into deep left center, for Mitchell.... and we'll see you tomorrow night!" was the famous call of CBS sportscaster Jack Buck as Puckett's drive carried into the seats, giving the Twins a 4–3, eleven-inning victory over the Braves in the sixth game of the series.) From last to first. Kent Hrbek's pro wrestling move. The tomahawk chop. Tribal culture clashes. It all happened over an eight-day period in October. The greatest World Series ever. Who could argue?

The big drama was the sum of many smaller dramas.

St. Paul native Jack Morris was the Twins starting pitcher in the classic Game 7. Inning after inning, the thirty-six-year-old pitcher mowed down the Braves. But the Twins couldn't score, either, and after nine innings the game was tied, 0–0.

Twins manager Tom Kelly was restless and tempted to remove Morris from the game. Kelly sent his pitching coach, Dick Such, to speak to Morris at the end of the bench. The conversation, as Morris recalls it, went like this:

The 1991 World Series, called by many the best in baseball history, was dramatic on and off the field. Twin Cities American Indian leaders organized demonstrations outside the Metrodome to protest the "Braves" nickname and gestures such as the tomahawk chop, which they believed demeaning to American Indians. COURTESY OF THE *ST. PAUL PIONEER PRESS*.

"You had enough?" asked Such.

"I'm not leaving this game," Morris said. "It's my game."

Such returned to Kelly.

"He says he's not leaving this game," Such said.

Kelly looked out at the field for a moment.

"What the hell, it's just a ballgame," said Kelly. "Let's go get 'em."

The game ended in the bottom of the tenth when pinch hitter Gene Larkin hit a fly ball over the drawn-in outfield of the Braves to drive in Dan Gladden. The Twins had gone from last place in 1990 to champions again in '91. There was delirium in the Upper Midwest.

Outside the stadiums there were extraordinary moments, too.

In Minnesota, American Indian leaders had been protesting the use of Indian nicknames in sports for years, saying they degraded the heritage of a great people. The leaders, including the Bellecourt brothers, Vernon and Clyde, found the chants and motions of Braves fans especially offensive.

The fans called it the "tomahawk chop," and whenever their team was in the midst of a rally—or in need of a rally—they would start chanting, "Oh, oh, ohohoho, oh" and moving their hands in a chopping motion. The sight and sound of 50,000 people "oohing" and chopping was impressive.

Hundreds of Ojibwe, Dakota, other Indian people, and their sympathetic supporters held rallies outside the Metrodome before each of the World Series games.

In a wise marketing move, the Bellecourts and other Indian leaders invited people in the media to make a daytime visit to "real Indians" on Lake Street during the series. Dozens of the country's more thoughtful sports journalist took them up on the offer, visiting an Indian center where they met Indian children and were treated to fry bread and ceremonial drumming and singing. Even jaded old sportswriters were moved by the scene.

In the meantime, though, in Cherokee, North Carolina, only a few hours from the home stadium of the Braves, leaders of the impoverished Cherokee had quite a different take on the whole issue of team nicknames. Tribal members had established a relationship with the baseball team. The Cherokee had the contract to produce all of the "official" Indian trinkets—little tomahawks and headdresses—for Braves games. They were perplexed by the attitudes of the Indians in Minnesota, pointing out their industry was vital revenue for tribal members. They were cranking out the trinkets as fast as they could. Every tomahawk chop was money in the bank.

This was a series that had something for everyone, including celebrities. Braves owner Ted Turner, a minor celebrity himself, was married to movie

Did he or didn't he? To this day, Braves fans are convinced that Kent Hrbek pushed Ron Gant off first base before tagging him out in a key play in the second game of the World Series. COURTESY OF AP IMAGES.

Kirby Puckett became a legend in Game 6 of the World Series, first with his dramatic catch of a Ron Gant drive and then with his homer in the bottom of the eleventh inning, which gave the Twins a chance for a Game 7.
PHOTOGRAPHS COURTESY OF THE *ST. PAUL PIONEER PRESS*.

star Jane Fonda. Caroline Lowe, a news reporter for WCCO-TV, got the off-the-field scoop of the Series. She had been tipped by a cop friend as to when and where Turner and Fonda would be entering the Dome, Gate E, across the street from Hubert's.

Lowe got to the gate early, with her cameraman. And sure enough, Turner and Fonda arrived. Lowe asked Fonda to demonstrate the "chop."

"She was almost shy about it, but she did it and she explained it," said Lowe. "You could see Ted, off to the side, just sort of shaking his head and rolling his eyes like, 'Let's get out of here.'"

Ah, even Fonda, known as a political leftist, saw nothing wrong with doing the chop. In Atlanta, where the Braves swept the Twins, Turner and Fonda were joined by former President Jimmy Carter, also a baseball fan. He, too, chopped, though shyly, as if knowing that this action wouldn't play well in some circles.

Eight months before the World Series, the Twins had gathered in spring training, feeling surprisingly good about themselves given their last place finish of 1990. The newcomers—Chili Davis, Mike Pagliarulo and Jack Morris—were fitting in nicely.

"I liked the character of this team," said Morris. "I knew guys like Hrbek and Puckett. They were winners. Chili and I talked about that during spring training. We kept telling each other that this team had the right kind of people to win."

One other significant newcomer was in spring training, too. Rookie Chuck Knoblauch, who had been the Twins' first-round draft choice in 1989, won the second base job in spring training. He played far beyond the high expectations, batting .281 and stealing 25 bases.

More importantly, he was Kelly's type of player. Competitive, feisty, and a gifted fielder. With Knoblauch at second, the always underappreciated Greg Gagne at short, and Puckett in center, the Twins were as strong up the middle defensively as any team in baseball.

"I think the thing people sometimes forget about that team is how good the pitching was," said Morris. "Three of us were pitchers of the month—[Kevin] Tapani one month, then [Scott] Erickson, and then me. You don't see that often."

Almost every game in the World Series was memorable.

With that quality of starting pitching—that Big Three won 54 games among them during the regular season—and Rick Aguilera in the bullpen, the Twins, after a slow start, were at times nearly unbeatable. During one regular-season stretch, Erickson, a sometimes sullen sinkerball pitcher, went 11–0. At another point, the Twins won 15 straight and 19 out of 20.

Ironically, after so much winning, they clinched the Western Division title after losing a 2–1 game to Toronto on September 29. Needing only a victory themselves or a loss by the second-place Chicago White Sox to win the division, the players boarded buses to head to the Toronto airport, not knowing of the outcome of the White Sox game against Seattle.

On the bus, Kelly was listening to the final outs of Seattle's 2–1 victory over Chicago via cell phone. When the game was over, Kelly stood up.

"Boys, boys. Congratulations. You're champions of the Western Division."

The news was relayed, via a dispatcher, to players on a second bus. There was cheering, hand-shaking and then the continuation of the trip to the airport, a flight to Chicago, another bus ride to the team's hotel, then, at long last, a drunken party. Ties and expensive suits were snipped by athletes armed with scissors. There was wrestling and broken tables. There were no injuries, other than hangovers. It was proving to be a fortuitous year for the Twins.

Because of the drama surrounding the World Series, it's been almost forgotten that the Twins had to defeat the Toronto Blue Jays in the American League playoffs before getting a chance to meet the Braves, who were beating the Pittsburgh Pirates in the National League playoffs.

After Jack Morris and the Twins prevailed in the bottom of the tenth in Game 7, celebrations occurred once again inside and outside the Metrodome. COURTESY OF THE *ST. PAUL PIONEER PRESS*.

Toronto was favored to win the '91 playoff series. The Blue Jays featured slugger Joe Carter and powerful starting pitching. They'd attracted more than four million fans while coasting to the more prestigious Eastern Division championship.

The playoffs were a reminder that superstars alone can't carry teams. Yes, Puckett was easily the most valuable player of what turned out to be a surprisingly quick series. He hit .429 in the series and drove in 6 runs.

But the biggest hit was delivered by Pagliarulo, that coming in the third game of the series in Toronto.

The Twins, always so dominant in the Dome, had won the opening game of the playoffs, 5–4, but had lost the second game, 5–2, a dire sign for a team which had won all of its postseason home games in 1987.

Game 3, in Toronto, was tied, 2–2, after nine innings, with Pagliarulo on the bench. But in the tenth, he was called on to pinch-hit. On the second pitch he saw from rookie pitcher Mike Timlin, Pagliarulo, who had been hitless in six at bats, homered to right. He nearly missed first as he started around the bases, later saying he had been wondering if his four-year-old son was watching the game back home. The homer gave the Twins a 3–2 victory and a 2 to 1 lead in the best-of-seven series.

Pagliarulo, of course, was mobbed by reporters after the game. Extra-inning, game-winning homers are the stuff of legend.

"It wasn't Reggie Jackson or Kirk Gibson," said Pags of his feat. "But it was pretty good."

A *Sports Illustrated* reporter noted how these joyful Twins dealt with heroes. Long after the game was over, reporters were still gathered around Pagliarulo and the rest of his teammates were ready to go back to the hotel.

"You got one hit," Hrbek yelled at Pags. "Big deal. You're holdin' up the bus."

That home run was a backbreaker for the Blue Jays. The Twins swept the Jays in the suddenly quiet Skydome, and were World Series bound. Seven players from the 1987 Twins—Puckett, Hrbek, Gagne, Dan Gladden, Larkin, Randy Bush, and Al Newman—were returning to the World Series.

What has likely never been appreciated by the Twins' loving fans is that the Braves were as big a Cinderella story in Atlanta as the Twins had been in 1987. To this day, Braves players talk of how special the 1991 season was.

"The people of Atlanta wrapped their arms around us and we just rode it like a wave," catcher Greg Olson told Jack Wilkinson, who wrote a retrospective piece for *Baseball Digest* about the '91 Braves ten years after the World Series. "It was like you were a prince or a president. We were kings of the town."

With good reason. Not only had the Braves finished last in 1990, they were nine and a half games out of first place in the National League West entering the All-Star break. Then, immediately after the break, the Braves won 7 of 8 while the Dodgers, the team they were chasing, lost 7 of 8. Now, they were just three games out of first. They clinched the division title on the last day of the regular season with a 5–2 win over Houston, then defeated the Pirates in a white-knuckle seven-game playoff series. All of Atlanta was jubilant.

"We captured a city," pitcher John Smoltz told Wilkinson. "It was hysterical, kind of like Elvis was back."

And the most dramatic was yet to come.

"To go from worst to first, then have the chance to go to the World Series," said Smoltz. "Wow! We played in some of the greatest games ever. Ever. Ever. How can there be a better game than the seventh game of the '91 Series?"

It all started calmly enough. Gagne hit a three-run homer and Hrbek a solo home run as the Twins, behind Morris, won the first game, 5–2, in the Dome.

Then, the wild, the weird, the wondrous started happening.

Game 2—the Dome was filled, of course. The Twins had a 2–1 lead entering the third inning. The Braves' Lonnie Smith was on first with two out when Ron Gant singled to left. Smith rounded second and made it safely to third as Gladden's throw from left sailed over the head of third baseman Scott Leius. But Tapani, the Twins' starting pitcher, had alertly hustled behind third to back up the play. He grabbed the overthrow. Gant had rounded first and was headed to second when he saw Tapani had the ball. He turned and hustled back to first. Tapani threw across the diamond to Hrbek, then—controversy.

Gant either stumbled, or was pushed off the bag by Hrbek, who promptly tagged him out. The Braves were irate. People all across Georgia were irate. Television announcers Jack Buck and Tim McCarver both were stunned. Braves, Georgians, and national telecasters were insistent that Hrbek had lifted Gant's leg off the base and pushed him.

The play still is argued. Hrbek, a monster of a man who has always loved pro wrestling, insists to this day that he was and is innocent of skullduggery.

In his book, *Tales from the Minnesota Twins Dugout*, Hrbek pleads his case.

"I tell everyone who will listen to watch the play in slow motion," Hrbek writes. "You'll see that Gant was falling backward, pushing me back. I did not pick up his leg. I knew he was going to come off the bag. That's why I kept my glove on him and held my ground."

Hrbek does admit he added fuel to the fire as he joked about his love of pro wrestling after the game.

"I said something to the effect that 'if you ain't cheating, you ain't trying,' which might have been the dumbest thing I ever said after a game because folks in Atlanta took it as a confession."

The play was huge. When first base umpire Drew Coble called Gant out, the Braves inning—and potential rally—was over. The Twins went on to win the game, 3–2, when Leius homered in the bottom of the eighth inning.

The Series moved to Atlanta, with the Twins holding a 2–0 lead.

If not for Games 6 and 7, Game 3 of this World Series might be considered the greatest in baseball history. The Braves led, 4–1, entering the seventh, when Puckett homered to cut the lead to 4–2. In the eighth, Davis hit a two-run homer and the game was tied, 4–4, and headed late into the night. Both managers emptied their benches as the game progressed through the tenth and eleventh innings. When the Twins loaded the bases with two outs in the twelfth inning, Kelly sent Aguilera to pinch-hit for pitcher Mark Guthrie. Aguilera was out on a fly to center and went in to pitch the bottom of the twelfth.

Four hours and four minutes after the game had begun, it was finally over. David Justice singled, stole second, and then slid home just ahead of Gladden's throw to the plate after Mark Lemke's single.

There was barely time for anyone to sleep before it was time for Game 4—and more drama. This time, the game was tied, 2–2, entering the bottom of the ninth when, with one out, Lemke tripled to left center. Pinch hitter Jerry Willard then hit a fly to right field. Lemke tagged up. Shane Mack fired home, the ball landing in the mitt of catcher Brian Harper before Lemke got to the plate. But he slid around Harper, was called safe by umpire Terry Tata, and no amount of arguing by the Twins over the call could change the fact that the World Series was tied, 2–2.

Game 5 was the breather everyone needed. The Braves blew open a tight game with 6 runs in the seventh inning and breezed to a 14–5 victory. For the second time in World Series play, the Twins had won the first two games at the Dome, then lost three straight on the road, but they were homeward bound.

So was Game 6 the greatest game ever played? This was the game in which Kirby Puckett was supposed to have said, "Get on my back boys, I'll carry you tonight." The fact is, the effervescent Puckett had said the same thing a hundred times before. It made his teammates laugh.

But on this night, he did carry the Twins into a Game 7. In the top of the third inning, he robbed Gant of what would have been a run-scoring extra-base hit as he leaped against the wall in deep left center, making a Dome-shaking catch. He drove in a first-inning run with a triple. He drove in another run with a fifth-inning sacrifice fly.

And then, with the game tied in the bottom of the eleventh, Braves manager Bobby Cox brought Charlie Liebrandt into the game. On a 2–1 pitch, Puckett homered.

The airwaves across the country were filled with exclamation marks.

"We'll see you tomorrow night," said Buck.

There was this from Twins broadcaster John Gordon: "Puckett swings and hits a blast! Deep left center! Way back! Way back! It's gone! The Twins go to the seventh game! Touch 'em all Kirby Puckett!"

The call was a little more somber for those listening to the game on Atlanta radio.

"Same two teams tomorrow night," said Braves announcer Skip Caray as Puckett's ball flew through the din.

In the Twins clubhouse, Morris, who would pitch Game 7, simply smiled.

"When Puckett hit that home run, I knew we would win the World Series," Morris said. "There was not one negative thought in my mind. I think it was the only time in my career I felt so absolutely certain about something. I wish I could have bottled that feeling and held onto it forever."

1992

Back to Earth

The World: The breakup of Yugoslavia turns into horror stories of ethnic cleansing in Bosnia and Herzegovina, as Serbians, Croatians, Christians, and Muslims, who once lived as neighbors, turn against each other.

The Nation: In the presidential election, Bill Clinton, the "Comeback Kid," defeats incumbent George H. W. Bush and independent candidate Ross Perot.

The State: The Mall of America opens. The Metrodome is the site of the Super Bowl; Washington defeats Buffalo, 37–24. It's also site of the NCAA men's basketball championship; Duke defeats Michigan, 71–51.

Pop Culture: Billboard's #1 Song: "End of the Road," by Boyz II Men. Best Picture: *Unforgiven*. Best Seller: *Dolores Claiborne*, by Stephen King. Johnny Carson leaves the *Tonight Show*; his final guest is Bette Midler.

The Season: The Twins compile a 90–72 record, but finish six games behind the Oakland A's. No Minnesota batter hits 20 homers or drives in 100 runs. For the first time, a Canadian team, the Toronto Blue Jays, wins the World Series, defeating the Atlanta Braves in six games.

Jack Morris was a 21-game winner in 1992 and for the second successive season was on a World Series championship team. The only problem for Minnesota fans was that Morris was wearing a Toronto Blue Jays uniform.

Following his incredible seventh game performance in the 1991 World Series, the pitcher from St. Paul rejected a Twins one-year contract offer, opting instead to take a two-year deal for nearly $10 million with the Blue Jays.

"When I came to Minnesota it was because I knew the players had the character to win," Morris said in an interview years later. "I saw the same sort of character in Toronto."

Morris wasn't the only player missing when spring training opened in 1992. Dan Gladden, one of seven players to have played on both the 1987 and '91 championship seasons, was gone too. He'd been released by the Twins two and a half months after scoring the winning run in Game 7 of the World Series. There were three reasons the Twins thought it was time for Gladden to go. The sparkplug outfielder was thirty-five years old, he was being paid $1.1 million, and the team had a young outfielder, Pedro Munoz, waiting in the wings. Munoz not only looked like a potentially powerful hitter, he would work for the major-league minimum, $155,000. Munoz did okay in several seasons with the Twins, but never managed the offensive numbers expected

Following the World Series, the Twins gather with President George H. W. Bush in the Rose Garden of the White House, where Tom Kelly presents the president with a Kirby Puckett bat autographed by the entire team. The Twins, from left: Gene Larkin, Randy Bush, Kent Hrbek, Chili Davis, Scott Erickson, Puckett, Paul Sorrento, Terry Leach, Brian Harper, and Lenny Webster. COURTESY OF THE ST. PAUL PIONEER PRESS.

of him. He spent the 1996 season with Oakland before disappearing from baseball.

Despite the departures, there was reason for optimism in spring training, especially after Andy MacPhail swung a deal with the Pittsburgh Pirates that was lauded as a steal. MacPhail acquired left-handed pitcher John Smiley, a 20-game winner in 1991, for two minor-leaguers, an outfielder, Midre Cummings, who had been the team's first round draft choice in 1990, and Denny Neagle, who had pitched at the University of Minnesota before becoming a third round draft choice of the Twins in 1989. The Twins also received $800,000 in the deal to help them pay the $3.4 million contract Smiley had just signed in Pittsburgh.

Murray Chass, the baseball columnist for the *New York Times,* reported that people throughout baseball were surprised that Smiley was available and that MacPhail could get him for so little.

"How did it happen?" Chass quoted Seattle general manager Woody Woodward as saying. "Nobody knew it was happening. You'd think they would shop him [Smiley] around. If they called around, they'd probably find six or eight clubs interested. Minnesota made a marvelous deal, one that has everyone baffled."

Among those baffled was Smiley. Like Tommy Herr before him, Smiley didn't want to leave his team; was not excited about moving to Minnesota. Tony Perez, a coach with the Cincinnati Reds, heard about Smiley's unhappiness and said, "John Smiley is going to change his name to John Frowny."

But, unlike Herr, Smiley did find himself laughing almost as soon as he joined the team. According to Chass, when Kelly introduced Smiley to the team, Randy Bush had only one question: "It said we got Smiley and $800,000. I see Smiley, but I don't see the $800,000. Where is it? Do we get to split it up?"

Smiley turned out to be a suitable replacement for Morris. In fact, his record in 1992 (16–9, 3.21 ERA in 241 innings pitched) was almost identical to Morris's 1991 record (18–12, 3.43 ERA in 246 innings). But the price MacPhail paid turned out to be high. Smiley pitched just one year for the Twins, then signed as a free agent with Cincinnati. Neagle ended up winning 124 games in his thirteen-year career with Pittsburgh; Atlanta, where he was a 20-game winner in 1997; Cincinnati; and Colorado. All of those victories, of course, came after being traded from the Twins. Though never becoming a starting outfielder, Cummings did play for eleven seasons.

As was the case in 1988, 1992 showed just how hard it is for a team to repeat. The Twins of '92 were very good, winning 90 games, only five fewer than they'd won the year before. They were immensely popular, drawing 2,482,428 people, the second highest attendance total in team history. The only real problem was that the Oakland A's, behind bulky Mark McGwire's 42 home runs, won 96 games.

There were memorable moments, as there are in every season.

On July 5, Chili Davis hit a monster fly toward right field against Baltimore pitcher Rick Sutcliffe. There were 36,927 people in the Dome and every one of them was sure that Davis's drive was going to go far over the fence. It was headed out, until it hit a speaker hanging from the roof. The ball caromed off the speaker and all the way back to Orioles second baseman Mark McLemore, who caught the ball. It was the longest fly out to second base in baseball history. The Twins did hang on for a 2–1 victory in the game.

On September 27, Shane Mack and Brian Harper each homered and John Smiley pitched a complete game shutout as the Twins defeated the Kansas

Tom Kelly was grouchy with fans, smoked cigars, and wore Zubaz, but he also was the manager of two World Series champion teams. COURTESY OF THE *ST. PAUL PIONEER PRESS.*

City Royals, 4–0, in a game that lasted just 2 hours, 11 minutes. It was victory number 523 for Tom Kelly, pushing him ahead of Sam Mele as the winningest manager in Twins history. He made no long speeches after the game. Kelly would finish his managerial career with 1,140 wins; his successor, Ron Gardenhire, is now second on the Twins wins list.

The season ended with a victory and smiles in Kansas City. There were high hopes for next year. But this would prove to be the Twins' last winning season until 2001.

The Twins never expected to turn the 1991 championship season into a dynasty. Given the economics of the game, few teams can afford to hold good teams together. Nonetheless, team president Jerry Bell thought that the team would be competitive for more than a season.

"We thought with Kirby and Herbie, we'd have a solid nucleus to build around well into the '90s," he said. "But then things you just don't think about happening happened. Kent retired early [1994] and one day Kirby woke up and he could only see out of one eye [spring training 1996]. How do you figure on things like that?"

1993

Baseball and Economics

The World: Israeli Prime Minister Yitzhak Rabin and the PLO's Yasser Arafat shake hands after signing a peace agreement in Washington. The North American Free Trade Agreement, promoting free trade between the United States, Canada, and Mexico, is ratified.

The Nation: A fifty-one-day siege of the Branch Davidian compound in Waco, Texas, ends with an inferno in which seventy-six members of the cult die, including twenty-seven children. Five people are killed when terrorists attempt to destroy New York's World Trade Center. President Clinton announces his "don't ask, don't tell" policy for dealing with issues of sexuality in the military.

The State: Norm Green moves the Minnesota North Stars to Dallas. In a legal dispute, Prince changes his name to a symbol. Sharon Sayles Belton becomes the first woman and the first African-American to be elected mayor of Minneapolis.

Pop Culture: Billboard's #1 Song: "I Will Always Love You," by Whitney Houston. Highest-Grossing Movie: *Jurassic Park*. Best Seller: *The Bridges of Madison County*, by Robert James Waller. The final episode of *Cheers* airs on NBC.

The Season: The long decline begins, with Twins falling to 20 games below .500 (71–91). Eddie Guardado is a young pitcher, trying to make it in a broken-down starting rotation. The Toronto Blue Jays end baseball's season with a second consecutive World Series title—this time over the Philadelphia Phillies. Paul Molitor is MVP of the series.

Following the 1992 season, Jerry Bell, Andy MacPhail, and Tom Kelly had a somber meeting. Bell explained his dilemma. The Twins had two key players without contracts, Kirby Puckett and Greg Gagne. "We can't sign both and we have to sign Kirby," Bell said.

Kelly nodded his head. He understood. But Kelly, always a man of few words around management, did have one comment, Bell recalled. "He said, 'I wonder who will make all those catches down the third base line?'"

The Twins did sign Puckett to a five-year, $30 million deal. Gagne remembers being offered a one-year contract that wasn't close to being acceptable and so he signed a three-year, $10 million deal with the Kansas City Royals.

"It was one of the best things I ever did," said Gagne. "It was time for me to go. In Kansas City, there was a lot more respect for me as a player and a person."

Baseball people will tell you that after Puckett and Hrbek, there was one key player in the Twins' two championship seasons, the shortstop, Gagne. The Twins simply never could have been champions without a sure-handed, strong-armed, wide-ranging shortstop. But Gagne said he never felt that he was perceived as being of much importance.

"Maybe it was because I was young, or maybe it was because I'm thin-skinned," Gagne said. "Some people have thick skin, I'm thin-skinned. I was a sensitive guy—I just never felt respected."

Gagne was seventeen years old when he was drafted in 1979 out of Fall River, Massachusetts, in the fifth round by the New York Yankees. He became the property of the Twins in one of Calvin Griffith's salary-dumping moves of 1982. Roy Smalley was sent to the Yanks for Gagne and pitchers Ron Davis and Paul Boris.

"I was told later that George Brophy [the head of Griffith's scouting operation] said the only way the Twins would do the deal is if they got me," said Gagne. "I don't know if that's true but it always seemed like those guys respected me."

Gagne learned of the trade to the Twins from his Yankees minor-league manager, Stump Merrill, who approached him and said, "I've got some good news and bad news."

"Let's hear it," said Gagne.

"The bad news, you've been traded to the Minnesota Twins," Merrill said, according to Gagne. "The good news is that you've got a chance to get to the big leagues faster."

Early in his minor-league days, Gagne had become a born-again Christian. That conversion had come in his second year of pro ball, in Greensboro.

"There was no one moment," said Gagne. "But there were a lot of Christians on the team. They sat around and talked, had Bible studies, and I felt like it was something I needed. It touched the spirit inside me."

His faith, he believes, might have been one of the reasons he never felt totally accepted by Kelly and some of the other core Twin players when he finally became the Twins' starting shortstop in 1985, which was a year later than Gagne thought he should have been a major-league starter.

Coming into that Twins locker room, surrounded by the class of 1982, made Gagne feel like "the new kid in school."

"Bushie, Brunansky, Gaetti, Hrbek, Laudner, they had their little group," said Gagne. "That was okay. I understood, it just felt different, and sometimes they were a little tough on me."

Not only was Gagne the new guy, there was the matter of his religion. Gagne didn't wear it on his sleeve, but in a locker room filled with boisterous, beer-drinking, devil-may-care players, Gagne was different.

"Sometimes in Minnesota, being a born-again Christian, wasn't easy," said Gagne. "Puckett was pretty good to me, but some of the others, it was just tough. They'd say things. Gaetti, before he became born-again, could be tough."

Gagne, looking back, knows he might not have been easy for a manager like Kelly to handle. Gagne was a Bible reader, but cocky. He was convinced that he should play every game, take every at bat. Despite the cockiness, he was insecure and sensitive. Little things upset him deeply. For example, Kelly frequently used a pinch hitter for Gagne late in games. Every time it happened, Gagne fumed.

The most comfortable Gagne ever felt in a Twins uniform came at a crucial time for the team, down the stretch in 1987. The Twins, searching for a veteran right-handed hitter, had acquired Don Baylor from the Boston Red Sox on September 1, for a minor-league player. Baylor, Gagne said, became a personal hitting mentor, filling Gagne with confidence.

"Every day he'd talk to me about hitting," Gagne said. "Instead of tearing me down, he'd build me up. TK seemed to tear me down. I'd get three hits in a game and TK would say, 'Well, tomorrow's another day.' It was just the opposite with Baylor. We'd talk, we'd do some soft tosses [a pregame drill in which a player tosses underhand to a hitter, who works on the mechanics of his swing]. I'd go into a game all pumped up after spending time with Baylor."

Perhaps it was mere coincidence, but in the Twins' surprising playoff triumph over the Detroit Tigers in 1987, Gagne had 5 hits; 3 doubles and 2 home runs. Though he hit just .200 in the World Series against the St. Louis Cardinals, he did have 2 hits in the Twins 4–2 Game 7 victory, driving in a run and scoring a run.

He was, of course, the shortstop on the 1991 championship season as well. But one year after that championship season, Gagne was gone and when he departed, the Twins collapsed, falling to 21 games below .500 in 1993.

The 1993 team had no power, despite the fact that St. Paul native Dave Winfield had been brought home as he was making his push to 3,000 hits. There is a word to describe Winfield: Extraordinary. He was a two-sport star, a power forward in basketball and a pitcher in baseball, at the University of Minnesota. Following his last season at the University in 1973, Winfield was not only a first-round draft choice of the San Diego Padres, but was drafted by the Atlanta Hawks of the National Basketball Association, the Utah Stars of the American Basketball Association, and the National Football League's Minnesota Vikings. That had never happened before.

St. Paul's own hitting machine, Dave Winfield, posed with 3,000 baseballs after collecting his 3,000th big-league hit on September 16. COURTESY OF THE *ST. PAUL PIONEER PRESS*.

He never played an inning in the minor leagues despite the fact that the Padres drafted him as a pitcher and immediately decided to make him an outfielder. He had power and speed and seven Gold Gloves in his twenty-two years. And he hit. Year after year, he hit.

On September 16, 1993, Winfield singled against the A's star relief pitcher, Dennis Eckersley. It was career hit number 3,000. But for whatever reason, Winfield never created the buzz Twins management had expected. There were just 14,654 people on hand to see the local guy become only the nineteenth player in baseball history to reach the milestone.

That hit, it should be noted, drove home Kirby Puckett and the two were together again in 2001 when they were inducted into the Baseball Hall of Fame together.

While the Twins were falling far from their World Series pedestal, Gagne was having the time of his life in Kansas City. He hit .280, had 10 homers and was reunited with Gaetti, whom he had become good friends with following Gaetti's 1988 religious conversion.

After leaving the Twins, Gaetti had only mediocre seasons in California and was released by the Angels in June 1993. Royals manager Hal McRae approached his shortstop. "Can Gaetti still play?" McRae asked.

"That was really special to me," Gagne said. "Here was the manager coming to me to ask a question. It showed tremendous respect. I told him, 'Yes, he can still play.' And so Gary and I were reunited again."

Gaetti was rejuvenated, hitting 14 homers in the last half of the '93 season, a season that saw the Royals finish thirteen games ahead of the Twins.

Gagne and Gaetti had two more productive years in Kansas City, then headed in separate directions, Gaetti to the Cardinals and Gagne to the Dodgers where he finished his fifteen-year big-league career.

The Twins' search for a shortstop continued into the twenty-first century.

1994

Herbie's Farewell

The World: Nelson Mandela, once a prisoner, becomes president of South Africa. Hutus slaughter more than 500,000 Tutsis in war-torn Rwanda. After seven years of construction, the Chunnel, connecting England and France, is open.

The Nation: "The Gingrich Revolution" puts Republicans in control of both houses of Congress. Nicole Brown Simpson and Ronald Goldman are murdered in Brentwood, California, and O. J. Simpson leads police on a low-speed chase in a white Bronco. The average income in the Unites States is $37,070. Minimum wage is $4.25.

The State: Though he doesn't have the endorsement of his fellow Republicans, Arne Carlson easily defeats DFLer John Marty to win a second term as governor. The legislature approves funding for the "Mighty Ducks Program," to help communities build sports facilities. At the same time, the state's High School League sanctions hockey as a sport for women. The NBA All-Star Game is played in the Target Center; The Timberwolves' Isaiah Rider wins the "slam dunk" contest.

Pop Culture: Kurt Cobain commits suicide. Best Picture: *Forrest Gump*. Pulitzer Prize for Fiction: *The Shipping News*, by E. Annie Proulx. *Friends* debuts on NBC.

The Season: With team owners demanding a salary cap, a players' strike beginning August 12 wipes out the rest of the season. For the first time since 1904 there is no World Series. In Kent Hrbek's final season, the Twins were 53–60 when strike began.

Kirby or Herbie. Among fans and players it would be difficult to select who was the heart and soul of the Twins. Kirby Puckett was Hall-of-Fame sensational. Yet, Kent Hrbek brought a let's-have-fun style of play that represented all that was enjoyable about the Twins for more than a decade.

In the field and at the plate, Kent Hrbek was always fun-loving and colorful. He retired at the end of the strike-shortened 1994 season. COURTESY OF THE *ST. PAUL PIONEER PRESS*.

Though Hrbek and Puckett weren't particularly close, they had much in common. Both loved to laugh. Both loved playing the game. Both played hard. Both were indifferent to off-season conditioning. Both took their defense seriously. Both had a flare for the dramatic. (Puckett had far more impressive postseason statistics and the unforgettable Game 6 performance in the 1991 World Series, but Hrbek had huge moments, such as his grand-slam home run in Game 6 of the 1987 World Series.) Both loved fishing. Both were stars, but never acted the part.

At the start of the 1994 season, Hrbek, who was just thirty-four, made it clear it would be his last. He was hurting from shoulders to knees to ankles. Diving around on the rock-hard Dome surface had taken its toll on Hrbek's 260-pound body.

That he didn't take better care of himself—French fries dipped in gravy were a Hrbek favorite certainly contributed to his aches and pains. But had he taken better care of himself he wouldn't have been Herbie. He played and ate with reckless abandon. His bulk was part of the man's personality and it was his personality that made the Twins clubhouse a joyful place. He was T. rex. He was Shamu. He laughed with others and at himself.

At the time of Puckett's death, for example, there was this comment to reporters from Hrbek: "I think the biggest thing I remember was there are so many animals in this state named Kirby and if somebody had a cow or a horse they named it Herbie."

For Twins fans, the fact that he was "one of their own" made everything better. He grew up in Bloomington and could see the lights of Met Stadium from his childhood home.

Hrbek, among so many other things, is proof that major-league scouting is not an exact science. He was not drafted by the Twins in 1978 until the seventeenth round, meaning hundreds of amateur players were selected before him.

"I can't tell you why he lasted so long," said Jim Rantz, who has spent a lifetime in the Twins' scouting and minor-league baseball departments. "I do know that he was on our board. We knew he had had a heckuva high school career. My guess is that he just hadn't had much exposure. All I know is that I'm sure glad we got him."

As it turned out, 1994 was a train wreck season for baseball and a lousy year for a swan song. It was the year of baseball's most devastating strike. This time owners were insistent that they would stand up to the Players' Association (they didn't). The strike started on August 12 and lasted until April 1995. The strike blew away the World Series, the only time the event had not occurred since 1904. It destroyed baseball in Montreal. (At the time the strike began, the Montreal Expos were baseball's best team, but when the season of so much promise was wiped out, Expos fans never returned to the ballpark. The Expos are now the Washington Nationals.)

The strike also meant that there was no way of acknowledging that Hrbek's career had ended. On August 10, a Wednesday night, he had a hit in five at bats, drove in three runs, caught a pop fly for the final out of the game that the Twins won, 17–7, over the Boston Red Sox before 23,492 fans at the Dome. The Twins had an off day on Thursday, the strike began on Friday and Hrbek's career was over. He was tired of hurting, tired of leaving his wife and child behind. He had more money than he'd ever dreamed of having and it was time to go hunting and fishing.

He was a natural. There were no big secrets to his success. He always said that he was born with the ability to hit a baseball.

The first time Roy Smalley saw Hrbek swing a bat, he was envious. "I hope he never starts to think," Smalley said. "Thinking would just get in the way of that swing." Even Ted Williams admired his swing, nodding approvingly as he watched Hrbek launch home runs during batting practice during spring training in 1982.

There was a big-boy ruggedness to Hrbek, but a sweetness, too. In 1982, his rookie season, he was the Twins' only representative on the American League All-Star roster. He showed up in Montreal, pushing his father, Ed, a big man who was slowly being torn apart by amyotrophic lateral sclerosis (ALS), in a wheelchair. Ed Hrbek died a few months later at the age of 53. At the time of his retirement, Hrbek acknowledged his father, noting, "He never had a chance to retire." Hrbek and his wife, Jean, have been tireless workers for ALS causes.

Hrbek's departure meant the final member of the class of '82 was gone from the Twins. Of that group—Hrbek, Tim Laudner, Randy Bush, Frank Viola, and Gary Gaetti—only Viola and Gaetti still were playing when Hrbek retired.

"I don't know if you'll ever see that again," said Hrbek. "You had a group of guys who grew up together in the minor leagues, stayed together, won championships together. It was the way baseball used to be."

Clearly, Hrbek was bigger in the Twins' history than his statistics. He didn't put up Hall of Fame numbers. His name was on the Hall of Fame ballot just once, five years after his retirement. He got only five votes, not even close to the 5 percent threshold needed to stay on the ballot in future seasons. (The Hall of Fame's veterans committee will have a chance to look at Hrbek's career in 2015 and decide whether he is Cooperstown worthy.)

Hrbek appeared in only one All-Star Game, that 1982 game with his dad at his side. Despite the fact that he was a graceful fielder, he was never awarded a Gold Glove. The Yankees' Don Mattingly had the lock on Gold Gloves during Hrbek's career. Gaetti, disgusted at what he considered an East Coast bias toward Mattingly, gave Hrbek one of his four Gold Gloves, noting that Hrbek had spared him countless throwing errors.

Twins fans always understood there was something more to Hrbek than statistics. The Twins recognized that, too. In 1995, they retired Hrbek's number 14. That puts him in company with Harmon Killebrew, Rod Carew, Tony Oliva, and, of course, Kirby Puckett.

1995

Decline Again

The World: Israeli prime minister Yitzhak Rabin is assassinated while attending a peace rally in Tel Aviv. For first time in twenty-six years, no British troops patrol the streets of Belfast, Northern Ireland.

The Nation: On April 19, the bombing of the Alfred P. Murrah Federal Building in Oklahoma City kills 168 people. Ultimately Timothy McVeigh and Terry Nichols are convicted; McVeigh is sentenced to death, Nichols receives life in prison. O. J. Simpson is found not guilty of murder. In February, the Dow Jones Industrial Average is higher than 4,000 for the first time ever. Later in the year, it surpasses 5,000.

The State: In Alexandria, members of an extremist antitax organization, the Minnesota Patriot's Council, are convicted of attempting to manufacture the toxin ricin. They apparently intended to use it to kill IRS and other federal agents.

Pop Culture: Jerry Garcia, the soul of the Grateful Dead, dies. Singer Selena Quintanilla-Perez is murdered. After a long hiatus, James Bond returns to the big screen with Pierce Brosnan as 007 in the movie *Goldeneye*. Best Seller (nonfiction): *Men Are from Mars, Women Are from Venus*, by John Gray. Top-Rated Television Show: *ER*.

The Season: In the top of the first inning of the last game of the season, Cleveland Indians pitcher Dennis Martinez hits Kirby Puckett in the head. This would prove to be Puckett's last appearance in a regular-season game. "I felt like the lowest man in baseball," Martinez tells reporters after the game. This is a dismal end to a dreary 56–88 season. (The season was shortened due to the carryover of the strike of 1994.)

Kent Hrbek wasn't alone in departing from the Twins in 1994. After the strike-shortened season, Andy MacPhail left, too, and became president and CEO of the Chicago Cubs. He still looked like a Boy Scout, but there would be no triumphant parades in Chicago, and after twelve years there, he stepped down.

"This is the first thing I've ever done in baseball that I didn't have a high level of success at," he told reporters when he left the Cubs in 2006. "The clock on the MacPhail o-meter has run down."

But the magic he helped to create in Minnesota was not forgotten in baseball. In the summer of 2007, he was named the president of baseball operations of the Baltimore Orioles. Most news accounts of his hiring started like this: "Andy MacPhail, who led the Minnesota Twins to championships in 1987 and 1991...."

Back in Minnesota, Terry Ryan, MacPhail's first hire with the Twins, succeeded MacPhail as vice president and general manager. He stepped into a mess. Not only were the Twins in serious decline, but baseball was in turmoil. The strike that had brought the 1994 season to a halt didn't end until April 2 of the following year, and it only ended then because a judge issued an order barring owners from trying to open the season with replacement players.

The Twins started the season, which was reduced from 162 to 144 games, in Boston on April 26, getting just two singles in a 9–0 loss. They opened their home season a day later and won, 7–4, over Baltimore but the crowd was small for an opener. Just 26,426 people showed up. Minnesotans, like people in the rest of the country, were disgusted with baseball. Placards reading "greed" were common in ballparks across the country. In New York, two fans jumped on the playing field and threw handfuls of dollar bills at players. Attendance and television ratings were down.

But the strike didn't just cost the Twins goodwill in Minnesota. It also cost them a chance to keep Shane Mack, a hard-hitting outfielder who had been a dependable force for the team for five seasons.

At thirty-one, Mack was at the peak of his career when he got caught up in the chaos of the strike. Following the '94 season, the Twins had offered Mack a two-year, $6.6 million contract but before Mack could make a decision, the players' union imposed a contract moratorium on its members. This move was in response to the owners' unilaterally placing a salary cap on its payroll structure.

Mack, who had been an All-America ballplayer at UCLA, was a practical man. A career .300 hitter, he understood that athletes don't hold on to their peak abilities for long. Not knowing when—or even if—the strike would end, he signed a two year, $8.1 million contract with Japan's Yomiuri Giants. It was the biggest contract in the history of Japanese baseball and also marked the first time that a U.S. player, in the prime of his career, opted to leave major-league baseball to seek fame and fortune in Japan.

In his years with the Twins, Mack was almost lost amid the excitement that always surrounded his best friend on the team, Kirby Puckett. But playing in Kirby's large shadow was just fine with him. Mack did not seek the limelight and Puckett brought out the best in a player who sometimes lacked confidence despite all of his skills. Puckett always was there for him, lifting his spirits and making him laugh.

On the day in 2006 that Puckett suffered the massive, fatal stroke, Mack was one of two former Twins players who dropped everything and headed to Arizona to be by Puckett's side. Kent Hrbek was the other.

In 1995, it was Puckett who offered Mack encouragement to take the Japanese deal and run. In an interview with *Sports Illustrated*, Mack said Puckett told him, 'I'm gonna miss you but you got a better deal.'"

So this was the state of baseball and the Twins when Ryan succeeded MacPhail: Hrbek was retired; Mack was headed to Japan; Puckett was slowing down and being shifted to right field, leaving center field open; Scott Erickson, so talented a pitcher when healthy, seemed to constantly be battling arm problems. On top of that, the fans were in a foul mood and bitter stadium politics were just around the corner.

Unlike MacPhail, there was nothing flashy about Ryan. Unlike MacPhail, he'd worked his way up through baseball's ranks the old-fashioned way. He was a minor-league pitcher, a scout, a scouting director, and then a vice president under MacPhail. Unlike MacPhail, Ryan liked nothing so much as going to a minor-league park to evaluate players and gab with scouts; other "baseball lifers" from other teams. "You're always looking five years out," was his approach to the job.

He needed all of those five years to right the Twins again. Even the good things that happened in 1995 didn't have much staying power.

Marty Cordova appeared to be one of the few good things the Twins had going for them. He joined a long list of Twins players when he became Rookie of the Year in 1995, hitting .277 with 24 homers, 84 RBI, and 20 stolen bases. Other Twins who had won the honor included Tony Oliva (1964), Rod Carew (1967), John Castino (1979), and Chuck Knoblauch (1991).

But Cordova never became a big star. He was good enough so that he built his salary to $3 million by 1999, his last season with the Twins. But he was often injured, missing 240 games between 1997 and 2000.

An obsessive weightlifter, rock hard and vain about his body, it was assumed by many that Cordova's name would be among the players listed in the damning steroid report of former Senator George Mitchell. Several players who had been with the Twins, including Knoblauch, Chad Allen, and Rondell White, were named in the report. Cordova was not.

His baseball career ended up being remembered for promise unfulfilled and a couple of strange events.

In 1997, the Twins used Cordova in one of their television ads designed to build public support for a new stadium. In the ad, Cordova was shown visiting a young child with cancer, while a voice said, "If the Twins leave Minnesota, an eight-year-old from Willmar will never get a visit from Marty Cordova." The public was offended by the ad, then, outraged when it was learned that the child had died.

After leaving the Twins, Cordova sustained an injury he'll always be remembered for. He was playing with the Baltimore Orioles in 2002 when he fell asleep in a tanning bed and was burned so badly he had to sit out several games.

But in 1995 he was the Twins' hope in a year when there wasn't much hope. On June 15, with a 13–33 record, they traveled to Salt Lake City to play an exhibition game against their top minor-league affiliate.

Here are the opening paragraphs of the story Loren Jorgensen wrote for the *Salt Lake Desert News*:

"It was business as usual for the Minnesota Twins Thursday afternoon— they lost yet another baseball game.

"Only this time it wasn't against the Cleveland Indians or the California Angels. Thursday the Twins were handed a 4–3 loss by the AAA Salt Lake City Buzz in an exhibition game in front of 14,596 fans at Franklin Quest Field. 'At least nobody got hurt,' said Twins manager Tom Kelly."

1996
From Cheers to Tears

The World: The Taliban seize the Afghan capital, Kabul, and take control of the country. Chechen rebels attack Russian government headquarters. Seventy Russian soldiers and 130 Chechen fighters are killed.

The Nation: President Bill Clinton is elected to a second term, defeating Kansas Senator Bob Dole. A bomb explodes in Atlanta's Centennial Olympic Park during the Olympic Games. One person is killed, hundreds are injured. The median household income in the United States is $35,492.

The State: The release of the movie *Fargo* has people across the country talking "Minnesotan." The coldest official temperature ever, negative sixty degrees Fahrenheit, is recorded on February 2 near Tower, Minnesota.

Pop Culture: Gangsta Rapper Tupac Shakur dies six days after being shot in a drive-by shooting; Janet Jackson signs a record $80 million deal with Virgin Records. Best Picture: *The English Patient.* Pulitzer Prize for Fiction: *Independence Day,* by Richard Ford. Top-Rated Television Show: *ER.*

The Season: Marty Cordova is the top home run hitter on the team with 16. Not surprisingly, the Twins rank dead last in the American League in homers, and slip to fourth in the A.L. Central.

Everybody loved Kirby Puckett. But few really knew him. He shielded whatever was going on inside that unique, round body with a huge smile and a steady line of chatter. Clichés bubbled from him and everybody around him smiled. Even opponents turned into starry-eyed fans when Kirby Puckett stepped onto the field.

"He never had a bad day," said former White Sox star Frank Thomas. "I don't care how bad things were going for him on or off the field. Kirby found a way to make you laugh. He was a breath of fresh air in this game."

Even on July 12, 1996, the day he came out of surgery at the Retina Institute of Maryland and learned that he'd never again step to the plate, Kirby tried to lift the spirits of those around him.

Following the fifth and final surgery to restore blood flow to the retina of Puckett's right eye, Dr. Bert Glaser entered Puckett's room. In an interview with *Ebony* magazine, Puckett recalled the conversation like this:

Glaser: "Kirby, there has been irreversible eye damage and you'll never be able to play baseball again."

Puckett: "My wife was crying and I looked up and shouted, 'Thank you, Jesus.' I was just so happy that it was all over; I was no longer in limbo and I could now go on with the other part of my life."

The worst day in Twins history? The day in July 1996 when Kirby Puckett, seated with his wife, Tonya, announced he was retiring from the game after a diagnosis of glaucoma in his right eye. Puckett and Twins fans had held out hope that surgery would make it possible for him to play again, but the surgery revealed that the damage to his eye was irreversible. Life for Puckett and for Twins fans was never quite the same again. COURTESY OF AP IMAGES.

When Puckett returned to Minneapolis, a press conference was held at the Metrodome. Puckett, wearing a patch over his eye, again shielded himself with that big smile of his. He looked around the room, filled with Twins players, front office personnel, and members of the media.

"Kirby Puckett's going to be all right," he said. "Don't worry about me. I'll show up and have a smile on my face. The only thing I won't have is this uniform on. But you guys can have the memories of what I did when I did have it on."

There wasn't a dry eye in the place.

We all would learn that when Puckett didn't have his uniform on, his life was a mess. He was acquitted of a criminal sexual conduct charge of groping a woman in an Eden Prairie bar. There were accusations of domestic abuse surrounding his 2002 divorce and ugly public disclosures of his longtime mistress. His weight swelled to over 300 pounds despite warnings from his friends that he was killing himself.

By the time of his 2006 death, all of that seemingly was forgiven, or at least ignored. Puckett had always said that his life—from the projects of Chicago to the Baseball Hall of Fame, where he was inducted in 2001—was "a fairy tale." And we all still want to believe.

It was the joy of being around Puckett—and the salesmanship of manager Tom Kelly—that drew Paul Molitor to the Twins in 1996. Kelly convinced Molitor that with Chuck Knoblauch at the top of the batting order and Puckett and Molitor in the middle of the lineup, the team could rebound from its miserable 1995 season.

The veteran, who had grown up in St. Paul and played at the University of Minnesota, had overcome some personal problems of his own. There'd been drug use issues when he was a young player in Milwaukee. But he'd become the consummate pro, starring in Milwaukee and Toronto before signing on with the Twins for 1996.

Molitor never looked like a superstar. In his first season with Milwaukee in 1978, he didn't feel like one, either, despite the fact he hit .273 and finished second in Rookie of the Year voting to the Detroit Tigers' Lou Whitaker.

"You have doubts about yourself when you start," said Molitor after his career was over. "It takes two or three years before you start to eliminate the doubts and are able to tell yourself, 'I belong here.' The first time you stand up there against somebody like Nolan Ryan you're convinced you don't have much of a chance. But over the years, your attitude changes. Somebody like Randy Johnson is pitching and it's pretty well known you haven't had much success against him. But you step in the box and you're thinking, 'No matter who throws it, something's going to come over the plate.'"

On September 16, Paul Molitor tripled in Kansas City, becoming the first player ever to hit a triple for his 3,000th hit. Molitor's all-around skills were extraordinary. He's one of four players in baseball history to have 3,000 hits, a .300 lifetime batting average, and 500 stolen bases; the others are Ty Cobb, Honus Wagner, and Eddie Collins, who all played prior to 1930. COURTESY OF AP IMAGES.

Spring training had gone well for Molitor, Puckett, and the Twins. Optimism was growing until the morning of March 28, the last day of training camp. That was the day Puckett woke up with blurry vision in his right eye. Initially, few thought this could be serious. After all, Puckett had hit .360 during spring training. How could everything just change overnight?

Incredibly, it wasn't so much the absence of Puckett that turned the Twins season of promise into a fourth-place mess. It was the absence of pitching. The Twins staff was the worst in the American League, allowing 5.5 runs per game.

Through all the losses, through all the attention that had been placed on Puckett, Molitor quietly went to work every day and put together an amazing—though largely unnoticed—season. At thirty-nine, he played in 161 of the 162 games, had 660 at bats, 225 hits, 113 runs batted in, and a .341 average, and he scored 99 runs and stole 18 bases.

Years before, he said, he'd learned a big secret about the game.

"You never give away an at bat. If you're losing 10 to 1 and it's the seventh inning, you still don't give away that at bat. If it's 41 degrees out, you don't give it away. Let's say you're going to get 500 at bats in a season. When you're younger, it's scary to remember how many of those you give away. No matter what's going on around you, when you go to the plate you stay in the moment."

Through all of the sadness and losses in the '96 season, Molitor stayed in the moment and the hits kept piling up.

On September 16, the Twins limped into Kansas City to play the Royals, another woebegone team. Molitor started the game with 2,998 hits. In his first at bat, he singled against Kansas City's Jose Rosado.

Rosado was on the mound when Molitor stepped to the plate again in the fifth. The young pitcher was thinking "I don't want to give him a strike." He threw a fastball, high in the strike zone. Molitor hit the ball to right center, between Jon Nunnlly and Rod Myers. Both closed in. Fearing a collision, both stopped. The ball fell between them, rolling away.

Molitor was on the run, slowing only momentarily at first to make sure he touched the bag. He ended up sliding into third, becoming the first player ever to triple for hit number 3,000.

"It wasn't the crispest I've hit over the years,'" he admitted.

The game was halted briefly. Twins players raced onto the field, mobbing the old star who had reached 3,000 exactly three years to the day from when David Winfield, also from St. Paul and also wearing a Twins uniform in the waning years of his career, had reached the 3,000 hit milestone. They are the only two players from the same city with 3,000 hits.

The congratulations over, Molitor continued to stay in the moment. He singled again and also drove in a run with a sacrifice fly in a game lost by the Twins, 6–5, before a crowd generously announced at 16,893.

After the game, reporters circled him.

How, one asked, after all the years, could he still be motivated?

"Tomorrow, I get to put on this uniform and play a major-league baseball game,'" he said.

1997
Who's Don Beaver?

The World: Mother Teresa dies of heart failure in Calcutta, India. The United Kingdom hands over Hong Kong to the People's Republic of China. Princess Diana is killed in a Paris car crash.

The Nation: Madeleine Albright becomes the country's first female secretary of state. In San Diego, thirty-nine members of the cult Heaven's Gate commit mass suicide.

The State: On April 18, Red River floods devastate Grand Forks, North Dakota, and portions of East Grand Forks, Minnesota. Andrew Cunanan begins a murder spree in Minneapolis and Rush Lake that extends all the way to Miami, where he kills fashion designer Gianni Versace in July. Eight days after the Versace murder, Cunanan kills himself.

Pop Culture: Billboard's #1 Song: "Candle in the Wind 1997," by Elton John. Best Picture: *Titanic*, the highest-grossing film in history. *Cold Mountain*, by Charles Frazier, wins the National Book Award for fiction. Top-Rated Television Show: *ER*.

The Season: Thank heaven for the Kansas City Royals. The Twins, despite a 67–94 record, manage to avoid last place in the Central Division because the Royals are a half-game worse. Torii Hunter appears in his first major-league game, but doesn't get a chance to bat. Mark McGwire takes his muscles from Oakland to St. Louis two-thirds of the way through the season and finishes with a combined 58 home runs.

The hero stage of ownership was long over for Carl Pohlad. He'd "saved" the Twins by purchasing them from Calvin Griffith in 1984. He'd triumphantly ridden in World Series parades in 1987 and 1991, fans cheering him as he waved.

But the cheers had stopped long ago. Pohlad's demands for a new stadium had gotten off to a terrible start when his first proposal for a $360 million, retractable roof stadium had included a promise of an $80 million contribution from the Pohlads. It turned out that the contribution was a loan. Disgust over the idea of public funding for a billionaire turned to utter contempt.

1997 would be another year of stadium politics and more mediocre Twins baseball. This was the year of Rich Becker in center field for the Twins and the year of Don Beaver, a North Carolina businessman with $250 million in his pocket and a hankering to move the team to his home state.

In his book, *Stadium Games*, Jay Weiner states the deal was always a bluff, a foil to get the Minnesota legislature to take Pohlad's demands for public money seriously. Jerry Bell, president of the Twins, denies that.

"He was a real buyer," Bell insists. "For heaven's sake, Carl was a banker. He wasn't going to make a deal with someone who couldn't pay off a loan.

The most tension-filled baseball in town was typically played at the state capitol, where politicians listened to the likes of commissioner Bud Selig, Kent Hrbek, and Kirby Puckett testify to the importance of a new stadium. COURTESY OF THE *ST. PAUL PIONEER PRESS.*

What happened is that Carl wasn't any different than the rest of us. Sometimes, he got angry. He was tired of everything and decided the only thing to do was sell the team and be done with it and then he changed his mind. Deep down, he really didn't want to sell."

In either event, Bell says, the most significant thing that happened in 1997 had nothing to do with the performance of the team, the actions of the legislature, or Don Beaver.

This was the year that revenue sharing came to baseball. That didn't just save the Twins, but Kansas City, Tampa, San Diego, Pittsburgh and other smaller-market teams as well. Pohlad, Bell says, was the owner who made revenue sharing happen.

Throughout baseball's history, baseball teams essentially kept whatever revenues they collected. This worked okay until the combination of free agency and local radio and television contracts exploded. Suddenly, the New York Yankees, with huge local TV and radio deals, had far more money to spend than such teams as the Twins. When baseball players in 1975 won the right to sell their services to the highest bidders, the rich teams obviously had more to spend. Disparities between revenues and team payrolls soared through the 1980s and into the 1990s.

In the early 1990s, Bell said, Pohlad called a group of owners of small-market teams together to talk about the problem.

"They happened at owners' meetings," Bell said. "All the owners would get together for a big dinner and then Carl would meet with a small group of owners. Each year, the attendance at those meetings grew. Carl was sort of a conspiracy buff. When the attendance kept getting bigger at his meetings, he started getting concerned. 'I bet there are spies from the big market teams sitting in on these meetings to see what we're up to,' he'd say. But then he'd laugh and say, 'Ah, so what.'"

The plan devised by the small-market owners roughly works like this: At the start of each season, each team puts money into a big pot, and then at the end of the year, it's distributed based on total revenues collected by each team. The rich teams, such as the Yankees, Boston Red Sox, Los Angeles Dodgers, and Chicago Cubs, get nothing back. But the low revenue teams receive millions of dollars.

There were two stumbling blocks to the socialistic plan inspired by the old capitalist banker. First were the owners of baseball's wealthiest teams. "Why should we give away money?" Second was the Players' Association. The union feared that any sort of revenue sharing plan would diminish the market value of free agent players; that teams such as the Yankees no longer would feel free to spend so much.

In time, however, the union was convinced by small-market teams that under revenue sharing, the total number of dollars for free agent players would be the same. It simply would be distributed differently. The superstar might not get quite as much as under the old system, but there would be more money for more players.

The players relented and in 1997 the owners voted, 28–2, in support of the system. By 2005 more than $300 million a year was flowing from the richer teams to poorer teams. Typically, the Twins get $20 million more from the revenue sharing pot than they put in.

Critics call it the "Robin Hood" plan. George Steinbrenner hated it. "Everybody else is living off the Yankees and I'm tired of it," he told *USA Today*'s Hal Bodley in 2005.

Some teams have abused the system, with owners using the money to enrich themselves rather than to improve their teams. For example, the Florida Marlins won the World Series in 2003 but by 2006 had dumped all of their star players, cutting their total payroll to $14.9 million. That same year, the Marlins collected $31 million in revenue-sharing dollars and reported the best profit margin in major-league baseball.

Bell insists the Twins have always used their revenue-sharing checks as they were intended. The money goes into the same pool as the rest of the team's revenue and then 50 to 52 percent of that total is used for paying the team's players.

In Bell's eyes, then, 1997 was a very good year for the Twins.

"It saved us and a lot of teams like us," said Bell.

There wasn't much to save on the field. The Twins had one of the oldest teams in franchise history, with such players as catcher Terry Steinach, thirty-five, designated hitter Paul Molitor, forty, and pitcher Bob Tewksbury, thirty-six, trying to lift younger players. They failed. The Twins finished 26 games under .500.

But there were a few bright spots beyond the Pohlad plan. Brad Radke, in just his third season in the big leagues, had the best season of his career, compiling a 20–10 record. (The problem was that the number two starting pitcher was Rich Robertson and he was 8–12.) There was a rookie, Torii Hunter, who showed up for a single game. He didn't come back, as the owner of center field, until 1999.

One other thing about 1997: Don Beaver disappeared almost as rapidly as he had emerged.

1998
Old and Bad

The World: Europeans agree on a single currency, the euro. India conducts three nuclear tests; Pakistan responds with five nuclear tests.

The Nation: President Clinton signs the first balanced-budget bill in thirty years. The President denies allegations of having an affair with White House intern Monica Lewinsky and is impeached by the House on a party-line vote.

The State: Jesse Ventura "shocks the world" by being elected governor over Republican candidate Norm Coleman and DFLer Skip Humphrey. A series of March tornadoes rips through St. Peter and the surrounding area, causing more than $200 million in damage. The *Grand Forks Herald* receives the Pulitzer Prize for Public Service for its coverage of the blizzards, flood, and fire that destroyed the *Herald*'s building. Minnesota becomes home to the largest Hmong population in the country.

Pop Culture: Frank Sinatra dies at the age of eighty-two. Best Picture: *Shakespeare in Love*. Pulitzer Prize for Fiction: *American Pastoral*, by Philip Roth. The final episode of *Seinfeld* is watched by seventy-six million people.

The Season: In another grim season (70–92), Matt Lawton leads the Twins with 21 home runs. In the meantime, in the National League, Mark McGwire and Sammy Sosa play home run derby in pursuit of Roger Maris's single-season home run record of 61. McGwire finishes the season with 70 homers; Sosa with 66. Baseball celebrates—until steroid questions start being asked a few seasons later.

Otis Nixon, an ancient center fielder, showed up to play for the Twins. He was thirty-nine years old and had previously played for the New York Yankees, Cleveland Indians, Montreal Expos, Atlanta Braves, Boston Red Sox, Texas Rangers, Toronto Blue Jays, and the Los Angeles Dodgers.

The signing of Nixon as a free agent for $2 million showed how desperate the Twins had become. He was, by all accounts, a good man but he was burdened with a long list of serious problems. He'd been arrested on drug charges in 1987 when he was with Cleveland, and there had been another problem that had had an impact on the World Series in 1991.

He was the Braves center fielder that year, a beloved figure in Atlanta, but late in the 1991 season, he failed a drug test and was suspended for sixty games. His suspension carried through the post-season, meaning the Braves played the Twins in that wonderful World Series without the services of their suspended center fielder.

But by the time he arrived in Minnesota, Nixon was sober and in most ways he fit right into a clubhouse that also included designated hitter Paul Molitor, who was forty-one; catcher Terry Steinbach, who was thirty-six; and pitchers Mike Morgan, thirty-eight, Bob Tewksbury, thirty-seven, and Greg Swindell, thirty-three. There may have been older teams around, but they played in senior citizen's leagues.

Nixon performed nobly in 1998, especially considering his age and his lifetime of woes. As the team's leadoff batter, he hit .297 and stole 37 bases. But he had no power—he hit 1 home run and had 20 RBI—and he didn't exactly have a bright baseball future.

This old team proved that veteran savvy can be overrated. The Twins finished 22 games under .500 and in fourth place in the Central Division, five games ahead of the last place Detroit Tigers, but nineteen behind the first place Cleveland Indians.

There had been a purpose behind the Twins' strange, old-age movement.

"After the strike [of 1994] we were trying to get the new ballpark," said Jerry Bell, who was the team's president at the time. "Our thought was that we wanted a veteran ball club that would be credible enough so that when we went to the legislature, they could see that we were a viable organization. But it was pretty clear this wasn't working."

Indeed, the Twins were not impressing either the legislature or their dwindling fan base. Every financing idea being tossed up in front of the legislature to get public money for a new ballpark was being quickly shot down, and the Twins finished last in the American League in attendance with 1,165,976.

Following the dismal '98 season, Jim Pohlad, Bell, general manager Terry Ryan, and manager Tom Kelly met to formulate a Plan B. And so began the great fall housecleaning of 1998. Molitor retired, Nixon was released and returned to play another season in Atlanta, Tewksbury retired, Morgan and Swindell were released, with both ending up with the Arizona Diamondbacks.

The age of the Twins changed dramatically. In 1998 the team's average age was almost twenty-nine years. In 1999, the average age would be closer to twenty-six.

Most of the departures were greeted with yawns by Twins fans. But one move stirred at least a bit of fan resentment. That came when shortstop Pat Meares was lost to free agency to, of all teams, the Pittsburgh Pirates, a team even more dismal than the Twins.

Meares had succeeded Greg Gagne as the Twins' shortstop in 1993 and had at least shown competence. He'd batted .270, hit 9 homers and driven

Wally McNeil has been donning vendor's attire as Wally the Beer Man since the opening of the Metrodome, through good times and bad. 1998 was filled with a lot of bad times. Here he serves up soft drinks at a pro-stadium rally at the state capitol. COURTESY OF THE *ST. PAUL PIONEER PRESS*.

in an impressive 70 runs, almost 10 percent of the team's 1998 total. The six years he'd spent with the team also made him the Twins player with the most longevity, meaning most fans at least knew his name.

Meares was even a footnote in baseball history. He made the last out in the perfect game that the Yankees' David "Boomer" Wells had pitched against the Twins on May 18 in Yankee Stadium. Most accounts of that game started like this: "David Wells threw a no-hitter against the hapless Minnesota Twins." Years later, in his book, *Perfect I'm Not! Boomer on Beers, Brawls, Backaches & Baseball,* Wells wrote that he had been "half drunk" in pitching the perfect game.

Half drunk, half sober, it didn't take much to beat the Twins, and now they refused to even try to sign Pat Meares, who at least didn't have gray hair.

What's it like in the clubhouse of a team that's not good enough to compete?

"You're still a major-league baseball player," said Ron Coomer, who was a twenty-eight-year-old rookie in 1995. "Most of us know we're very fortunate. You never look at baseball like it's going off to a job, you get to go play another game. Even when things are going tough, there are times that it's still exhilarating."

Though he never played on a Minnesota team with a winning record, Coomer, with his slow-pitch softball body and his ability to at least occasionally hit a home run, became a fan favorite in his six years with the Twins. When Coomer recalls his years with the Twins, he thinks about the little things.

In 1997, the Twins were playing their last game of the season in Cleveland. Entering the game, Coomer was batting an even .300, the gold standard for hitters at any level of ball.

"TK asked me if I wanted to sit out the game and protect the average," Coomer said. "I said, 'When there's a game, I want to play.'"

So he played in that final game of the season and in his first four trips to the plate, he had one hit. His batting averaged had slipped to .299 with one more chance to swing the bat.

"Sandy Alomar was catching for Cleveland," Coomer said. "Jose Mesa was pitching. Alomar says, 'You need one more for .300, don't you?' I nodded my head. Next thing I know Alomar's saying, 'We're coming fastball.' I hit a bullet, but right at the shortstop. Finished at .298."

Coomer laughed as he told the story. Even in losing seasons there are lifelong memories.

Coomer was among the handful of players to survive the clubhouse clearing of 1998. Despite unimpressive minor-league numbers, Torii Hunter would replace Nixon in center for the Twins in 1999. He'd work for $200,000, 10 percent of the cost of Nixon. Another rookie, Cristian Guzman would replace Meares at short and work for the $200,000 big-league minimum as opposed to the $2.5 million Mears had been paid. Corey Koskie would also get $200,000 and replace Coomer at third, while Coomer would be the designated hitter for $1.1 million in place of Molitor, who'd been paid $4.2 million. Doug Mientkiewicz would move in at first, again for the minimum salary. The same sort of changes would take place on the pitching staff, with young, inexpensive pitchers such as Eric Milton, Joe Mays, and Mike Lincoln filling spots once held by vets.

"The primary reason for changing our direction was baseball," said Bell. "It was obvious to us that we needed to go a different direction. But the second part of it was economic. It turned out to be the right thing to do."

For his part, Otis Nixon returned to the Braves for one last season. After his playing days were done, there was an ugly assault charge in 2004. But in recent years, Nixon says he's found a new passion. He runs an organization called On-Track Ministries. "My life today is Christ-centered," he says on the On-Track Web site.

1999
Oh, Canada

The World: There is international angst over "Y2K." What will happen to computers when the year changes from 1999 to the new millennium, 2000? There turned out to be very little disruption. The world population surpasses six billion. Boris Yeltsin resigns as president of Russia, and Vladimir Putin steps in as acting president.

The Nation: Two teenagers kill twelve of their fellow students and a teacher at Columbine High in Littleton, Colorado. For the first time, the Dow Jones Industrial Average surpasses 10,000, then 11,000.

The State: The new governor, Jesse Ventura, arrives at his Target Center inaugural ball, wearing a fringed leather jacket, a bandana covering his head, a Jimi Hendrix T-shirt, and his famed feather boa from his pro wrestling days. The governor joins performer Warren Zevon on stage for rousing version of "Werewolves of London." Sara Jane Olson, aka Kathleen Soliah, is arrested at her St. Paul home and charged with conspiracy to commit murder from her days in the 1970s as a member of the Symbionese Liberation Army.

Pop Culture: Prince's 1983 hit song, "1999," has a resurgence as a millennium theme song. Highest-Grossing Movie: *Star Wars: Episode I—The Phantom Menace.* Pulitzer Prize for Fiction: *The Hours,* by Michael Cunningham. Top-Rated Television Show: *Who Wants to Be a Millionaire?*

The Season: Last in home runs, last in runs scored, last in American League attendance, last in the A.L. Central Division with a 63–97 record.

In the first round of the amateur draft, the Twins, with the fifth pick overall, selected a high school kid out of Moses Lake, Washington, B. J. Garbe. He'd been a high school superstar, All-State in football and baseball. He was out of the game a few years later, after experiencing a number of health problems. A bust.

In the second round of the draft, the Twins selected a catcher from Texas, Rob Bowen, another high school kid. Bowen has had a more productive career than Garbe, actually making it to the Twins, briefly, in 2003 and 2004, before bouncing around to a number of major-league teams as a backup catcher.

On the field, the Twins had little to offer, finishing last in their division. But, after the fall housecleaning of '98, the team certainly was younger—and cheaper. Torii Hunter, Doug Mientkiewicz, Cristian Guzman, Corey Koskie, and Eric Milton were learning on the job.

But the lessons came hard. By season's end, the young Twins had proven to be seven games worse than the old Twins of 1998 and it was time for the Pohlads, Jerry Bell, TK, and Terry Ryan to meet again.

"I mentioned to Carl and Jerry that I thought, all things considered, we'd had a pretty good year," recalled Ryan. "Carl looked straight at me and said, 'We lost 97 games and you're telling me we had a good year?'"

These were nerve-wracking times for everyone in management. Would the Pohlads continue to show patience with the team?

"If you're a thinking person at all you know that things aren't going well," said Ryan. "You know there are no guarantees that you'll keep your job."

Off the field, the future of the team seemed to remain very much in doubt. Norm Coleman, mayor of St. Paul at the time, had pushed hard for voters to pass a half-cent sales tax that would have given the city the revenue to build a new ballpark for the Twins. Coleman's dream was crushed by the voters. The public again made it clear that it wanted no part of paying for a ballpark for millionaire players and a billionaire owner. Would the Twins really leave Minnesota? Was all the talk a Pohlad bluff?

Inside the Twins scouting offices, it was business as usual through all the politics and losses. In the third round of the 1999 amateur draft, the team selected another high-school-age catcher, a Canadian named Justin Morneau. For years, he'd been hitting baseballs out of parks in New Westminster, British Columbia. Why, he'd won a batting title when he was four years old, playing against kids who were six and seven years old.

Twins scout Howie Norsetter liked him because he was big, strong, and a left-handed hitter. Picking Morneau was a gamble, but big left-handed-hitting catchers don't just fall from the sky in either the United States or Canada. The Twins made their pick and called the Morneau home.

"We've selected you in the third round," the kid was told.

Moreneau and his father, George, were both surprised. They hugged, smiled, and hugged again.

"We didn't think he'd be picked until the fifth or sixth round," George Morneau said. "And I think the Twins were about the only team we hadn't talked to before the draft."

George Morneau coached both of his sons, Geordie and Justin, from the time they were two, though George's sport was fast-pitch softball. He'd been a member of the Canadian national team in the early 1970s, a pitcher and a hitter. His great joy as a competitor was beating the Americans, who seemed to think that Canadians couldn't play the game.

His sports hero, though, was a U.S. baseball player, Mickey Mantle. A baseball with Mantle's autograph was proudly displayed on a shelf in the Morneau living room. Or, at least, that was where it was supposed to be. One day, George came home from work and the Mickey Mantle ball was missing. He looked outside and saw his two young sons playing with it.

"I hung 'em from the rafters for that one," George recalled.

But the ball and the boys recovered. And in June 1999, Justin signed his contract with the Twins. But just before heading to the farm team in the rookie Gulf Coast League, he decided to do something he wasn't supposed to do after signing. He played with his local team in a tournament in the States and suffered a broken arm when he was hit by a pitch. Morneau showed up in Fort Meyers with his arm in a cast.

"Howie told me he really caught hell from the Twins for that," said George.

The eighteen-year-old did heal in time to play a few games and show some promise, but not as a catcher. The team didn't think he had a strong enough arm to catch. He was moved to the outfield, then first base.

As a little bonus, the Twins brought Morneau to the Metrodome near the end of the '99 season so he could work out with big-leaguers. His father and mother, Audra, came to the Dome to watch the workout. The kid put on a show, driving several pitches deep into the second deck in right field.

Watching it all, was Twins manager Tom Kelly.

"Hurry up and learn, kid, we want you up here," he said as he watched.

The Morneaus, father and son, were elated by the whole experience. So was a fellow Canadian, Koskie. As Morneau was leaving the Dome, Koskie loaded up the young slugger with prime, big-league bats and told him he'd stay in touch until he returned to the Dome full time.

Midway through the 2003 season, the two Canadians were united on the Twins. Ron Gardenhire, who had succeeded Kelly as manager, frequently batted the two back-to-back in the lineup.

"So they can talk Canadian to each other," he explained.

George Morneau makes frequent appearances at Twins games. He'll offer advice to the kid he coached for years, "but only if he asks." Mostly, George sits in the stands feeling incredibly proud.

"He's playing with the best in the world," he said. "I just marvel that he's out there with those guys. He's out there playing against guys like Mickey Mantle."

The Mantle autographed baseball shares space with dozens of other baseballs signed by old Twins, current Twins, and stars from throughout the major leagues.

The draft of 1999 turned out pretty well.

A young slugger, Justin Morneau, was drafted in the third round by the Twins in 1999. By 2003 he had advanced to the AAA Rochester Red Wings, and played in his first big-league game on June 10. Doug Mientkiewicz was traded to Boston in 2004, and Morneau has been the Twins starting first baseman ever since. COURTESY OF THE ROCHESTER RED WINGS.

2000
Bobblemania

The World: Oil prices soar to $37.38 a barrel, causing international concern. Oil producing nations increase production and prices fall to $22 by December. The National Action Party's Vicente Fox is elected president of Mexico, ending seventy-one years of rule by the Institutional Revolutionary Party.

The Nation: The presidential election is held on November 7, but the outcome is not determined until December when the Supreme Court halts Florida's vote recount, giving the White House to George W. Bush over Al Gore, who won the popular vote. Vermont legalizes civil unions for same-sex couples.

The State: An academic scandal at the University of Minnesota wipes out all post-season men's basketball records from 1993–98, meaning the Final Four team of 1997 didn't exist, according to the NCAA. *St. Paul Pioneer Press* sportswriter George Dohrmann, who broke the story in 1999, receives the Pulitzer Prize for Beat Reporting, the newspaper's third Pulitzer in fourteen years.

Pop Culture: Billboard's #1 Song: "Breathe," by Faith Hill. Best Picture: *Gladiator.* Best Seller: *The Brethren,* by John Grisham. Top-Rated Television Show: *Who Wants to Be a Millionaire?*

The Season: The Twins have a losing record (69–93) for a franchise record eighth straight year. Cristian Guzman offers some hope for a brighter future by hitting 20 triples. The Yankees win their third straight World Series, beating the Mets in the Subway Series, 4 games to 1.

There was little to celebrate on the field as the 2000 season began. The Twins were in a funk that had begun in 1993. The payroll had been slashed to $15 million and pitcher Brad Radke, who was being paid $3.5 million, was the one credible big-leaguer the organization was building around.

"The job engulfs you," said general manager Terry Ryan of trying to put the pieces together on a shoestring budget. "You end up with baseball as 100 percent of your life. The one time you get to settle back and just enjoy the game is when you're in the playoffs. There's nothing else to do then but enjoy."

The first bobbleheads date back to the 1960s, but it was a Twins promotion of a Harmon Killebrew bobblehead on June 9, 2000, that created chaos in the Dome and a national bobblehead passion. That giveaway showed Killebrew in home whites with his bat on a shoulder and the promotion's sponsor, Mountain Dew, on the base. The Killebrew bobblehead shown here in road grays was a prototype for a version that was to be given to anyone who purchased two full sets of season tickets in 2001. In the end, what they received was the 2000 version, except with Killebrew's name on the base. FROM THE COLLECTION OF CLYDE DOEPNER; PHOTO BY ROBERT FOGT.

Enjoyment was still a couple of years away. In 2000, the Twins were still wandering in baseball's wilderness. There were rays of hope. For example, Eric Milton had a breakout season, compiling a 13–10 record and giving the Twins a strong one-two pitching punch. Radke, the right-hander, then Milton the lefty. The two were talented, media shy, and close friends. They'd leave the Dome and head to Lake Minnetonka to fish.

But mostly there were bumbling young players on the field and apathy in Twins Territory. The one thing that inspired enthusiasm was the arrival of a phenom in June.

The phenom: A bobblehead. A little figurine, in this case of Harmon Killebrew. The Twins announced they were going to give away 5,000 of the bobbleheads, the first of a series.

What happened was almost terrifying. The day before the bobbleheads were to be given away, the *Star Tribune* ran a front-page story quoting Dave Mona, a sports memorabilia expert, saying that the bobblehead would have an immediate value of $100 on eBay.

Hours before the game began, fans started lining up outside the Dome.

"Oh, oh," was the thought that went through the mind of Patrick Klinger, the Twins' marketing executive who'd made the decision to order the bobbleheads.

Klinger had come across bobbleheads in 1999. It was among the hundreds of promotional proposals that arrive at his office each season.

"A company in Seattle had developed a prototype for it," he said. "They'd sent me a Willie Mays bobblehead that the Giants were considering using. I saw it and thought, 'This is interesting.' I wanted to use it in 1999 but there just wasn't enough time to find a sponsor."

By giveaway standards, this was a fairly expensive product, costing $2.50 each. (Bats for bat days are the most expensive, costing the team or sponsor $4 each.)

So, while Klinger sought a sponsor—Mountain Dew ultimately became the sponsor—it was the San Francisco Giants that first unveiled the new-age bobblehead, but it didn't cause nearly the stir in the Bay Area that the little Harmon Killebrew bobblehead created in Minnesota.

"We saw the lines start forming in the morning," recalled Klinger. "The lines kept growing and the gates didn't open until five o'clock. Within five minutes after the gates opened, they were gone. There were a lot of very unhappy people. We just weren't prepared because we'd never seen anything like it. There were gate-crashers. There were adults snatching them from little kids. People would go to buy a hotdog, set their bobblehead on the counter and somebody would reach out, grab it, and run."

The bobblehead concept, which proved to be a hugely successful marketing gimmick for the next nine years, wasn't really new. When Calvin Griffith arrived in Minnesota in 1961, the team had a similar device sold at its concession stands.

"It was called a bobbing head," said Clyde Doepner, a retired high school history teacher who probably has the largest collection of Twins documents and memorabilia of anyone around. For a few decades, Doepner, his attic jammed with old uniforms, bats, bobbing heads, and bobbleheads, has been Twins unofficial, unpaid archivist.

Doepner ended up in this position because of his friendship with Griffith, which was based on two words: "Thank you."

Back in 1967, Doepner was a high school baseball coach. That year, Griffith had sent all of the region's high school coaches a free season pass to all Twins games.

"I was thrilled," said Doepner. "I stopped by Calvin's office one day and asked to see him. The secretary said he was busy and wasn't seeing anybody but she asked me what I wanted. I said I was there to thank Mr. Griffith for his wonderful gift. She was surprised and said she thought Mr. Griffith would see me. So I went into his office and he was kind of grumpy. 'What do you want?' I said, 'I just want to thank you for this pass. It's a wonderful gift. Thank you.' He said, 'I don't know how many of those we sent out, but I do know you're the first son of a bitch who's come by to say thank you.'"

Griffith was so impressed by the courtesy that he escorted Doepner from his office to the executive booth used by Twins executives for watching games.

"You're welcome to sit here anytime you come to a game," Doepner said Griffith told him. "Let the rest of those ungrateful son of a bitches sit out there."

Doepner said he accepted the Griffith offer only a couple of times a year. ("I didn't want to take advantage of his kindness.") But as the years went by, he became close to Griffth and Griffith's brothers.

Through his relationship with the Griffith clan, Doepner developed a relationship with many of the Twins' old stars, who would give him bats, signed balls, even uniforms.

One of his great treasures, for instance, is the bat Killebrew used in hitting that five-hundred-foot monster home run in 1967. It's covered with pine tar.

"Harmon explained to me why it had so much pine tar on it," Doepner said. "He kept using that bat for a month after he hit the homer before he finally cracked it. Then the batboys used it to stir the pine tar for good luck for everybody else on the team."

Doepner hit the mother lode of Twins stuff when the team was making the move from the Met to the Metrodome. Griffith had stored tons of stuff, including boxes and boxes of documents the team had brought from Washington, at the old ballpark. There was no space for it in the new stadium. So Griffith unloaded. Doepner, the history teacher, was offended.

"Do you mind if I go through anything you're throwing out?" he asked Griffith.

"Have at it," said Griffith.

Doepner hauled out box after box of stuff, including everything from letters from presidents who had attended games when the team was in Washington, to old programs.

Jim Kaat helped select the version of his bobblehead for a Twins promotion. After seven tries the company came up with the final version to give to fans. One bobblehead looked like Kaat was wearing lipstick. FROM THE COLLECTION OF CLYDE DOEPNER; PHOTO BY ROBERT FOGT.

"Calvin thought it was funny," said Doepner. "One day he saw me carrying boxes of stuff and he said, 'I'm paying people good money to throw this shit away and you're bringing it all back in to show me.'"

Among the treasures Doepner received from Griffith was an original and rare bobbing head. It shows the little Twins doll on a pedestal inscribed with the words "Minneapolis Twins."

"When they were in the process of moving here, the team's original documents called them the Minneapolis Twins," Doepner said. "It wasn't until a little later they switched to Minnesota."

But no promotional gimmick—not halters, nor bats, nor baseballs, nor caps—ever stirred the passions of Twins fans like the bobbleheads. So enthusiastic was the response that Klinger started receiving calls from teams throughout baseball, then basketball and hockey. Everyone wanted to get a piece of the bobblehead action.

So, in 2000, there were two lineups for the Twins.

The typical lineup on the field was filled with still-unknown players who in future years would turn the fortune of the team around: catcher Matt

LeCroy, first baseman Ron Coomer, second baseman Jay Canizaro, shortstop Cristian Guzman, third baseman Corey Koskie, leftfielder Jacque Jones, center fielder Torii Hunter, right fielder Matt Lawton, and designated hitter David Ortiz. This lineup finished last in the American League and drew only 1,000,750 fans, fewest in the league.

And then there was the bobblehead lineup: Harmon Killebrew, Kent Hrbek, Tony Oliva, and Kirby Puckett. That group stirred the passions of Twins fans and started a national craze.

2001

Hot Dog! A Revival

The World and Nation: On September 11, the world stands still as terrorists fly passenger aircraft into the World Trade Center towers in New York and the Pentagon outside Washington, D.C. A third plane is crashed, by the heroic passengers on board, into a field near Shanksville, Pennsylvania. Nearly 3,000 people are killed in the attacks. On September 18, letters containing anthrax are opened at ABC, NBC, CBS, the *New York Post,* and the *National Enquirer.* Five people die and seventeen become ill. On October 7, the United States, with participation from other nations, invades Afghanistan, host of terrorist training bases.

The State: Thomas Burnett Jr., who grew up in Bloomington, is believed to have been among the heroes of United Airlines flight 93 when he and passengers attacked the hijackers of the flight, forcing it to crash near Shanksville, Pennsylvania. The actions of Burnett and others may have prevented the plane from being used to crash into a target in Washington, D.C. All aboard the plane perished. Warned of concerns by instructors at a flight training academy in Eagan, FBI agents arrested Zacarias Moussaoui on August 16 for immigration violations. FBI headquarters in D.C. turned down repeated requests by Minnesota agents to conduct searches of Moussaoui's laptop computer. He was in a Minnesota jail at the time of the terrorist attacks, but was later found guilty of conspiring to take part in the attacks and is serving a life sentence.

Pop Culture: Grammy Song of the Year: "Fallin'," by Alicia Keys. Highest-Grossing Movie: *Harry Potter and the Sorcerer's Stone.* Best Seller: *Desecration,* by Jerry B. Jenkins and Tim La Haye. Top-Rated Television Show: *Friends.*

Season: The Twins end their run of eight sub-.500 seasons with an 85–77 record, and are actually in first place with a five-game lead in the Central Division at the All-Star break. Shortstop Cristian Guzman leads the league with 14 triples and is an All-Star, along with pitchers Joe Mays and Eric Milton. Their second-place finish renews excitement for baseball in the region. San Francisco's Barry Bonds electrifies baseball with 73 home runs, a single-season record that later became stained by questions of steroid use.

This was the season of the Twins' greatest-ever comeback. Hot dogs flew from the stands. Guzy flew around the bases. Fans poured back into the Dome. Major-league baseball owners threatened to close down the Twins, and a Hennepin County district court judge saved the day. Oh, what a season!

It started on the field. A trade that had been maligned in 1998 by the media and fans—wealthy but disgruntled All-Star second baseman Chuck Knoblauch going to the Yankees for some kids nobody ever had heard of—

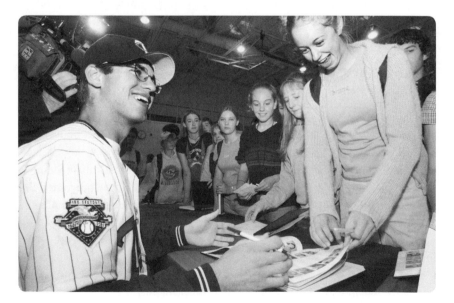

On the day the Twins made Joe Mauer the first pick of the 2001 draft, he signs autographs at St. Paul's Cretin-Derham Hall, the high school where he was a three-sport star. COURTESY OF THE *ST. PAUL PIONEER PRESS.*

After signing with the Twins, Mauer headed to Elizabethton, Tennessee, for his first season of professional ball, living at the home of "Miss Jane," a home he shared with players Richard Smart, brother Jake Mauer, Kahaulua Kaulaua, and Jason Miller. COURTESY OF THE *ST. PAUL PIONEER PRESS*.

suddenly was paying off. The Twins had received minor-leaguers Cristian Guzman and Eric Milton, along with Brian Buchanan and Daniel Mota, in the trade that they really had not wanted to make.

Knoblauch, Rookie of the Year in 1991, had become bitter playing for an organization that had gone sour in 1993 and was showing no signs of getting better. Knoblauch was hard to get along with in the clubhouse and at home.

"Sometimes Chuck would sit in silence for hours," his former wife, Lisa, told a *Sports Illustrated* reporter shortly after he was traded. "He was sad, desolate, miserable."

There was an ugly incident in a Seattle hotel. A fifteen-year-old kid sought an autograph. Knoblauch blew him off. The kid responded, "Knoblauch you suck!" Knoblauch countered by backing the kid against a wall and cursing at him. Police were called. Though there were no charges filed, Twins fans were disgusted with their second baseman. He had signed a five-year, $30 million contract. He could at least sign autographs.

His teammates and the Twins' coaching staff struggled with Knoblauch, too. He'd become obsessive about his diet and weight lifting. A decade after the trade, Knoblauch was one of the players interviewed by a Congressional committee about using banned substances, in this case human growth hormone. Perhaps use of the substance was an outgrowth of his desire to turn his stocky body into a no-fat machine. It should be noted that Knoblauch only admitted to using the hormone in 2000, after being traded by the Twins.

As spring training of 1998 approached, Knoblauch let the Twins know he wanted to be traded, and general manager Terry Ryan obliged.

"It wasn't that we wanted to trade Knoblauch," he said early in the 2001 season. "He wanted to be traded and when we made the deal, people were concerned we didn't get enough back. The Yankees won three World Series and Knoblauch's been a part of that. And you have some players here that give us the ability to grow. We both got what we were looking for."

Guzman and Milton had become key parts of an emerging team. Because of his sprinter's speed, any ground ball that Guzman hit had the potential to be at least a single. Milton was turning out to be one of the best left-handed pitchers in the league. These two parts of the Knoblauch trade of four years earlier blended perfectly with Torii Hunter, who was becoming a star, and fan favorite Doug Mientkiewicz, who could catch anything anywhere near first base and sat on the dugout floor, his cap turned inside out, when the Twins were rallying.

With this group, baseball suddenly was fun again in the Upper Midwest. TV and radio ratings soared, as did attendance at the Dome.

The Twins marketing department was on a roll, too. To bolster a slogan—"Get to Know 'Em"—the organization worked to attract young fans to the Dome, offering discounted tickets to students showing a school ID. The Twins, on some weeknights, also offered hot dogs for a buck. The Dome became the cheapest place in the metro to take a date.

There was one other thing needed to create the perfect hot dog storm on May, 2, 2001. Starting in the 2000 season with the Yankees, Knoblauch, the once brilliant fielder, suddenly couldn't make a simple throw from second base to first. "The yips," is how ballplayers describe this otherwise unexplainable behavior.

In fact, he told the Congressional committee that the reason he started using the banned hormones was in an effort to regain trust in his arm. But no amount of hormones, coaching, or practicing could solve the problem, so Yankee manager Joe Torre moved Knoblauch to left field.

All of this set the stage for the night the hotdogs rained on left field in the Dome. With the Yankees in town, with the Twins playing well, with cheap seats and cheap hot dogs available, there were more than 36,825 people in the park for the weeknight game. Many of them were young and seated in the left field bleachers.

In one of the most memorable games at the Dome, manager Tom Kelly went to left field with the Yankees' Chuck Knoblauch to discourage fans from pelting the former Twins star with $1 hot dogs. COURTESY OF AP IMAGES.

Those fans had come to party. Beach balls were bouncing through the stands. Fans were booing Knoblauch each time he stepped to the plate or moved to left field. In the fifth inning of a game the Twins were winning, a few of the dollar dogs started landing in left field. By the sixth, there was a downpour of 'dogs, plastic beer bottles, and coins.

Torre pulled his team from the field.

Bob Casey, the team's venerable public address announcer, was furious.

"Please!" he said. "This is a championship game. Let's act like it."

His voice, rumbling through the Dome, sounded like the ultimate scolding grandfather. Some of the fans in the crowd laughed and tossed more stuff onto the field.

"If the trouble does not stop in left field, this game will be forfeited and the Yankees will win," said Casey, more angrily than ever. "Now quit that!"

Forfeit? To the Yankees? This seemed to catch the attention of the fans. As security people rushed to the scene, fans in the bleachers started pointing out the troublemakers. Forty people were evicted.

The Yankees took the field again, with Twins manager Tom Kelly personally escorting Knoblauch to left, his arm draped on Knobby's shoulder.

"Hang in there," Kelly said he told Knoblauch. "Do the best you can."

After a twelve-minute delay, the game resumed, though it was stopped

Kirby Puckett (*right*) and St. Paul's Dave Winfield were inducted into the Baseball Hall of Fame on the same day in August 2001. COURTESY OF THE *ST. PAUL PIONEER PRESS*.

BUDDY BOY

There were all sorts of baseball passions in 2001: joy was created on the field by a new generation of Twins players, and rage was directed at baseball commissioner Bud Selig, who was threatening to contract the Twins unless a new ballpark was constructed. PHOTO BY JERRY HOLT. COPYRIGHT 2009 *STAR TRIBUNE*/MINNEAPOLIS–ST. PAUL.

again in the eighth when more junk was tossed on the field.

That the young Twins won the game, 4–2, was almost forgotten. Kelly apologized profusely to the Yankees.

Sports columnists, such as the *Star Tribune*'s Dan Barreiro, scolded the fans. "It's more than a shame. It's a disgrace," he wrote in the next day's paper. "A low point in Minnesota sports history."

After the hot dog game at the Dome, Knoblauch was perplexed.

"They just seriously need to turn the page," he said of the fans. "Seriously. It's been four years. I'm not mad. It's just silly."

Hunter, the Twins center fielder, wondered what it might be like when the Twins played in Yankee Stadium, a place notorious for rough treatment of opposing players.

"They started a war," said Hunter of the hot dog throwers. "When we go to Yankee Stadium, I think I'll wear a hard hat."

Throughout the rest of the season, the Twins continued to achieve beyond expectations, thrilling the fans and finishing in second place in the Central Division, six games behind the Cleveland Indians. More than 1.7 million fans came to the Dome, close to double the attendance of the 2000 team that had the worst attendance in baseball.

But the excitement of the winning season was overshadowed on November 6, when the owners of the major-league teams voted to eliminate two teams: The Montreal Expos and, with the consent of Twins owner Carl Pohlad, the Twins.

It's unknown if the owners would have followed through on this threat, or if it was just another gambit to allow Pohlad to pressure Minnesotans to help finance the construction of a new stadium. Certainly, throughout the business world, Pohlad was known as a hard-nosed dealer, who would go to any extreme to get what he wanted.

Pohlad was respected by his fellow owners, in part because he had more money than most of them. And he was liked by baseball's commissioner, Bud Selig, who once had been the recipient of a Pohlad loan. Now, with contraction talk filling the air, Selig had arranged for Pohlad to receive $250 million if he gave up the team.

There was another reason owners were willing to play the contraction bluff: They had been unable to get concessions from the players' union to do something to get skyrocketing salaries under control. Contraction was an obvious threat to the players. Suddenly, there were would be eighty fewer union members. Suddenly, the market would be flooded with free agents, as players from the contracted teams sought employment elsewhere.

Whatever Major League Baseball's motive, the plan was blown up on November 16 by Hennepin County district court judge Harry Crump. In response to a request from the Dome's governing body, the Metropolitan Sports Facilities Commission, Crump issued an order requiring the Twins to fulfill their contractual obligation to play in the Dome in 2002.

"The welfare, recreation, prestige, prosperity, trade, and commerce of the people of the community are at stake," Crump wrote. "The Twins brought the community together with Homer Hankies and bobblehead dolls. The Twins are one of the few teams in town where a family can afford to take their children to enjoy a hot dog and peanuts and a stadium. The vital public interest or trust of the Twins substantially outweighs any private interest."

2002

From Contraction to Playoffs

The World: On March 1, the United States–led forces throw the Taliban out of Afghanistan during a three-week operation that leaves Hamid Karzai as "interim president" of the country.

The Nation: The federal government begins an investigation of bankrupt Enron Corporation in Houston. *Wall Street Journal* reporter Daniel Pearl is kidnapped in Pakistan. His body is found days later, his murderers claiming Pearl was a CIA agent.

The State: On October 25, a plane carrying U.S. Senator Paul Wellstone crashes, killing Wellstone, his wife, Sheila, their daughter, Marcia, and four others. The crash occurs eleven days before Wellstone is to stand for re-election against Republican candidate Norm Coleman. The DFL selects former Vice President Walter Mondale to replace Wellstone on the ballot, but in the wake of an outcry over the tone of a Wellstone memorial service, Coleman defeats Mondale to win the Senate seat.

Pop Culture: Billboard's #1 Song: "How You Remind Me," by Nickelback. Best Picture: *Chicago*. Best Seller: *The Summons*, by John Grisham. *American Idol* makes its debut on Fox.

The Season: It's the most remarkable season in the team's history, as the Twins go from being the center of contraction talk into the playoffs. Torii Hunter—29 homers, 94 RBI—becomes a star, and a young pitcher, Johan Santana, moves into the starting rotation late in season, compiling an 8–6 record. The Twins extend the excitement by winning the Divisional playoff series against Oakland, but lose to the eventual World Series champion Anaheim Angels in the League Championship Series.

Tom Kelly, in typical style, retired following the 2001 season. "It's just been a fantastic ride for me. But now I just feel it's a good time for me to step aside and let somebody else take over," he said. And then he was gone.

Kelly had made no big production of his decision within the Twins organization. One day, shortly after the season was over, he'd stopped by to see general manager Terry Ryan.

"He just dropped into my office and told me that it was time," said Ryan. The general manager made little effort to talk Kelly out of his decision. "You know how it is with TK. Once he's made up his mind about something there's not much you're going to be able to do to change it."

Most fans—and members of the media—could never understand what made Kelly so special. But most of his players understood.

"He was one of the few who could be both your friend and still get tough when he had to get on you," recalled Frank Viola. "And fundamentals. The stuff I learned from TK has stuck with me my whole life. He'd probably laugh if he knew that. Every spring we would have to put up with fundamentals. We thought it was crap when we were doing it. Same stuff, over and over again. But he understood that if you're not as good as the other teams, you have to beat them in other ways. His way was fundamentals. If you out-fundamental the other teams you're going to beat them more often than not."

He was a character. Players were never sure what to expect. Most days he was just happy to be at the ballpark.

"He was a regular guy, down to earth, a guy who loved putting the uniform on," said Viola.

Only once could Viola remember Kelly getting red-necked, out-of-control angry. That came when Viola was pitching in the minor leagues for Orlando, in 1981. The team had played a miserable game in Nashville. Randy Bush had missed a sign in a crucial situation. The team walked into the clubhouse, hungry, ready to eat the turkey sandwiches that were spread out on a wooden table.

"If we were getting any meal money at all, it wasn't much," said Viola. "We were all thinking about those turkey sandwiches on a wooden table. I'll never forget it. We're about ready to go for the sandwiches and all of a sudden, they're flying through the air. It was like slow motion. The sandwiches, the table, TK sent everything flying through the room. We're all sitting there thinking, 'Wow! There goes our meal.' Next day, we went out and kicked the crap out of whoever we were playing."

Usually, though, in his fifteen-year run, he was laid-back. He'd throw an arm around a player's shoulder. He'd laugh. He let his players have fun—as long as they were playing fundamentally sound baseball.

The first big issue in the minds of Twins fans following Kelly's surprising announcement was not about who would replace him. It was whether there would even be a team. Talk of contraction was everywhere, including in the Twins' offices. Ryan tried to block out all of the talk. "There was nothing I could do about it." He went through a list of possible successors to Kelly. Paul Molitor, bench coach under Kelly, and Ron Gardenhire, Kelly's third base coach, were the two leading candidates. Scott Ullger, another Twins coach, was also under consideration. Molitor eventually withdrew his name.

But everything was on hold as the contraction battle played out in the courts. The days passed. Spring training was coming closer. Finally, Ryan went to Jerry Bell and Pohlad and said the team could wait no longer.

"We had all these coaches out of work, wondering if they were going to have a job with the Twins or what," said Ryan. "We had to make a move."

Pohlad gave him the nod. Though the contraction issue was still in the courts, Ryan could go ahead and name a manager. On January 4, 2002, he called Gardenhire to his office.

"I'm gonna name you as my manager," said Ryan.

Gardenhire's heart was pounding. But he was trying to act calm.

"Thank you," Gardenhire told Ryan. "I don't think I'll disappoint you."

Gardenhire said that though he felt like jumping for joy, he calmly walked out of Ryan's office, then sprinted to a place where he could call his wife.

"It was one of those incredible moments in your life," said Gardenhire. "How do you describe it? So happy, so excited."

The national media saw the hiring as bizarre. Wrote Murray Chass of the *New York Times:* "Ron Gardenhire was named manager of the Minnesota Twins yesterday. That was the easy part. Now he has to have a team to manage.... If the Twins do not play, the forty-four-year-old Gardenhire will become the first manager in major-league history not to manage a game."

But Gardenhire refused to believe the opportunity that he'd long wanted—in previous years, he'd interviewed for managing jobs with the Chicago Cubs and Kansas City Royals—was going to simply disappear.

Twins President Jerry Bell insists the contraction threat was real. What wasn't an absolute certainty, he said, was whether the Twins would be one of the two teams contracted under the plan concocted by a handful of owners during the 2001 World Series. "I can tell you there were a number of teams interested (in being contracted)," Bell said.

The owners didn't put the contraction plan in play until November 6, when they voted 28–2 in favor of contraction. A day later the Players' Association filed a grievance, and on November 14, Minnesota Senator Paul Wellstone and U.S. Representative John Conyers of Michigan introduced legislation that would end baseball's longstanding exemption from antitrust laws. On November 16, in Hennepin County District Court, Judge Harry Crump stepped to the plate and ordered that the Twins were contractually obligated to play in the Dome in 2002. On February 5, 2002, a month and a day after Gardenhire had been hired, the Minnesota Supreme Court backed Crump's decision. Even obtuse baseball owners were getting the message. The day after the Supreme Court ruling, baseball announced it would table contraction for at least a year.

The Twins were headed to spring training, a Cinderella story. Typical of the national coverage they received was this from *Sports Illustrated:* "Darlings for much of the 2001 season, darn near dead in the off-season, the Minnesota Twins eke into 2002 with a new lease on their baseball life."

After a winter of "Save the Twins" rallies and angst among hardcore fans, the Twins were alive—and, as it turned out, very well.

They opened the season at Kansas City. Outfielder Jacque Jones led off for the Twins and homered. In the first inning of his first game, Gardenhire had a 1–0 lead. But entering the seventh, the team trailed 6–4. Jones came through again, hitting a three-run homer, and Gardenhire was a winner.

They won five of their first six games, then dropped four straight at Cleveland before finally making their home debut. They won eight of nine games in the Dome, and the Twins were on their way to a first-place finish in the Central Division.

The key to this team, beyond spectacular defense, was the bullpen. The combination of LaTroy Hawkins and J. C. Romero setting up Eddie Guardado was the best in baseball. Guardado saved 45 games, Romero, appearing in a staggering 81 games, had a 1.89 ERA, and Hawkins was nearly as impressive, appearing in 63 games and compiling a 2.13 ERA.

The Twins faced Oakland in the first round of the playoffs. In previewing that first game, which was played in Oakland, television baseball analysts went on and on about how the Twins represented the best of fundamentally sound baseball. Those words were still echoing through the airwaves when the Twins started stumbling. In the first two innings, the Twins committed three errors—one each by shortstop Cristian Guzman, catcher A. J. Pierzynski, and

Jacque Jones was among the players who took special delight in sipping champagne following the Twins' first-round playoff win over the Oakland A's in 2002. He had moved up from the team's farm system in 1999, when the club was still in the doldrums. Jones holds the team record for leading off a game with a home run, a feat he accomplished 20 times from 1999 through 2005. Chuck Knoblauch hit 14 lead-off homers, Dan Gladden 12. COURTESY OF THE *ST. PAUL PIONEER PRESS*.

third baseman Corey Koskie—giving Oakland four unearned runs and a 5–1 lead after two innings.

But this was the team that had come back from the dead. It came back and won Game 1 of the series, lost the next two games before evening up the series with an 11–2 victory over the A's in the Dome. In Game 5 at Oakland, the Twins took a 2–1 lead into the ninth and added three more runs, with Pierzynski hitting a two-run homer and David Ortiz driving home a third with a single. It turned out they needed all of them. Guardado gave up three runs to the A's before getting the final out that set off celebrations on the field and in the Twin Cities.

But unlike 1987 and 1991, there was another playoff series that stood between them and the World Series. Following the 1993 season, baseball had restructured itself. In the old format, there had been two divisions in each league, East and West. But in 1994, the two divisions were divided in three divisions, East, West, and Central, with the division winners, plus the team with the best second-place record (the "wild card"), each winning a playoff spot.

After their victory in Oakland, the Twins had to deal with the California Angels in a best-of-seven American League Championship Series.

Minnesotans, so fond of the din in the Dome, so enthusiastic about waving white "Homer Hankies," were not amused by what Southern California had done to the game. Angel fans not only ate sushi at the ballpark, they got excited about something called the "rally monkey" as they pounded plastic thunder sticks handed out as they passed through the turnstiles. Oh, such a racket. What were these people doing to the national pastime?

The series, though, did open in Minnesota. And there was huge noise and there were 55,562 people waving Homer Hankies as the Twins won, 2–1.

But then things turned ugly for the team that had survived so much. The Angels, who had defeated the Yankees in their divisional playoff series, won the second game at the Dome, 6–3, despite the fact that Governor Jesse Ventura and Tony Oliva sang "Take Me Out to the Ballgame" in the seventh inning. The series never returned to Minnesota.

In the third game, which was filled with breathtaking defensive plays, the Angels needed just two swings to beat the Twins, 2–1. In the third inning, Garret Anderson homered against Twins starter Eric Milton, and in the eighth, Troy Glaus homered against Romero. Glaus pumped his fists as he rounded first, the rally monkey danced and Angels fans made a racket with their thunder sticks. The fourth game was tight until the eighth, when the Angels again beat the Twins' strength, their bullpen, to take a 3–1 series lead.

Game 5 was a nightmare. The Twins led, 2–1, after three innings and 5–3 headed into the bottom of the seventh. Johan Santana, in relief, started the inning. Hawkins, Romero, and Bob Wells all would pitch before it was over. The Angels scored 10 runs en route to a 13–5 victory.

Still, Gardenhire had fulfilled his pledge to Ryan. He didn't disappoint, and the Twins, near dead in the winter, had played ball deep into October.

2003

A Star Who Got Away

The World: On March 19, the first U.S. bombs begin falling on Baghdad, and a day later ground troops from the United States, the United Kingdom, Australia, and Poland begin the invasion of Iraq. On March 22, the "shock and awe" air campaign begins and on April 9, allied land forces enter Baghdad. On May 1, President Bush lands on USS *Abraham Lincoln* and declares "mission accomplished." On December 13, former Iraqi president Saddam Hussein is captured in Tikrit.

The Nation: The Department of Homeland Security is open for business. Eric Rudolph, a suspect in the 1996 Centennial Olympic Park bombing in Atlanta, is captured near Murphy, North Carolina. Californians recall Governor Gray Davis and elect Arnold Schwarzenegger to replace him.

The State: Republican Tim Pawlenty, after defeating DFLer Roger Moe and independent Tim Penny, is inaugurated, succeeding Jesse Ventura as governor.

Pop Culture: Billboard's #1 Song: "In Da Club," by 50 Cent. Best Picture: *The Lord of the Rings: The Return of the King.* Best Seller: *The Da Vinci Code*, by Dan Brown. Top-Rated Television Show: *CSI: Crime Scene Investigation.*

The Season: Even with only one player, closer Eddie Guardado, selected for the All-Star Game, the Twins win the division for the second year in a row. Trailing the White Sox by seven games midway through the season, the Twins acquire outfielder Shannon Stewart from Toronto and move into first place by early September. After winning the opening game of their first-round playoff series with the New York Yankees, the Twins drop three straight, ending their season. Major League Baseball's one hundredth season ends with the Florida Marlins beating the Yankees in six games in the World Series.

On March 31, the Boston Red Sox opened their season at Tampa Bay. Smiling, as always, David Ortiz slipped into his Red Sox uniform. Ever since, Twins fans have been asking, "How the hell did that happen?"

Simple answer: Nine days before Christmas 2002, the Twins gave Ortiz his release. He was free to go anywhere he wanted. The franchise had made one of the game's biggest blunders ever.

The team has little defense, other than that offered by Mike Radcliff, a vice president of player personnel, who headed the team's scouting department and is a key person in evaluating the organization's players at both the major- and minor-league level.

"The only thing you can say is that a lot of other teams made the same mistake we did," said Radcliff. "The entire world had a chance to take David Ortiz."

David Ortiz was loved by his teammates in Minnesota and then he became a beloved superstar in Boston. PHOTOS COURTESY OF AP IMAGES (LEFT) AND THE ST. PAUL PIONEER PRESS (RIGHT).

The difference is that the Twins had the man who became one of base-ball's best hitters and most popular performers. They had Ortiz in their club-house, where he was immensely popular with his teammates. They saw his potential before he became Big Papi, the hero of Red Sox Nation. They let him go and got nothing in return.

The Twins weren't the first team to blunder in regard to Ortiz. If the Twins are going to be long remembered as the team that released Ortiz, they deserve at least a little credit for being the organization that plucked him from deep in the Seattle Mariners farm system in 1996. At the time, Ortiz was called David Arias and was playing in Appleton, the first baseman of the Wisconsin Timber Rattlers.

The Mariners, involved in a race for the A.L. West Division title, were looking for a veteran hitter. The Twins, in decline, were looking to unload old players. They traded Dave Hollins, a veteran third baseman, to Seattle for a player to be named later.

Player personnel departments and scouts don't just follow the players in their own systems, they study the performances of every minor-leaguer, hoping to find a nugget in someone else's organization. The Twins knew about Arias.

"You saw the power, you saw the leverage in his swing," said Radcliff. "He wasn't the kind of hitter who strikes out a lot."

David Americo Arias Ortiz was the player the Twins wanted in the Hollins deal. The one request that he had when he moved into Minnesota's farm system was that he be called Ortiz, not Arias.

From the beginning, the young Dominican slugger impressed the Twins. In 1997, he was the organization's minor-league player of the year, hitting 31 home runs and driving in 124 for three different farm clubs. After several brief call-ups to the majors, Ortiz finally made it to the Twins in 2000.

Prior to finally getting to the top, there had been some flare-ups with Twins manager Tom Kelly. At one point, the Twins manager didn't think the young first baseman was working hard enough on his defense. In later years, there would be earnest discussions about his approach to hitting. Kelly was a big believer in young hitters learning to control their swings; to drive the ball to all fields.

Years later, Ortiz famously described, in an interview with the *Boston Globe*, what he thought of the TK approach: "Whenever I took a big swing in Minnesota they'd say to me, 'Hey, hey, what are you doing?' So I said, 'You want me to hit like a little bitch, then I will.'"

But, in fairness to Kelly, he was not the team's manager when the Twins made the decision to release Ortiz. Kelly had stepped down as manager following the 2001 season. Ron Gardenhire was the manager in 2002, a season in which Ortiz showed his potential by hitting 20 home runs and driving in 75 runs. Not only could he hit, he was loved by his teammates. This was a man who came to work with a smile on his face. Practical jokes between him and Torii Hunter, Jacque Jones, and Corey Koskie kept everyone alert and laughing.

"He was one of my favorites," said Gardenhire. "He's a wonderful guy."

But then he was simply released.

"Nobody wanted that," said Gardenhire. "But he was arbitration eligible. I told David, 'If you get to arbitration, you'll kill us.' The other thing was that David got beat up pretty bad playing on the turf [in the Dome]. Ankles, knees. Always beat up. But nobody wanted to see him go. It was one of those things."

Ortiz was being paid $900,000 a year in 2002, but the Twins feared, his salary could jump to $2 million in 2003 if an arbitrator came down on his side. They had another young, promising slugger, amiable Matthew LeCroy, who could swing the bat for a fraction of the cost.

It appeared the Twins were set for years to come with a double play combination of Cristian Guzman (*left*) and Luis Rivas—but both soon were gone. COURTESY OF THE *ST. PAUL PIONEER PRESS*.

The team decided Ortiz had to go. They tried to trade him, but nobody was interested.

Following his release, the Twins point out, Ortiz was not a hot commodity. The Red Sox might not have been interested, either, if their star pitcher, Pedro Martinez hadn't pushed them to sign Ortiz. Before spring training, the Red Sox signed Ortiz to a one year, $1.2 million contract, and after one month, according to the Twins, Boston was so unimpressed they put Ortiz on waivers. No other teams showed any interest and Ortiz hung on with Boston.

Few Minnesotans were second-guessing the Twins' decision to release Ortiz after the first month of the 2003 season. Ortiz never even got off the bench in eleven of the twenty-seven games the Red Sox played in April. By the end of the first month of the season, he was batting just .228 with 1 home run. It wasn't until the second half of his first season in Boston that Ortiz started to become Big Papi, hitting 20 of his 31 home runs after the All-Star break.

In the meantime, the Twins were doing just fine without him. True, the team, ahem, didn't have much power, but it was funky group, proving that 2002 hadn't been a fluke.

The 2003 team is also a symbol of how incredibly rapidly things change in baseball in the twenty-first century. The Twins infield, the key to the success of the 2002 and 2003 teams, was young, sure-handed, and fun. But all of them were gone in a matter of a few seasons.

Catcher A. J. Pierzynski was gone by 2004. First baseman Doug Mientkiewicz was gone halfway through the '04 season. Cristian Guzman was gone by 2005 as was third baseman Koskie. Second baseman Luis Rivas made it until 2007. The outfield of Dustan Mohr (gone by 05), Jacque Jones (out by 2006), and Torii Hunter (gone by 2008) didn't exactly grow old in Minnesota, either.

But they were fun while they lasted. The Twins won the Central Division by four games over the Chicago White Sox, but had to meet the Yankees in the Division Series.

The series opened in New York, and the Twins used a committee of pitchers, starting with Johan Santana. In the second half of the season, Santana had moved from the bullpen to the role of staff ace, winning 12 games. Against the Yankees, Santana pitched four shutout innings and Rick Reed, J. C. Romero, and LaTroy Hawkins finished up. The Twins were 3–1 winners. But that was it. The team would score 3 runs the rest of the series, losing three straight.

They could have used one more big bat in the lineup.

2004

Who to Pick?

The World: On December 26, a large earthquake in the Indian Ocean triggers a tsunami that kills more than 225,000 people in eleven countries.

The Nation: In May, Massachusetts legalizes gay marriage; in the November elections, eleven states ban gay marriage. Abuse of prisoners at an Iraqi prison, Abu Ghraib, is exposed on *60 Minutes*. President Bush is reelected, defeating John Kerry.

The State: After losing in the first round of the National Basketball Association playoffs for seven straight seasons, the Minnesota Timberwolves, behind Kevin Garnett, Latrell Sprewell, and Sam Cassell, advance to the Western Conference finals before losing to the Los Angeles Lakers.

Pop Culture: Grammy Song of the Year: "Daughters," by John Mayer. Best Picture: *Million Dollar Baby*. Bill Clinton publishes his autobiography, *My Life*. Top-Rated Television Show: *csi: Crime Scene Investigation*.

The Season: Johan Santana is the unanimous choice for the Cy Young Award after winning his final 13 decisions, completing the season with a 20–6 record while striking out 265 batters in 228 innings and compiling a 2.65 ERA. Behind Santana, the Twins win their third successive Central Division title, but lose to the Yankees in first round of the playoffs. The Boston Red Sox are baseball's story of the year, overcoming a 0–3 deficit to the Yanks in the playoffs and winning the World Series for the first time since 1918.

Baseball is a game of patience, wisdom, foresight, economics, and luck. It was a decision made in 2001 that allowed the Twins to reshape themselves going into the 2004 season.

Immediate reshaping was necessary because, following the playoffs in 2003, the Twins knew they would lose two key pitchers to free agency. Beloved closer "Everyday Eddie" Guardado signed a three-year, $16 million deal with the Seattle Mariners, and starting pitcher Kenny Rogers, who the Twins wrongly believed was nearing the end of his career, signed a $2.5 million contract with the Texas Rangers. The Twins also knew they'd be attempting to get rid of pitcher Eric Milton, who was injured throughout 2003. He was due to receive $9 million in 2004.

A month after the 2003 playoffs were over, Twins general manager Terry Ryan made a trade designed to cover those holes inexpensively. Catcher A. J. Pierzynski was sent to San Francisco for three pitchers, Joe Nathan, who was to fill Guardado's spot, Boof Bonser, who was to replace Rogers, and, as a throw-in, a kid pitcher, Francisco Liriano. Milton also was traded, to Philadelphia for pitcher Carlos Silva and infielder Nick Punto.

Though not popular with the fans, the Pierzynski deal was possible because of a decision that had been made in the draft of June 2001.

The Twins had the first pick in the draft that year and were looking at three "can't miss" prospects: Mark Prior, a pitcher from the University of Southern California, Mark Teixeira, a slugging first baseman from Georgia Tech, and a high school kid from St. Paul, Joe Mauer, who had been offered a football scholarship at Florida State.

For months, Twins scouts debated among themselves and with Twins general manager Terry Ryan about whom they should pick. Prior and Teixeira tried to help the Twins with their dilemma. Prior told the team that under no circumstances did he want to be drafted by the Twins. With painfully predictable regularity Ryan would get calls from Prior's father, "Don't draft my son!" Teixeira hired Scott Boras, an agent most small-market teams found impossible to deal with.

But Mauer presented two problems. Just out of high school, he was less of a sure thing than either Prior or Teixeira, and he had that football scholarship in his hand.

The week before the draft, Ryan and his assistant, Wayne Krivsky, moved in with the scouting department. They spent most of their time on the phone with the young players or their agents. On a couple of occasions, they went to the Mauer home in St. Paul, but they could get no commitment from Mauer that he would sign with the team if he was drafted. On the day before the draft, Ryan told the scouts that they should decide whom they would pick

Johan Santana, Brad Radke, and Joe Nathan gave Twins fans scores of reasons to smile. COURTESY OF THE *ST. PAUL PIONEER PRESS*.

based on talent alone. Toss out the agents, relatives, money as factors, Ryan said. Just think baseball. Whom would you want to draft?

"The room was split in half," said Mike Radcliff, director of the scouting staff. "Half wanted Prior. Half wanted Mauer."

On the day of the draft, Joel Lepel, a supervising scout who knew the Mauers well, made one last call to the Mauer family to see if the Twins would be able to sign him. Moments before the Twins were to announce their selection, Lepel hustled into the room where the draft was being held and told Radcliff, "We got *no* deal."

Radcliff nodded grimly, and the Twins announced that they were selecting Mauer.

The Twins—and Carl Pohlad—were blasted by many in the media. The only reason they'd picked Mauer, sports columnists wrote, was because they wouldn't be willing to pay the signing bonus Prior would demand.

Even though the Twins were able to sign Mauer—for a then-record $5 million signing bonus—the criticism of the Twins got more intense as time went on. While Mauer was in his second year in the minor leagues, Prior was a starting pitcher with the Cubs, winning 6 games, and showing great promise in 2002. In 2003, Mauer was still in the minors and Prior was a star, winning 18 games for the Cubs.

But the Twins were confident that Mauer would be their starting catcher on opening day of the 2004 season, thus the trade of Pierzynski.

The plan seemed to be working beyond even the highest hopes of the Twins. Nathan was both younger and more reliable than Guardado. Bonser showed promise and, in 2006, Liriano would become a momentary star. Silva was a reliable starter who worked much cheaper than Milton. And Mauer was ready to be the starting catcher when the 2004 season opened. Before 49,584 fans at the Dome on opening day, Mauer had a couple of hits, a couple of walks, and the Twins had a 7–4, eleven-inning victory over Cleveland.

In the second game of the season, bad luck got in the way of a good plan. Mauer suffered a knee injury that required surgery. He came back to the Twins in June, experienced pain and swelling in the knee in July and was done for the season.

But not all of the Twins' luck was bad.

In 1999, at Major League Baseball's annual winter meetings, the Twins had made an unnoticed minor-league trade with the Florida Marlins. To understand the deal the Twins made, you need to understand a Major League Baseball rule—Rule V—which is in existence to prevent teams from hoarding talented minor-league players. Under the rule, a minor-league player who signs with a team before his nineteenth birthday must be added to the signing team's forty-man roster by his fifth year or he can be drafted by another major-league team for $50,000. The catch to Rule V is that the team that drafts another team's minor-leaguer must put the drafted player on their twenty-five-player active roster for a full season.

In 1999, the Twins drafted a pitching prospect, Jared Camp, from the

Cleveland Indians system. But, in a prearranged deal, they immediately turned around and traded Camp to the Florida Marlins, who had drafted a young pitcher, Johan Santana, from the Houston Astros system. Santana was suddenly a member of the Minnesota Twins. He had been a fifteen-year-old Venezuelan center fielder when he was spotted by the Astros. They signed him and turned him into a pitcher.

"I'd like to tell you we saw Cy Young potential in him when we drafted him," said Radcliff. "But that's not true. We knew he could throw hard, he was left-handed, and we saw that he'd made normal progress in the Houston system. Our thought was that he might be good someday. We'll take him, stack him in the bullpen and see how it works out."

It worked out well. Under Rule V, the Twins were required to keep Santana on the twenty-five-man roster for the 2000 season. He was the team's least valuable pitcher, appearing in 30 games. He was sent back to the minors in 2001 and for part of 2002 before returning to the Twins.

By the second half of the 2004 season, he was baseball's best pitcher, compiling a 13–0 record over one amazing stretch. By season's end, he had a 20–6 record, led the American League in strikeouts and earned run average, and was easily voted the A.L.'s Cy Young Award winner. Nathan was just as impressive, saving 44 games with a 1.62 earned run average, while Guardado struggled in Seattle.

The changes that had begun following the 2003 season kept on coming during the summer of 2004. Doug Mientkiewicz, who had played such a big role in the rebirth of Twins excitement, started the season at first but ended up losing the job to a rookie, Justin Morneau. While Morneau pounded the ball—19 home runs and 58 RBI in just half a season—Mientkiewicz sulked. Before the season was over he was traded to Boston in a complex four-team deal. That meant that Mientkiewicz, Pierznyski, Rogers, Guardado, Milton, and LaTroy Hawkins all were gone from the 2003 Central Division championship team, and Mauer, who was supposed to be a key figure in the middle of the lineup, played in only 32 games. Still, the Twins won two more games in '04 than the '03 team, and for the third successive year were the Central Division champions.

Throughout baseball, they were hailed as the consummate "budget ball" team. But then, they had to play the budget-busting New York Yankees in the first round of the playoffs. The comparative salaries of the starting lineups told the story of what twenty-first century baseball had become.

The Yankees: catcher, Jorge Posada, $9 million; first base, Jason Giambi, $12.5 million; second base Miguel Cairo, $900,000; third base, Alex Rodriguez, $22 million; shortstop, Derek Jeter, $18 million; left field, Hideki Matsui, $7 million; center field, Bernie Williams, $12.5 million; right field, Gary Sheffield, $13 million. Starting pitchers: Mike Mussina, $16 million; Kevin Brown, $15 million; Jon Lieber, $2.5 million. Closer, Mariano Rivera, $10.9 million.

The Twins: catcher, Henry Blanco, $750,000; first base, Justin Morneau, $300,000; second base Luis Rivas, $1.5 million; third base, Corey Koskie, $4.5 million; shortstop, Cristian Guzman, $3.7 million; left field, Lew Ford, $340,000; center field, Torii Hunter, $6.5 million; right field, Jacque Jones, $4.5 million. Starting pitchers: Santana, $1.6 million; Brad Radke, $10.7 million; Carlos Silva, $340,000. Closer, Joe Nathan, $440,000.

In the end, money trumped patience, wisdom, and luck. But just barely.

Santana shut out the Yankees in the first game of the series in New York. And, for a moment, things looked bright for the Twins in the second game. With the score tied, 5–5, in the twelfth inning, Hunter homered to give Minnesota a 6–5 lead. Nathan, starting his third inning of work, struck out John Olerud to start the bottom of the twelfth, but walked two batters and gave up a run-scoring double to Rodriguez. With the game again tied, J. C. Romero replaced Nathan and gave up a sacrifice fly to Matsui. The Yankees had dodged a bullet and the series was tied, 1–1.

The Twins returned to the Dome full of hope, but promptly lost 8–4. Still, they weren't quite done. The Twins took a 5–1 lead into the eighth inning of Game 4 when New York came back. Sheffield singled against Juan Rincon, Matsui walked, Williams singled, driving home Sheffield. It was 5–2 when aging Ruben Sierra stepped to the plate. It was 5–5 after he homered. It stayed tied until the eleventh when Rodriguez doubled against Kyle Lohse, stole third, and scored on a wild pitch. The Twins went down—1, 2, 3—against Rivera in the bottom of the eleventh inning.

But Mauer's knee was healing.

2005

Press Box under Siege

The World: Pope John Paul II dies on April 2 and more than four million people go to the Vatican to mourn. His successor, Pope Benedict XVI, is named on April 19. The trial of former Iraqi president Saddam Hussein begins on October 19.

The Nation: On August 29, Hurricane Katrina strikes the Gulf Coast from Louisiana to Alabama, killing 1,836 people. New Orleans is hardest hit when floodwaters breach the city's levee system, flooding 80 percent of the city. The storm causes more than $81 billion in damage and leaves many questioning the competence of the federal government's response.

The State: On March 21, after killing his grandfather and his grandfather's girlfriend, sixteen-year-old Jeffrey Weise enters Red Lake High on the Red Lake reservation and kills an unarmed security guard, a teacher, and five students before killing himself.

Pop Culture: Billboard's #1 Song: "We Belong Together," by Mariah Carey. Best Picture: *Crash*. Best Seller: *The Broker*, by John Grisham. Top-Rated Television Show: *American Idol*.

The Season: While leaping to catch a drive hit by David Ortiz on July 29, Torii Hunter catches his spikes in the padded fence in Boston's Fenway Park and suffers an ankle injury that knocks him out of the lineup for the rest of the season. Without Hunter, the Twins fade to third in the Central Division. The

Public address announcer Bob Casey was the voice of the Twins at the Met and in the Dome. He also made a great target for practical jokes. The only public address announcer Twins fans had ever heard, he died on March 27, 2005. COURTESY OF THE *ST. PAUL PIONEER PRESS*.

Chicago White Sox jump into the void and go on to not only win the Division but also their first World Series title since 1917.

Shortly after Alexander Cartwright's Knickerbockers lost their first game to the New York Nine in 1845, the first sportswriter came along to pen the first cliché about the game. And for more than 150 years, newspaper baseball writers were the kings of sportswriting, the official historians of America's game.

They had the best seats in the house. They selected the Rookies of the Year and the Most Valuable Players and the Cy Young Award winners and the Hall of Famers. Baseball writers even have their own wing at Cooperstown.

There were sportscasters on television and radio. But, like the fans, they tended to rely on the sportswriters for the inside dope. Who was bickering with whom. Who was about to be traded. Why the cleanup hitter was struggling.

But in the 1990s, the Internet began to change how the rest of us received our information. And by the twenty-first century, even baseball fans were turning to their computers to follow the game. The poets of the press box were under siege by a ragtag army of bloggers.

In Minnesota, that army was led by John Bonnes, also known as Twins Geek, whom most credit with being the first to put up a serious baseball blog in Minnesota, though to his credit, he didn't take himself terribly seriously. The full title of his blog, which began in 2002: "Twins Geek.com. He's a Twins fan. He's a geek. It's kinda sad, really."

"People ask me how Twins Geek started and I have to admit, it was mostly driven out of disdain for local baseball coverage in late 2001 and early 2002," Bonnes once said.

The Geek was happier with the new breed of sportswriters, in part, because they blogged, too, and accepted the role of people like the Geek. Older sportswriters despised the bloggers and hated watching the media revolution undermine their importance to the game.

Old-timers had been dealing with change for decades. In the 1960s, the growth of televised sporting events forced sportswriters to change the way they covered games. No longer was it good enough to sit in the press box and write about what they had seen. Their readers had seen it, too. Now, they had to go into the clubhouse, talk with the players, report what they had to say.

In the 1970s, a federal law, Title IX, had not only opened playing fields for women, it had brought the first wave of women into the press box. They were not treated kindly by many of their male colleagues, or by many of the athletes they covered. But in time there was grudging acceptance.

Computers replaced typewriters as the means of writing stories. Cigar smoke, alcohol, dirty jokes, and foul language all slowly disappeared from the press box, though ugly rumormongering about female sports writers was a constant. ("She's screwing the shortstop.")

But bloggers were causing the most frightening change of all. The Internet was eating away at newspaper revenue and circulation. The old scribes were losing their place as voices of the game.

In these early years of the twenty-first century, the bloggers still did not have a seat in the press box. Baseball is an institution that changes more slowly than much of our culture. But bloggers began to understand that even baseball would have to catch up with the rest of the world; that even baseball and the old scribes would have to accept the legitimacy of bloggers.

"My basic take on the whole mainstream versus new media thing is that we're closing in to the point that there won't be a difference," said Aaron Gleeman, whose site went up a few months after the Geek's. "Newspapers are collapsing and more content is moving online every day. Within a couple of years the vast majority of people will get just about every form of media online."

But even Gleeman was surprised by the how fast the media revolution was happening. The speed of change changed his own goals.

"In 2002, my site was essentially my attempt to practice for a mainstream media job," he said. "From an early age, my goal was to be a sports columnist for a newspaper. But somewhere around 2004, it started to become clear that the Internet was creating some pretty interesting, new opportunities for people like me and holding out hope that a newspaper gig was no longer necessary. In terms of sports coverage, mainstream media has always done a solid job at reporting news. However, for someone interested in something beyond that, whether it's analysis of trades or simply discussion of the day-to-day goings on with a team, it was severely lacking. Space limitations in the newspaper makes discussing the daily minutia of a team impossible. And columnists generally seem more interested in making jokes and creating controversy instead of offering up actual analysis."

John Bonnes, also known as the Twins Geek, put up the first serious blog about the Twins in 2002. As a lark, Anne Ursu, an author and baseball lover, started her Batgirl blog in 2004. Batgirl, promising "more sass than stats," quickly attracted an audience of thousands. Female fans especially were attracted to the site, though Twins players embraced it, too. The birth of a child and book deadlines led Ursu to retire Batgirl prior to the start of the 2007 season. COURTESY OF ANNE URSU.

This media change was in full swing by 2005.

On the field, the Twins were undergoing fundamental generational changes, too. The M & M boys, Joe Mauer and Justin Morneau, were moving from the minors to the Dome. Mauer replaced Henry Blanco and Morneau replaced Doug Mientkiewicz, who had been so instrumental in the surprising success of the Twins from 2001 through 2004.

Mientkiewicz hadn't only ignited the Twins on the field. His style had helped rekindle fan enthusiasm, too. Among those drawn closer to the Twins by Mientkiewicz was a Minnesota author, Anne Ursu.

"I love Mauer and Morneau," she said, "but not as much as I loved Doug Mientkiewicz."

In 2004, she started a blog, Batgirl, on a whim.

"My husband and dad were watching a game with me and they said I should start a blog," she said. "I thought that would be kind of fun but I really thought the only person who would read it would be my brother."

She started the site and was amazed.

"My God, there were sixty people reading it," she said. "I wondered who they were. And the next thing I knew there were 150 people reading it. By 2005, there were a few thousand. Sometimes, there were in the tens of thousands."

With the slogan "less stats, more sass," Batgirl had tapped into a huge female audience, which for 150 years had been ignored by the men in the press box. To Batgirl and her followers, baseball was actually fun.

For example, a Batgirl account of a 2005 game between the Twins and the Kansas City Royals started like this:

"Oh my battlings, there's really no way to describe today's game, except perhaps for Batgirl to take all the cans in her pantry and open them up and throw the contents against the wall and then take a picture of the wall and print it up and feed the picture to one of the Batkitties and wait a few hours and then go to the Batkitty litter box then throw the result on the wall too and try to clean the whole thing up, accidentally mixing ammonia and chlorine bleach, which my dears you should never ever do, and then having Jeb find her and the Batkitties passed out on the floor and he has to take them to the hospital where they all are miraculously revived, but not before vomiting various substances into a puddle on the floor that one of the orderlies trips on and skids down the hall, through the operating room doors, and lands head first in someone's right breast implant, which promptly explodes in everyone's faces. The game was like that. Sort of."

In other words, the Twins had finally won, 6–5, over the Royals in eleven innings, in a game that they nearly blew on several occasions.

Batgirl offered such features as "if the Twins were chicks, who would be the hottest?" She attached the faces of Twins players to the bodies of super models to illustrate the question. She used Legos to display key plays. Her father and brother photographed the uniformed posteriors of Twins' players and had a "name that butt" contest. And her audience kept growing.

At one point, she was taken on a tour of the Twins' dressing room.

"I saw Matt Guerrier naked and Torii Hunter gave me a hug," she said. "A number of players came up to me and said they read 'Batgirl' every day."

The Twins fell from first in 2005. It was the year of the White Sox. But Batgirl wasn't down about her team. She was sad only that the season was over.

"The season's been over about fifty-five hours and I'm already bored out of my Bat Gourd. What the hell am I supposed to do, read? Have meaningful conversations with my friends? Bah."

Following the birth of a child in 2007, Batgirl put away her Legos and laid down her pen. She left her blog, never claiming to have been a sportswriter. But then, most sportswriters left her perplexed.

"It's just a game," she said, "a beautiful game."

2006

Nibble, Nibble, Nibble

The World: Israeli prime minister Ariel Sharon suffers a massive stroke and his powers are transferred to Ehud Olmert.

The Nation: Democrats regain control of both the U.S. House and Senate in off-year elections. Warren Buffet donates $30 billion to the Bill and Melinda Gates Foundation.

The State: Amy Klobuchar becomes the state's first elected female Senator, easily defeating Republican Mark Kennedy by twenty points in the general election. Governor Tim Pawlenty, meanwhile, wins a second term, edging DFLer Mike Hatch by a point. On March 7, Kirby Puckett dies at the age of 45 at a Phoenix hospital after suffering a massive stroke at his home. "Something about the guy just makes you feel good," Puckett's former manager Tom Kelly told *Sports Illustrated* in a 1987 interview.

Pop Culture: James Brown, the Godfather of Soul, dies on Christmas day. Best Picture: *The Departed*. Best Seller: *For One More Day*, by Mitch Albom. Top-Rated Television Show: *American Idol*.

The Season: The Twins return to first place with a cast of stars. Joe Mauer wins the batting title (.347), Justin Morneau is MVP (.321, 34 HR, 130 RBI), and Johan Santana, for second time in three years, is the Cy Young Award winner (19–6). Still, they can't get past the first round of A.L. playoffs, getting swept by Oakland.

Ozzie Guillen became manager of the Chicago White Sox in 2004. He became an ex-officio member of the Twins marketing department two and a half years later. Surrounded by sports writers on August 19, he was asked about the surging Twins. It was suggested that the Twins, who had pulled to within a game of the second place White Sox in the Central Division, weren't really all that good.

"This team beats you so many ways," said Guillen. "They look like piranhas. You wake up [he points to his left arm] you ain't got no meat. [He adds nibbling sound effects to his monologue.] All those piranhas—blooper here, blooper here, beat out a ground ball, hit a home run, they're up by four. They get up

Late in the 2006 season, White Sox manager Ozzie Guillen said that the Twins lineup was filled with "piranhas." Luis Castillo, leading off, Nick Punto, batting second, Jason Tyner, batting eighth, and Jason Bartlett, batting ninth, could nibble an opponent to pieces, Guillen said. The Twins turned Guillen's comments into part of their advertising campaign. FROM THE COLLECTION OF CLYDE DOEPNER; PHOTO BY ROBERT FOGT.

by four with that bullpen? See you at the National Anthem tomorrow. When I sit down and look at the lineup, give me the New York Yankees. Give me those guys because they've got holes. You can pitch around them, you can pitch to them. These little guys? Castillo and all of them? People worry about the catcher, what's his name, Mauer? Fine, yeah, good hitter, but worry about the little guys, they're on base all the time. Morneau has 106 RBIs and nobody talks about that guy. It's Big Papi. How does he have all those RBIs? Because of those little piranhas."

The piranhas: second baseman Luis Castillo, batting first; third baseman Nick Punto, batting second; spare outfielder Jason Tyner, batting eighth; and shortstop Jason Bartlett, batting ninth. On first hearing the description, they scratched their heads over the label.

"We didn't know if it was a compliment or derogatory," said Punto. "But we decided it was Ozzie just being Ozzie and that he meant it as a compliment. We started to like it. We can't hit balls over the fence, but we can go out and play hard."

The Twins marketing department took Guillen's label and ran with it. Within a few days, there were "piranha" T-shirts on sale at the Dome. There were "piranha" commercials. And the fans loved it. Whenever the Twins put a runner on base, they would hold up their hands and bring their fingers and thumbs together in a nibbling motion.

For all of its popularity, the label was a rather large overstatement. You had to go back to 1987, a World Series championship year, to find a Twins team that had more home run power or that scored more runs. Morneau became the team's first player to hit 30 home runs since Tom Brunansky, Gary Gaetti, and Kent Hrbek reached that number in '87. Torii Hunter, torrid in September, eventually reached 30 homers, too.

This was the only Twins team ever to have the batting champion (Mauer was the first American League catcher ever to win the title), the Most Valuable Player, and the Cy Young Award winner (Johan Santana won pitching's triple crown by leading the majors in victories, earned run average, and strikeouts).

This was hardly a group of nibblers. They led the major leagues in hitting and resilience and quick decision-making.

Early in the season, the team was playing under .500 and seemed listless. Manger Ron Gardenhire and general manager Terry Ryan decided the team had to get faster. Two old pros who had been brought in during the off-season, third baseman Tony Batista and shortstop Juan Castro, were dumped, Bartlett was brought up from the minors to play short, and Punto was installed at third.

Most important, Francisco Liriano was promoted from the bullpen to the starting rotation in May and for nearly three months he was even better than Santana. Liriano, with a history of arm injuries in the minor leagues, had been a throw-in from the San Francisco Giants in one of the best trades in Twins history: Joe Nathan, Boof Bonser, and Liriano for catcher A. J. Pierzynski following the 2003 season.

Between May 3 and May 13, Liriano started three games, went 3–0, and gave up 1 earned run. From May 19 to May 31, he went 3–0 again, giving up just 3 earned runs in 24 innings while striking out 26. Then, he got warmed up. He was named the American League's pitcher of the month in June and July, becoming only the second pitcher ever to accomplish that feat. He was named to the All-Star team. His teammates started calling him "Francisco the Franchise."

But pitchers live in a fragile world. Every pitch could be their last, which was why Calvin Griffith never could tolerate the idea of signing a pitcher to a long-term contract.

In August, Liriano was placed on the disabled list. The diagnosis was a strained collateral ligament in his left elbow. In September, he was sent to the minor leagues for a rehabilitation start and pitched three scoreless innings. He was brought back to the Twins for a start on September 13, but lasted just two innings against Oakland before complaining of pain in his left elbow. He was finished for the season, after setting a Twins rookie strikeout record (144) in 121 innings. Following the season, he underwent "Tommy John" surgery and was out for all of 2007.

Despite the loss of Liriano, the Twins refused to fold. A team that had been eight games under .500 on June 7 passed the defending World Series champion White Sox and moved into second place in late August and started closing in on the Detroit Tigers, who had led the division from opening day.

On August 10, 2006, Colby Schroeder, five, (*foreground*), and brother Jacob, eight, proudly wear their Joe Mauer sideburns, a unique Twins giveaway item. Alas, on that day Mauer, with his sweet swing and real sideburns, went 0-for-4 and the Twins were defeated by Toronto, 5–0. COURTESY OF AP IMAGES.

On September 26, the Twins clinched a playoff spot with a 3–2 victory over the Kansas City Royals before 24,819 in the Dome. The players doused themselves with champagne. It appeared they would be the wild card team in the playoffs, headed to New York for a first-round series against the Yankees.

"It ain't done yet!" vowed Hunter in the midst of the raucous celebration.

He was right. The Tigers couldn't close the deal. They kept losing and losing and three games before the end of the season, the Twins moved into a first place tie with Detroit, a team they had trailed by 12 games at the All-Star break.

But then, the Twins started losing, too. The Twins lost game number 160 at home to the White Sox. At the same time, the Tigers were losing to the Royals in Detroit. Entering the 161st game of the season, the two teams were still tied for first. The Twins lost again to the White Sox. The Tigers again lost to Kansas City.

There were 45,000 people in the Dome for the regular season's last game. The Twins defeated the White Sox, 5–1, with Hunter hitting a two-run homer. And then everybody waited. The players went to the clubhouse. As many as 35,000 of the fans stayed in the Dome, watching the Tigers blow a six-run lead to the Royals, a team that lost 100 games in 2006. Finally, in the top of the fourteenth, the Royals scored twice. The Tigers couldn't answer and lost, 10–8.

In the stands and in the clubhouse, the delayed celebration began. For the second time in a week, champagne flowed. The Twins were Division Champions for the fourth time in five years.

"It's sweeter than before because we were written off," said Hunter.

The Twins had become the first team in major-league history to clinch first place on the last day of the season after never having had sole possession of first. Instead of meeting the Yankees in round one of the playoffs, the Twins would get to open the playoffs in their loud, lovely Dome, where they were 54–27 in the regular season, against Oakland.

Even the long stadium debate had ended in this season of comebacks for the Twins. In May, the Minnesota legislature had authorized Hennepin County the right to levy a half-cent sales tax for construction of a new stadium.

Destiny seemed to be smiling on the team.

But then came a big, bad hop. Destiny left the building.

The playoffs started on a disappointing note, with Barry Zito outpitching Santana in the first game of the best-of-five series. The A's pulled off a surprising 3–2 victory, with Frank Thomas hitting two home runs for the A's.

Still, there was confidence the Twins could come back, though confidence took a roller coaster ride on that October 4 day. It dimmed when Oakland took a 2–0 lead. It soared into a Homer Hanky waving frenzy when Cuddyer and Morneau tied the game with back-to-back homers in the sixth. Ah, surely the magic was back.

In the seventh, Oakland catcher Jason Kendell was on first when Mark Kotsay stepped to the plate.

ESPN's Dave O'Brien's call of what ensued went like this: "Line shot center field, coming on Hunter. That's gonna drop down, he dives and misses it! It's gonna bounce and roll all the way to the warning track and up against the wall. The run will score, Kendell is in, here comes Kotsay, rounding third, the throw won't get him! Mark Kotsay comes all the way in, an inside-the-parker! A stunning development in Minnesota!"

Hunter was stunned.

"I'm telling you, I had the ball," he told reporters after the game. It took a funny hop, he said, just as he was diving. Perhaps there was spin on the ball, or it hit a seam in the turf. For whatever reason his dive was futile and Kotsay raced around the bases saying, "I need oxygen" as he laughed on the bench with his Oakland teammates.

Shouldn't he have played it safe? Kotsay would have had a single, Kendell would have gone no farther than second base.

"I can't play it safe," Hunter said. "That's not me."

The A's went on to win the game, 5–2, to take a 2–0 lead in the series. The trip to Oakland for the Twins was a formality. With sore-armed Brad Radke making his last big-league start, they were beaten, 8–3.

2007

Good-bye, Everybody

The World: On December 27, former Pakistani prime minister Benazir Bhutto is assassinated at an election day rally. Vietnam joins the World Trade Organization.

The Nation: Seung-Hui Cho kills thirty-one people at Virginia Tech University in Blacksburg before killing himself. The killings, by a mentally ill man, cause President Bush to sign the first handgun control bill in thirteen years. The minimum wage is increased for the first time since 1997, from $5.15 to $5.85. Former U.S. Senator George Mitchell issues a report accusing eighty-nine former and current major-league baseball players of using steroids.

The State: During rush hour on August 1, the I-35W bridge in Minneapolis collapses, killing thirteen people and injuring scores of others. The collapse was caused by "a design flaw," according to federal investigators.

Pop Culture: Billboard's #1 Song: "Irreplaceable," by Beyoncé. Best movie: *No Country for Old Men*. Best Seller: *A Thousand Splendid Suns*, by Khaled Hosseini. Top-Rated Television Show: *American Idol*.

The Season: For first time in six years, and the first time in Ron Gardenhire's tenure as Twins manager, the Twins fall below .500 (79–83) as the offense slips, scoring 83 fewer runs than in 2006. The Twins finish third in A.L. Central, seventeen games behind the Cleveland Indians. The Boston Red Sox sweep the Colorado Rockies to win the World Series.

The Twins were to open the 2007 season on April 2, a Monday. Herb Carneal, the radio voice of the team since 1962, had been hospitalized with heart problems, and for the first time in his fifty-one-year major-league broadcasting career, he'd been unable to attend spring training. But he had been anticipating the opening game.

On the Friday before the team was to start the season with a home series against the Baltimore Orioles, Dave St. Peter, the team's president, called Carneal at his home.

"How you doing?" St. Peter asked.

"Dave, I can't go," said Carneal.

"That's okay," said St. Peter. "Let's just take it slow. Sit out the first home stand and when you're feeling better ..."

On Sunday, April 1, St. Peter received a call. Carneal had died of congestive heart failure. He was eighty-three.

"We always said that the day he could no longer broadcast would be the day he died," said Carneal's longtime broadcast partner, John Gordon. "That's exactly what happened."

Herb Carneal, beloved by all, was hugged by Twins manager Ron Gardenhire when Carneal celebrated his 50th season in broadcasting in 2005. Carneal died at the age of eighty-three the day before the 2007 opener. COURTESY OF AP IMAGES.

John Gordon became Herb Carneal's partner in the radio booth in time for the 1987 season. COUR-
TESY OF THE MINNESOTA TWINS.

This marked the third straight year the Twins had started the sea-
son in mourning. In 2006, Kirby Puckett had died in March. In 2005, Bob
Casey, the team's longtime public address announcer—"No smoking in the
Metrodome!"—had died.

Now Carneal, who had been the Voice of Summer through good times and
bad. Carneal was there from Lenny Green to Kirby Puckett to Torii Hunter to
scores of forgettable center fielders in between. In his soft Virginia drawl, he
never tried to draw attention to himself. He understood the effectiveness of
silence. He understood baseball is only a game. No matter how well, or how
poorly, the team played one day, there'd be another game the next, a game that
would begin with Carneal simply saying, "Hi, everybody."

Even the players—especially those who had grown up listening to the
Twins network—had a fondness for Carneal's style.

"To hear that voice was magic," Kent Hrbek, who grew up in Bloomington, listening to Herb, told the *Star Tribune.* "When I was a kid, it meant
school was almost out and spring was coming."

Carneal often was surprised by the niche he had come to fill in the passing of the Minnesota seasons.

"Sometimes I say to myself, 'What's an old man like me doing here announcing a kid's game?' But I'll get a letter from someone saying how much they look forward to hearing the games on the air. That's one of the things that makes me keep going."

Garrison Keillor paid tribute to Carneal's role in Minnesota in a song for *A Prairie Home Companion.*

> *Just give me two pillows and a bottle of beer*
> *and a Twins' game on radio next to my ear.*
> *Some hark to the sound of the loon or the teal.*
> *But I love the voice of Herb Carneal.*

Carneal's death brought about genuine mourning across the Upper Midwest. He'd been a constant. His voice was not just about a baseball game, it was about shared memories.

A writer, Double A, posted this comment on Batgirl's Web site on the day of Carneal's death: "My earliest memories of baseball, the Twins and my grandpa involve a transistor radio, 'cco and Herb Carneal. After supper was over and the kitchen cleaned, grandpa would turn on the radio, fiddle with the dial until 830 was as clear as it would get, pull out a deck of cards, then, relax by listening to Herb call the game while playing solitaire. Grandpa has been gone for nearly 25 years now, but I've been remembering him by playing solitaire and listening to the Twins for several years. Now, with Herb gone, it's like a little piece of grandpa is gone, too."

Carneal's death came at a time of more transition than usual for the team. The contract status of two of the team's superstars—Hunter and pitcher Johan Santana—became a subtext of the whole season. Would the team sign the two hugely talented and popular players?

This season also marked the first time the team's games would not be broadcast on wcco Radio. Money and power trumped sentiment in the Twins' decision to leave wcco and move to KSTP. The Twins wanted to control both the production of games, and more importantly, sell and collect revenue from all in-game advertising. Additionally, the team wanted to collect a rights fee. The station would make its money selling pre- and post-game advertising and, presumably, have higher ratings because it was broadcasting Twins games. Higher overall ratings would allow it to sell advertising for other programming at higher rates.

For all of its down-home, "good neighbor" sound, wcco is a corporation. The station is owned by CBS, and New York executives were not interested in losing either control or money to a mid-level, Midwest baseball team. They believed the Twins would not actually pull the plug on their longtime broadcast home. They were wrong. KSTP radio was willing to make the deal the Twins wanted, so the Twins signed a three-year contract with the station that always had played second fiddle to WCCO.

The season was a disappointment, with the team finishing below .500 for the first time in six years. The offseason brought major changes.

Terry Ryan, who had become general manager in 1994 and led the team out of one of the most dismal periods in its history and into the playoffs, stepped down, telling reporters, "This has been creeping in and creeping in. It got to the point where I knew I had to step aside. I didn't like seeing the way I had become, the way I treated people. I don't have it in me anymore."

Bill Smith became general manager as soon as the 2007 season ended. Smith understands that most fans know they are more capable of doing the job than he is.

"I get a steady stream of e-mails every day that let me know they're more qualified," said Smith, an East Coast French major who was the second-string catcher on his Hamilton College baseball team in New York.

Smith, who grew up a Red Sox fan, came into baseball through an experiment. Major League Baseball was seeking to attract young blood into its ranks, and in 1980 established an executive training program. Smith applied for an internship, got it, and, much like a player, started up through the ranks. Following the internship in New York, he got a low-level management job with the Chicago White Sox, then became the general manager of a White Sox Class A farm team in Appleton, Wisconsin.

The pay was awful, the hours long, "but it's a wonderful thing to look forward to going to work every day," said Smith.

He took a job as assistant director of minor leagues and scouting with the Twins in 1989, kept advancing, and following the 2007 season was suddenly, as general manager, faced with the contracts of Santana and Hunter.

Underlying all Twins decisions was the goal of fielding as strong a team as possible upon moving into the new ballpark being constructed across downtown Minneapolis from the Dome. Joe Mauer had been signed to a four-year, $33 million contract before the start of the 2007 season. Justin Morneau signed a six-year, $80 million contract following the season, and Michael Cuddyer signed a three-year $24 million deal at the same time. These three were seen as the core of the team that would move into the new stadium.

The sums are staggering, even to the players.

"You can't even think about the money," said Mauer of being young and rich. "My friends always said I was tight. I gained that reputation when I had to be tight. Now, I still am. The one thing all the money allows you to do is help your family. But I'm not the kind of person who goes out and buys fancy cars. My goal in sports was not about making a lot of money, it was about accomplishing things. That's still my goal."

Delightful as he was as a player and a person, Hunter would be almost thirty-five years old when the new park opened. Santana would be only thirty-one, but a bottom-line buster. Both would be gone before the 2008 season began.

After turning down a three-year, $45 million contract from the Twins, Hunter, a free agent, signed a five-year, $90 million contract with the California Angels. The Twins were determined to trade Santana before he became a free agent and on January 29, 2008, they made a deal with the Mets: Santana for a young outfielder, Carlos Gomez, and three minor-league pitchers, Phillip Humber, Kevin Mulvey, and Deolis Guerra.

"When you're making a deal involving minor league players, you have to get numbers," Smith said. "Too many things can happen to young players along the way. Let me say this about Johan. He told us, 'If you trade me, make sure it ends up being a good deal for the Twins.'"

2008

One-Game Season

The World: Raul Castro takes over as president of Cuba for his ailing brother, Fidel. Oil prices exceed $100 a barrel for the first time and cause worldwide economic chaos. Asif Ali Zardari, widower of Benazir Bhutto, becomes Pakistan's prime minister.

The Nation: With markets tumbling, the government takes control of mortgage lenders Fannie Mae and Freddie Mac. That's quickly followed by the collapse of investment bank Lehman Brothers. Congress approves a $700 billion bailout package for the stumbling financial industry. On November 4, Barack Obama is elected the first African-American president.

The State: St. Paul hosts the Republican National Convention, where John McCain accepts his party's nomination for president, and his choice for running mate, Alaska Governor Sarah Palin, wows the crowd. Incumbent senator Norm Coleman and challenger Al Franken stage the dirtiest and most costly U.S. Senate race in state history. No winner is determined for months. Despite questioning the patriotism of her Congressional colleagues in a nationally televised interview, incumbent Representative Michele Bachmann manages to win a second term. Jon Hassler, who wrote gracefully of small-town Minnesota life, dies at the age of seventy-four.

Pop Culture: Billboard's #1 Song: "Low," by Flo Rida. Highest-Grossing Movie: *The Dark Knight.* Best Seller: *The Appeal,* by John Grisham. Top-Rated Television Show: *American Idol.*

The Season: Lofty expectations disappeared with Johan Santana and Torii Hunter, but a young pitching staff, another batting title for Joe Mauer, and surprising performances by second baseman Alexi Casilla and outfielder Denard Span lift the team into a first place tie with the White Sox at season's end. A 1-0 loss in a one-game playoff in game 163 ends the dream.

Nick Blackburn thought he'd been prepared for everything. The Chicago White Sox and Twins had played the 162-game season and ended up in a first place tie in the Central Division. It was all going to come down to this one game, in Chicago on September 30. It was all coming down to Blackburn, a rookie pitcher in the biggest game of the year.

"It was his turn," said Twins manager Ron Gardenhire of why Blackburn, who had struggled in the last weeks of the season, got the start. "All season, we tell the guys, 'It's a long year, it's gonna take everyone doing their part.'"

Gardenhire practices what he preaches. So now Blackburn, who lives in Blanchard, Oklahoma, "because there's not much that happens there," was stepping out of the dugout.

"Go get 'em," Gardenhire said.

"Don't back away, use all your pitches," were the last words of advice from pitching coach Rick Anderson.

Blackburn started walking to the mound and that's when he got surprised. There were 40,354 White Sox fans in the park, most of them dressed in black for "blackout night," in Chicago. To Blackburn it seemed as if every one of those fans had studied his life story.

"Rough crowd," said Blackburn. "They'd done their research. They were yelling all sorts of stuff at me. They knew my whole season. They were yelling what I'd done in my last ten games. They were yelling a lot of other things, too."

His heart was pounding, until he got to the mound. Then everything was okay.

"I knew the White Sox," Blackburn said. "I knew their lineup. We'd played them, what?, nineteen times in the season. I knew they could beat me; they'd done that. But I knew I could beat them, too."

He took a deep breath and settled in.

Everything about the night was improbable. No one—except for Gardenhire and his players—had figured the 2008 Twins would be in contention for anything. Johan Santana was with the New York Mets. Torii Hunter, the old team leader, was with the California Angels. Shortstop Jason Barlett and top pitching prospect Matt Garza had been traded to Tampa by first-year general manager Bill Smith, who'd replaced an exhausted Terry Ryan—twice base-

Twins pitcher Glen Perkins lifts the spirits of kids during a visit to Crystal Lake Elementary School in Lakeville. Perkins grew up in Oak Park Heights, starred at Stillwater High and at the University of Minnesota, where over a two-year period he compiled a 19–5 record before being drafted in the first round by the Twins in 2004. Over the years, most Twins players have been willing participants in the team's community outreach programs. COURTESY OF THE MINNESOTA TWINS.

ball's Executive of the Year—following Ryan's decision to step down at the end of the 2007 season.

"Thirteen years is a long time in that chair," said Ryan of his decision to leave.

Carlos Gomez, wildly exciting and wildly unpredictable, replaced Hunter. Delmon Young, whom the Twins had received in the deal with Tampa, was supposed to give the team power in the middle of the lineup. And a bunch of old players who worked relatively cheap—third baseman Mike Lamb, shortstop Adam Everett, outfielder Craig Monroe, and pitcher Livan Hernandez—were supposed to fill in all of the other holes.

At the start of spring training, Gardenhire talked, once, about all the players who were gone.

"They're not here," he told his players. "We've got to get it done without them. I believe athletes are made to achieve. That's what we're going to do."

All of the old vets were a bust, and, with the exception of Everett, all were gone before the end of the season. In addition, Michael Cuddyer, who was counted on to have a big season, spent most of the year recovering from a series of injuries.

The year had started on such an upbeat note for Cuddyer. He'd signed a three-year, $24 million contract with the Twins, an acknowledgment that the team saw him as one of the core players heading into the future. But on April 4, Cuddyer dislocated his right index finger sliding into third base against the Kansas City Royals. Shortly after recovering from that injury, his strained his left index finger and was placed on the disabled list. Cuddyer could only fret as the injury lingered.

Finally, in early August, he was ready to swing the bat again. He was sent to the Twins farm team in Rochester to scrape the rust off of his game by swinging against live pitching. A couple of days before he was to rejoin the Twins, he was running between first and second in a Rochester game. A team-mate hit a ball, hard, toward right field. Incredibly, the ball struck Cuddyer on the left foot. A bone was broken. He returned to Minnesota wearing a cast. "Snakebit," he muttered.

Cuddyer's injuries did open the door to Denard Span, whom the Twins had drafted in the first round in 2002. A serious young man, a wonderful athlete, Span's hitting had been suspect throughout his long minor-league career. But Span kept plugging, buoyed in part by minor-league instructors who pointed out that Torii Hunter hadn't compiled impressive minor-league statistics, either.

Given a chance to play right field in place of the injured Cuddyer, Span was magnificent. He replaced Gomez as the team's leadoff hitter and, unlike Gomez, was patient and consistent, batting .297. Playing in 93 games, Span drew twice as many walks, 50, as Gomez drew playing in 153 games. A cen-ter fielder all of his life, Span moved to right field and made spectacular plays on a routine basis.

The Twins competed all year and with six games remaining in the sea-son, the White Sox came to town, holding a two-and-a-half-game lead over the Twins.

Before 35,225 fans on September 23, the Twins, with 2 home runs from Jason Kubel and 1 from Young, beat Chicago, 9–3. The White Sox had a one-and-a-half-game lead with five games left in the season.

Before 42,126 fans on September 24, the Twins won a nail-biter, 3–2 and the White Sox had a half-game lead with four games left in the regular sea-son.

Before 43,602 fans on September 25, the Twins showed off the new breed of piranhas, overcame a 5-run deficit, and defeated the White Sox, 7–6, in ten innings. The new piranhas—Gomez, Nick Punto, Span, and Alexi Casilla—combined for 9 of the Twins' 15 hits, had 3 triples and scored 5 of the 7 runs. With two out in the tenth, it was Casilla who singled to drive home Punto with the winning run. The first-place Twins raced onto the field, celebrating.

In the White Sox clubhouse, there was concern, at least among the Chi-cago sports media.

"What are you going to do?" a reporter asked White Sox manager Ozzie Guillen. "Are you going to call a meeting?"

Guillen responded with a thought worthy of study in business schools. "Winning teams have winners," Guillen said. "Losing teams have meetings."

The White Sox had no meetings. The Twins had a chance to hold the

Pitchers Craig Breslow *(right)* and Nick Blackburn visit with a young fan from Hawaii at the University of Minnesota hospital. COURTESY OF THE MINNESOTA TWINS.

lead and win the title with three home games remaining against Kansas City. Instead, they managed to lose two of three to the Royals, while the White Sox were at home, losing two of three to Cleveland.

With their 162-game season finished, the Twins had a half-game lead over Chicago. But the White Sox had one more chance to even up the standings, a makeup game against the Detroit Tigers to be played in Chicago on Monday, the day after the season was supposed to be over. The White Sox breezed, 8–2, over Detroit, a victory that gave them an identical record to the Twins. A coin flip determined that the deciding game would be in Chicago, which is how Blackburn got the ball in the biggest game of the season.

He got through the first inning without giving up a run. And the second, the third, the fourth.

"It was the most calm I'd been all season," said Blackburn. "It doesn't matter who's at the plate. You're not thinking, 'My God, it's Thome or Griffey.' You're thinking, 'What's their weakness?'"

The only problem was, the Twins were being held hitless by Chicago's John Danks. Then, in the fifth, Cuddyer, who had finally recovered from all injuries in the final days of the season, led off with a double and advanced to third on a deep fly to center by Young. Brendan Harris hit a fly to shallow center, Cuddyer tagged up and when Ken Griffey caught the ball, headed home. Everybody said Cuddyer's decision to run was a good play, but Griffey's throw, bouncing twice, was snagged by A. J. Pierzynski, who tagged Cuddyer out.

In the sixth, the White Sox's powerful Jim Thome stepped to the plate to start the inning. Blackburn worked the count to two balls, two strikes.

"We'd been pounding him all night inside," said Blackburn. "I was thinking, 'Change-up, he'll swing over it.' But I got the ball up. As soon as I released the ball I could see it playing out."

Thome swung hard, as always. The ball traveled 461 feet, flying over two rows of shrubs beyond the center field wall. The White Sox led, 1–0. That's all they needed.

"It was not a great ending to the story," said Blackburn.

The White Sox, by virtue of their 1–0 victory, were in the playoffs and the Twins were in the off-season.

It was a loss that hung in their minds for weeks, in some cases months.

"I wasn't fun to be around for a couple of weeks," said Gardenhire. "But then I went down to the instructional league to work with some kids. That was fun. Getting around the game again got me over it."

In the off-season, Justin Morneau gave Christmas gifts to every office worker in the Twins organization ("They work hard, thankless jobs so we can go out and play baseball") and got married, but still brooded about that 163rd game in a 162-game season.

"We were playing so well," said Morneau. "I thought we could get into the playoffs and do something, that's how well we were playing. To get that far and lose 1–0, it's not easy to get over. Nick pitched so well. We had a chance to do something special. You never know if you'll get that chance again."

2009

One Last Roar

The World: Starting in Mexico, an outbreak of "swine flu," quickly renamed the H1N1 virus, raises international concerns of a deadly flu pandemic. North Korea conducts a number of nuclear weapons tests, raising alert levels across Asia.

The Nation: On January 20, Barack Obama is inaugurated as the 44th and first African-American president. Four months later, he nominates Sonia Sotomayor to be the first Hispanic and only the third woman to be a justice on the U.S. Supreme Court. In the midst of a recession, the mighty continue to fall. First Chrysler, then General Motors declare bankruptcy. Chrysler is purchased by Italian automaker Fiat. As a cost-saving measure, General Motors stops manufacturing the once-popular Pontiac brand. Roxana Saberi, an Iranian-American journalist with North Dakota roots, is arrested in Iran and quickly found guilty of spying. International outrage over what appears to be a mockery of justice causes an Iranian appeals court to review the case and release Saberi.

The State: Governor Tim Pawlenty announces he will not seek a third term, setting off a flurry of speculation over whether he can eventually become the Republican nominee for president. Through the first half of the year, Senator Amy Klobuchar continues to be the state's only senator as the recount process continues in the race between Democrat Al Franken and Republican Norm Coleman. Finally, in June, the court appeals end and Franken is declared the winner by 312 votes. Denny Hecker, once the high-flying owner of twenty auto dealerships in Minnesota, files for Chapter 7 bankruptcy. In the filings, he claims $50 to $100 million in assets, but $500 to $1 billion in debts. After more than a quarter-century of playing in the Metrodome, the University of Minnesota football team moves back to campus on September 12, playing the Air Force Academy at their new TCF Bank Stadium.

Pop Culture: Scotland's Susan Boyle competes on *Britain's Got Talent* and wins over the world with her voice. Ultimately, she finishes second in the contest, but first in the hearts of millions. Highest-Grossing Movie: *Harry Potter and the Half-Blood Prince.* Pulitzer Prize for Fiction: *Olive Kitteridge,* by Elizabeth Strout. Top-Rated Television Show: *American Idol.*

When Walter Bush was president of hockey's Minnesota North Stars, he described the region's sports fans as "a bunch of phlegmatic Swedes." The Hubert H. Humphrey Metrodome changed all of that. Yes, the Dome was gray and plastic, but there was nothing impassive about the two generations of people who attended games there.

No longer was baseball a slow-moving game savored while enjoying a cigar. ("No smoking in the Metrodome!" public address announcer Bob Casey would say with gusto before every game. Sometimes, Kent Hrbek would pantomime Casey's words.) In the Dome, baseball became a video game. High hops became triples, lost fly balls led to rallies, and speed was essential on the artificial surface. And then there was the noise. Players talked about the electricity they felt from the fans. The noise at a ballgame no longer drifted into the sky, instead it was compressed in the massive building and enveloped fans and players. Noise begat more noise, more mistakes from the opposition, and more intensity among Twins players. "Now we know what noise feels like," said television sportscaster Al Michaels during the din of the 1987 World Series.

In the final days of the final season in the Dome, the din of '87 was back. Oh, what a finale for the place that purists loved to hate. It was joyful, raucous, incredible, stunning—and finally hushed, as a team that had staged a remarkable comeback to win the American League's Central Division gave away chances to beat the mighty Yankees in the playoffs.

There are two ways to look at the '09 season. The great sprint to the finish, or the disappointing flop in the playoffs. Presumably, most fans will recall all that was so much fun about the final days at the Dome.

And there is so much to remember. With the team floundering in mid-September, Justin Morneau's season ended because of a stress fracture in his lower back. When healthy, Morneau had been having his best year, hitting 30 homers and driving in 100 runs. But starting in August, his hitting had begun to fall and through the first two weeks of September, the pain in his back took over. He had just 3 hits in 39 September at bats when physicians told him it was time to give up the season and let his back heal.

News of Morneau being done hit the clubhouse at about the same time that the Twins learned that third baseman Joe Crede also was done for the year because of a bad back. This news came when the team was five games behind Detroit.

"It's tough," said manager Ron Gardenhire. "But we can't do anything about it. We still have a job to do, and we'll have to do it without them."

On the first night that Morneau was out of the lineup, Michael Cuddyer, who moved from right field to first base, hit a three-run homer in a come-from-behind win over Cleveland. The most exhilarating finish in Twins history was about to unfold. Without Morneau, the team won 16 of their last 20 games as the flawed Detroit Tigers stumbled, slowly but steadily blowing what had been a seven-game lead on September 6.

The Twins' finish set the stage for Minnesota's wildest-ever sports weekend. The Twins had a three-game series with the Kansas City Royals. The University of Minnesota football team played archrival Wisconsin in the Gophers' sparkling new stadium. There was the Twin Cities Marathon, and a Monday Night Football game between the Brett Favre–led Vikings and the Green Bay Packers at the Dome.

For a period of 120 hours, sports overwhelmed everything else in Minnesota. For five days, politics and economics and foreclosures and joblessness were set aside as the subjects of the day. The streets were filled with people wearing Badger red, or Gopher maroon, or Viking purple. But Twins baseball was the biggest story of all.

Nobody—not fans, not sports writers, not Twins management, not players—could have imagined any of this.

Throughout the year, this had been a team that never could get on track. It was a team bedeviled by injuries. A team that had seen three of its five starting pitchers—Kevin Slowey, Glen Perkins, Francisco Liriano—either become injured or flame out. Until Orlando Cabrera was acquired on July 31 from Oakland, it was a team with no real starting shortstop.

For most of the season, the organization had a two-pronged marketing plan: Come to the final games at the Dome, and get ready for the 2010 season in a brand-new, outdoor ballpark. That last regular-season series against the Royals at the Dome had been marketed as a nostalgia weekend, not a weekend in which the games would really matter.

The Dome, always primarily a football stadium, wasn't even dressed for baseball in the closing days of the improbable pennant race. Instead, huge purple murals, including one of Favre over the stadium's main entrance, covered the outside of the Dome. The Vikings had even sold naming rights to the place: "Mall of America Field" read the huge banner over the purple wrappings.

Julian Empson Loscalzo and Michael Samuelson, founders of the "Save the Met" organization, stood outside the Dome on what was to have been its last baseball weekend hawking "Save the Met" T-shirts and marveling at the passage of time.

"I wore a medium back then," said Loscalzo of being at the final game at the Met. "And Sammy had two arms." (Samuelson lost an arm to cancer. Loscalzo now wore a large.)

"We were right!" Samuelson yelled as people walked past. "They never should have moved indoors."

"We were right before they were wrong," chimed in Loscalzo.

Most of the fans, wearing Mauer and Morneau jerseys, hustled past the outdoor baseball purists, past all the purple and out of a cool, drizzly night and into the heat of a pennant race inside the Dome. Many were too young to remember the team had ever played anywhere but indoors.

Even Joe Mauer had talked earlier in the season about how he would miss the Dome, which made him different from most of his teammates.

"The first major-league game I ever saw outdoors was one I played in," said Mauer.

Now here it was: The last weekend of the regular season. The Twins trailed Detroit by two games, with three games remaining. While the Twins were playing the Kansas City Royals, the Tigers were in Detroit, playing a Chicago White Sox team that had been a disappointment.

The noise was inside. The Homer Hankies were there. The magic was there. The Twins swept the series with Kansas City while Chicago won two of three against Detroit, meaning the regular season ended, for a second year in a row, with two teams tied for first and needing a 163rd game to determine a champion. The Twins had become the first team in baseball history to make up a three-game deficit with just four games remaining to be played.

Game 163 turned out to be one of the most memorable games ever played in the Dome, ranking only behind Game 6 (the Puckett game) and Game 7 (the Jack Morris game) of the 1991 World Series. The game lasted twelve innings. It went on for and 4 hours and 37 minutes. 54,088 people, the most ever to watch a regular-season ballgame in the Dome, bit their nails and waved their hankies and watched in agony and ecstasy. The Twins would use eight pitchers before the night was over. The Tigers would use five.

There was an apparent blown call that cost the Tigers dearly in the top of the twelfth. With the bases loaded and one out and the game tied, 5–5, the Tigers' Brandon Inge appeared to be hit by a pitch by the Twins' final pitcher of the night, Bobby Keppel. Had umpire Randy Marsh ruled that Inge's jersey had been brushed by the pitch, the Tigers would have taken a 6–5 lead. But Marsh didn't see it that way. He called a ball.

Inge then hit a chopper toward second baseman Nick Punto. Punto, who would later become one of the goats of the playoffs, made a play that saved the season. With no chance to turn a double play, Punto fired home, forcing an out at the plate on an oh-so-close play. Again, the Tigers had missed out on a chance to take the lead.

"That kid—that play—won the ballgame for us," Gardenhire would later say.

It was another "kid," Alexi Casilla, who became the final hero in the epic game. Casilla, who had spent the season moving between the minor leagues and the Twins doghouse for disappointing play, stepped to the plate in the bottom of the twelfth inning and grounded a single into right field that drove home Carlos Gomez with the division-winning run.

The celebration was on. Twins players hugged and leaped and hugged, and fans hugged and waved Homer Hankies and hugged. They'd pulled it off. The Dome wasn't going to go away quietly.

Mauer, who won his third batting title (.365), led his teammates in a joy-ful victory lap around the field as the fans cheered on and on.

"My God, I've never seen anything like this," said Gardenhire.

Even the Tigers, who had seen the title slip through their fingers, were caught up in the drama of game 163.

"It was the best game I ever played in with the worst outcome," said Inge.

In fan memories, this game, with its tension and final joy, will likely be remembered as the way it all ended at the Dome. The team that once had been on the verge of contraction had won another division title and along the way, attracted 2.4 million fans, fourteenth best in major-league baseball.

Of course, that's not the way the season ended. Within hours of all the celebration, a playoff series with the Yankees began in New York. And that turned out to be all about might-have-beens. It was as if the Twins had used up all their good plays, and caught their quota of good breaks in the final weeks of the season.

Jason Kubel, a mighty component of the Twins stretch drive, suddenly stopped hitting against the Yankees, getting just 1 hit in 14 at bats. Delmon Young, also a key player in the final days of the regular season, was just as futile, going 1-for-12. But they weren't alone. Throughout what turned out to be a short but tense series, Twins hitters failed in the clutch, going 1-for-9 with runners on base in the first game of the series, and stranding 17 runners in Game 2. But the hitters weren't the only ones failing in the clutch. Twice, Joe Nathan, the Twins' mighty closer, had chances to bail out his team. But both times—in Games 2 and 3—he failed. And there were base-running blunders, by Nick Punto and Carlos Gomez, that took the Twins out of potentially winning situations.

In addition, there was the awful foul-ball call by left field umpire Phil Cuzzi in the eleventh inning of Game 2. With the score tied, 3–3, Mauer sliced a ball toward the left field line. Cuzzi, whose only job was to call fair or foul balls on the line, signaled foul. In fact, it was fair by a foot before it bounced into the stands. What should have been a ground-rule double was a strike.

Mauer did follow that blunder with a single, but he advanced to second (instead of third) when Kubel followed with his only hit of the series, and got no farther than third (instead of home with the go-ahead run) when Cuddyer singled. With the bases loaded and nobody out, the Twins failed to score and the Yankees' Mark Teixeira hit a walk-off, game-winning homer in the bottom of the eleventh.

So many might-have-beens. Instead, it was just another lost playoff series for the Twins, who didn't beat the Yankees all season. The sweep by the Yanks meant the Twins had lost nine successive playoff games dating back to 2004. The last season in the Dome was finally over.

For all of its ugliness and plastic, it was a special place.

Karol Ann Marling, a University of Minnesota professor, a student of pop culture, and a baseball fan, loved everything about the Dome.

"It was the one place in Minnesota where total strangers talked to each other," she said. "It was a place that made even Minnesotans passionate. You went in on a hot summer day and it was cool, and on a cold day it was warm. There was pleasure in the Dome."

Bill Lester, executive director of the Stadium Commission, which oversees the Dome's operations, called it "the state's recreation room," noting that virtually everybody in Minnesota had made at least one visit to the place for events ranging from tractor pulls to high school football games, to revivals, to World Series games.

One of the Dome's special beauties was that it was despised by the Twins' foes. Every time the late Billy Martin entered the place as manager of the Yankees, he seethed. His most memorable line was a head scratcher.

"It stinks," said Martin of the Dome. "It's a shame a great guy like Hubert Humphrey had to be named after it."

Wiser Twins players loved it when opponents complained. "We just figured it was to our advantage," said Gary Gaetti. "We knew the quirks of the place. It was ours."

Quirks did happen. The roof deflated for the first time on November 19, 1981, after heavy snow caused a tear in the fabric. Not surprisingly, Jerry Bell, who headed the Stadium Commission at the time, was concerned. He called one of the Dome's designing engineers.

"I told him, 'We've got a problem here,' Bell recalled. "He told me that if we blasted a hole in the roof with a shotgun, it would allow heat from the inside to get out and the snow would melt and it would work out. He said we could patch the holes from the shotgun blast in the spring. We decided that didn't sound like a very good idea."

Instead of a shotgun blast, temp workers were hired to shovel snow from the roof.

It deflated again, for the same reason, on December 30, 1982. And on April 14, 1983, it happened again. Heavy snow, a tear in the roof, and for the

The Dome became a stadium filled with memories, some of them quirky. For instance, in May 1984, the Oakland A's Dave Kingman hit a ball up ... and Twins infielders John Castino and Houston Jimenez waited for it to come down ... It never did. PHOTO COURTESY OF AP IMAGES.

one and only time in the Dome's history a game was postponed due to the weather—sort of.

There were humorous moments in the Dome. For example, with two outs in the fourth inning of a game being played on May 4, 1984, between the Twins and Oakland, A's slugger Dave Kingman hit a pitch from Frank Viola almost straight up.

Kingman, disgusted with himself, pounded his bat on the turf and started running to first. Viola looked up, as did catcher Tim Laudner, first baseman Mickey Hatcher, second baseman Tim Teufel, shortstop Houston Jiminez, third baseman John Castino, and 10,155 spectators. All were looking for the ball to come down. It didn't.

Kingman's mighty pop-up had gone up 180 feet and into one of the seven-inch drainage holes in the inner layer of the roof. The umpires gathered to discuss this event that had never before happened in a major-league baseball game. The umps decided to call the lost ball a ground-rule double. Viola retired the next batter, meaning no damage was done except to the Dome's reputation. In the ninth inning, Kingman homered for Oakland's only run, and the Twins won the game, 3–1.

The day after the Kingman pop-up got lost in the roof, Hatcher, always in search of a reason to laugh, concocted an elaborate scheme. Prior to the May 5 game, Hatcher was going to catch the lost ball, which was to be dropped from the roof by a Dome worker standing on a catwalk. At that point, an umpire would call Kingman out and Kingman would run from the dugout to protest the call.

One problem with the plan: Hatcher lost sight of the ball as it fell and was nearly beaned. The Twins and A's players roared with laughter.

There was terror in the Dome, too—and not just when Davis was summoned from the bullpen.

On April 26, 1986, the baseball gods seemed to express their outrage at the Dome. With a thunderstorm raging outside and 31,966 fans inside, the Twins built a 6–1 lead over the California Angels heading into the seventh inning.

Wind gusts outside were reaching sixty miles per hour. Thunder rumbled. Lightning flashes could be seen from inside. In the bottom of the seventh inning, the lights above right field started swaying. Water started pouring through the roof. It appeared the end was near as fans were evacuated from the right field stands and the Angels players fled from the field.

But the game was delayed for only nine minutes before it was decided that the Dome was more powerful than the forces of nature. With the Twins still leading, 6–1, entering the ninth, a new storm formed. This one from the Angels. George Hendrick homered off Viola. Davis was called in from the bullpen. He gave up a single to Rob Wilfong and a two-run homer to Ruppert Jones. Then the angst-producing reliever retired two batters before walking Reggie Jackson and giving up a two-run homer to Wally Joyner. By inning's end, the Angels had scored 6 runs and left the tattered Dome with a 7–6 victory.

For all the quirks, it should not be forgotten that magnificent baseball was played here.

The World Series of 1991 is considered by many to have been the greatest ever. Outfielders complained of how difficult it was to follow the ball, yet Kirby Puckett and Torii Hunter won a combined eleven Gold Gloves playing half their games under the Teflon roof. Until the turf was replaced in 2004, the Dome had the worst field in major-league baseball, yet Gaetti won four Gold Gloves, and Chuck Knoblauch and Doug Mientkiewicz each won one.

The place was filled with memories for millions of fans. It was the scene of that triumphant homecoming in 1987 after the Twins defeated the Detroit Tigers in the playoffs. It was the site of the sad farewell tribute to Kirby Puckett, who died on March 5, 2006. Seven days after his death, 15,000 people ignored blizzard warnings to attend the service for Puckett. Tears flowed when old Twins pitcher "Mudcat" Grant sang a soulful version of "What a Wonderful World."

More often than not, the Twins were winners playing inside. Over the years, they won 1,214 games in the Dome and lost 1,028. On the road during the Dome years, Minnesota was 981–1,243. Will the new ballpark, so lovely to look at, be as friendly to the hometown team?

Following the Yankees sweep, Nathan spoke with actions, not words about what a fine home the Dome had turned out to be. He picked up some dirt from the pitcher's mound with the idea of sprinkling it on the mound in the new ballpark.

2010

Blue Sky Again

For the Twins' fiftieth season in Minnesota, they will have a new ballpark. It is made with native Minnesota limestone and landscaped with Minnesota native flowers, shrubs, and trees. It has far more restrooms than the Metrodome; 40,000 seats, 18,500 of them surrounding the infield; real grass; no roof. It's here, but the man who begged, bluffed and bullied to get it won't be in attendance. Carl Pohlad died, at the age of ninety-three, on January 5, 2008, as the ballpark was being built between the Target Center and the Hennepin County garbage burner.

There were two fundamentally opposing views of Pohlad following his death.

Here's how Pat Borzi, a *New York Times* correspondent and contributor to an online publication, *MinnPost,* viewed Pohlad's life:

> Of all the words that could be used to described Pohlad, "beloved" probably would not be used outside his immediate family and friends. He was a billionaire ranked by *Forbes Magazine* as the second-richest man in Minnesota, but his notorious frugality with his baseball team left him an easy target for frustrated fans who branded him a skinflint.... But for now, as the Pohlad kids prepare to bury their father, let's remember that he kept baseball in the Twin Cities. You can't consider yourself a major-league sports town without base-

Carl Pohlad always said his wife, Eloise, was the true baseball fan of the couple, but Carl pushed, pleaded, and threatened for a new ballpark. He lived to see the groundbreaking for the new park but died on January 5, 2009, at the age of ninety-three. Eloise died, at eighty-six, in 2003. COURTESY OF THE MINNESOTA TWINS.

ball, and those of us who relish such things should be grateful. Above all else, that is Carl Pohlad's legacy.

Tom Powers, a sports columnist for the *St. Paul Pioneer Press*, wasn't so kind. He wrote:

Carl Pohlad won. That's the most fitting thing I can say about the Twins owner. He went to his grave knowing that a new ballpark, being built primarily with public money, was nearing completion. No doubt he heard the angels singing all the way to his eternal resting place ... Excuse me if I don't shed any crocodile tears. I'm not sure the old boy would like that anyway. Perhaps in private he was a big buttercup. In business, which was his lifeblood, he was ruthless. He was cutthroat. To him "the deal" was everything. Oh, I know what you're thinking: The guy's dead, give him a break and say something nice. But I am. He'd love being recognized as the master dealmaker. The ultimate compliment. His assets overwhelmed his debits. Amen.

No matter your view of the man who bought the Twins in 1984 for a bargain price, the ballpark is here. And it wouldn't be here without Pohlad.

There is another key figure in the opening of the new stadium. While two governors, Jesse Ventura and Tim Pawlenty ducked the issue, a Hennepin County Commissioner, Mike Opat, stepped to the plate and, in the face of public disapproval, took one more swing at getting a ballpark built. In 2002, Opat began pushing for a simple solution to a complex problem. The county, in his view, was the one government entity in Minnesota with the economic and political wherewithal to fund the public portion of a stadium. Unlike all other plans that had preceded it, Opat's plan was transparent. With state legislative approval, the county could levy a .15 percent sales tax in the county. Collected over as long as thirty years, that tax would generate the public's $392 million of the stadium project. The Twins were to contribute $130 million to the deal and pick up cost overruns.

There was one other thing that Opat demanded from the legislature. There could be *no* referendum attached to the legislation granting the county authority to levy the tax. Opat knew what the outcome of any referendum would be.

"I said we're not going to do all the work to bring this deal together only to have it all go down in a referendum," Opat said.

Though the state wasn't on the hook for any money, Governor Ventura and legislators were nervous about the arrangement that Opat and a handful of others had worked out with the Twins.

"We met with the governor a couple of times," Opat said. "I kept saying, 'No referendum' and then he'd get very noncommittal.'"

But Ventura and, later, Pawlenty, were of two minds on the whole ballpark issue. They didn't want to be part of any plan that put public money into a stadium without voter approval. But they also didn't want the Twins to leave town under their watch.

Despite strong support from such legislative leaders as Dean Johnson, a DFLer in the senate, and Steve Sviggum, a Republican and, for a time, the Speaker of the house, legislators kept balking at the Opat plan. A form of the plan failed to pass muster in 2002, 2003, and 2004, and Opat had to be convinced it would be worth his time to try again in 2006. Others who had worked with Opat, including members of the Minneapolis Downtown Council and business leader Jim Campbell, and even the Twins, understood the frustration.

"We all decided, 'We're not going to do it,'" said Opat. "Why bother?'"

But some supporting legislators urged them to try one more time. On

May 3, 2006, the Hennepin County Board of Commissioners, on a 4–3 vote, approved the stadium resolution that would be presented to the legislature. The vote on the county board broke along gender lines with Mark Stenglein, Peter McLaughlin, and Randy Johnson supporting it, Gail Dorfman, Linda Koblick, and Penny Steele opposing. Koblick was so upset that it was months before she again would speak to Opat.

Fifteen days later, the Minnesota Senate, after considerable posturing, voted 34–32 to grant Hennepin County permission to levy the tax. Twelve years of political debate was over with two votes to spare.

There were no parades for Opat. Quite the opposite. The immediate reaction was outrage.

Coming up with a plan did not make him a popular man. He received threatening letters. On three occasions, protestors stood outside his home in Robbinsdale. One night when he was at a meeting, protestors knocked on

With the team returning to an outdoor ballpark, fans in the Upper Midwest will again see scenes like this one from a photo from the early 1960s showing Bob Allison watching the grounds crew trying to make the Met baseball ready. COURTESY OF THE MINNESOTA TWINS.

Outdoors again: the view from behind home plate at Target Field, the Twins' third home in Minnesota. COURTESY OF THE MINNESOTA TWINS.

the door of his home. His wife, Kim, answered. The protestors started yelling at her.

"I'm sorry," she said, "I've got three kids in the bathtub right now." She shut the door and went back to supervising bath time.

The county resolution required that three public hearings be held before county commissioners would vote one more time to formalize the deal. In each case, the hearing rooms were jammed with people, most of whom were opposed to a public subsidy for a ballpark.

Former Twins players Tim Laudner, Kent Hrbek, and Scott Leius attended a meeting with Opat in Maple Grove. Opat recalls, "After the meeting, Leius said, 'I can't believe you can sit there and take it.' I told him it was just all part of being a public official."

Opat understood the anger. The son of an ironworker, he is not a wealthy man. He understands public ire about spending the public's money to benefit an extremely rich family and wealthy players.

"It's an easy issue to demagogue," said Opat. "I understand it's a tough sell. But I just think of my kids. Do I want them to be able to grow up and go to a ballgame? I don't look at it as subsidizing the Pohlads, I think of it as a magnificent public structure that we all will be able to enjoy."

But in the summer of 2006, most people didn't seem to share that view. On one occasion, Opat ran into Ventura, now a former governor, at a golf course. Opat said hello. The former guv wasn't interested in pleasantries.

"He started shaking, like he does when he gets mad and said, 'It's a good thing I wasn't governor when that thing passed,'" Opat said. "I told him, 'Well, governor, actually you did support it.' And he said, 'Oh no, I never did, and I tell you this, I'm never going to be spending another penny in Hennepin County.'"

The outrage wasn't limited to Hennepin County. Even in outstate Minnesota, the passage of the stadium levy created anger. When Ken Tschumper, a farmer from La Crescent in far southeastern Minnesota, was knocking on doors in his campaign for the legislature in the summer of 2006, he was surprised at what residents wanted to talk about. "The first thing most people wanted to talk about was the stadium," he said. "They were mad about it and they wondered what I could do to stop it."

But, Opat said, not everyone is upset. Sometimes, he said, he'd walk into a restaurant and someone would quietly say, "Good work, glad the Twins are staying."

There have been scores of other signs that the anger is dissipating. During construction of the stadium, the most popular office spaces in Minneapolis became those with a view of the ballpark. At Twins Fest, the annual January event where baseball fans can mingle with players, the most popular display was the model of the ballpark. Until the economic crisis of 2009, the luxury boxes were selling quickly. Sportswriters have written glowing reviews of the ballpark as it has taken shape.

The reality is that in most cities there has been resistance to public subsidies for stadiums. And in most cities, the resistance has disappeared the moment the home plate umpire yells, "Play ball!"

Then it will all get pretty simple. If the Twins keep building teams around players such as Justin Morneau and Joe Mauer, they'll probably be successful and the seats in the ballpark will be filled in foul weather or fair. If they become a team of Bombo Riveras and Terry Feltons, the seats will be empty no matter how blue the sky.

Stadium Timeline

Metropolitan Stadium

1953   Search for a site begins.

1955   161 acres in Bloomington is selected; construction begins in June.

1956   The three-tier version of Met Stadium, with a capacity of 18,200, opens as the home of the Minneapolis Millers.

1959   Capacity expanded to 22,000.

1961   The Twins arrive. Capacity is expanded to 31,637 with double-deck seating constructed down the right field line.

1964   Capacity expanded to 40,000 with improved and expanded bleacher seating down the left field line.

1965   Vikings construct a double-deck structure in left field, increasing capacity to 45,900 for baseball. (Football capacity roughly 48,000.)

1982   Stadium demolished to make way for the Mall of America.

Hubert H. Humphrey Metrodome

1973   A Minneapolis Chamber of Commerce Task Force is formed to study the possibility of building a domed stadium in Minneapolis.

1975   Governor Wendy Anderson warns that without a new stadium, the region would lose both the Vikings and the Twins.

1975–77   A "no-site" bill is debated in the state legislature, finally passing in 1977.

1977 A new Metropolitan Sports Facilities Commission is formed and accepts proposals from Minneapolis, St. Paul, Bloomington, Brooklyn Center, Coon Rapids, and Eagan as potential sites of a new domed stadium. The Commission narrows the site possibilities to Minneapolis and Bloomington, finally selecting Minneapolis.

1978 Minneapolis business leaders form Industry Square Development Corp. and raise $14.8 million to purchase the 20-acre site where the Metrodome will ultimately be constructed. In exchange, the business leaders get development rights surrounding the field.

1979 Construction begins on December 20. The Vikings build private suites and receive all revenues from those suites.

1981 The air-supported roof is inflated on October 2.

1982 Construction completed in time for the start of the baseball season. New stadium cost $68 million, $2 million under budget. Seating capacity: 40,000 baseball; 64,000 football; 50,000 basketball.

1983 Air-conditioning installed in the stadium that had quickly earned the name "the Sweat Box."

1984 AstroTurf surface installed to replace original, rock-hard SporTurf.

1996 Curtain hung to cover seats in the second deck in right center field for regular season baseball games.

2004 AstroTurf surface replaced with FieldTurf.

Target Field

1994 Twins owner Carl Pohlad tells the Stadium Commission he needs a new stadium in order to compete.

1996 A stadium plan that includes a metro-wide advisory referendum is defeated in the legislature.

1997 A stadium bill fails at the legislature. In a special legislative session, the legislature again defeats a stadium bill and Pohlad announces he's reached a deal to sell the team to North Carolina businessman Don Beaver. But a stadium bill in North Carolina is defeated by voters.

1999 St. Paul voters turn down a half-cent sales tax that would have funded a new Twins stadium.

2001 Contraction becomes the newest term in Minnesota baseball. Major-league owners agree to eliminate two teams, generally believed to be the Twins and the Montreal Expos. A Hennepin County judge orders the Twins to play the 2002 season in the Metrodome. The players' union balks at the contraction plan which is eventually tabled, then disappears.

2002   A stadium deal passes the legislature, but Hennepin County is excluded from competing for the ballpark and Twins are unable to reach a deal in St. Paul.

2004   St. Paul City Council votes against a plan that would use a 3 percent restaurant sales tax to fund a new ballpark.

2006   The state legislature approves a Hennepin County plan to use a sales tax to fund building a new park. The deal calls for the county to contribute $350 million and the Twins to contribute $130 million.

2007   Construction begins on what will be called Target Field on 8 acres of land near the Warehouse District at edge of downtown Minneapolis. The stadium is to have a capacity of 40,000; 18,500 of those seats will be on the first level of a three-tier grandstand that runs from foul pole to foul pole. The stadium is to include sixty private suites and 4,000 club seats.

2010   First game to be played.

Acknowledgments

Baseball is a game of shared memories of times, places, and people, both on and off the field. Thanks to all who shared their memories with me.

Todd Orjala of the University of Minnesota Press not only accepted the idea for this book, he helped direct it. He dug through hundreds of photos, he shared his own memories of the Twins, and, most important, he stayed excited about the project.

Liz Salzmann is a fantastic editor, who not only unmangled sentences but pointed out content holes that needed filling. Andrea Rondoni, editorial assistant at the Press, never complained—to me, at least—as she tried to keep me organized.

Clyde Doepner, a former high school history teacher and baseball coach who befriended Calvin Griffith shortly after the team arrived in Minnesota, was always willing to share his incredible collection of Twins' memorabilia and his stories.

Special thanks, too, to Hillery Shay, senior editor and director of photography at the *St. Paul Pioneer Press*, who was generous with her time and access to the storehouse of photographs at the newspaper. Thanks to the Minnesota Historical Society for help in sorting through its baseball photographs, and to Sandy Date, librarian at the *Minneapolis Star Tribune*, for her time, efforts, and smiles.

The Minnesota Twins organization was always helpful. Special thanks to Bryan Donaldson, the team's community relations manager, who was willing to help connect me with former players, and to members of the media relations staff who made it possible to have access to current players. Dozens of players, past and present, made themselves available for conversations about their days on the playing field.

Even those few who opted not to converse sometimes created a new, amusing memory. There was, for example, a manager from the 1960s. When reached by phone and asked to talk about his memories of the team, he said, "What the fuck's in it for me?"

"Everlasting fame and glory," I said.

"I've got enough of that already," he said, just before slamming down the phone.

Finally, thanks to my wife, Sheila. She is not a sports fan—except when the Twins have been in the World Series—but she supported a husband who spent almost twenty years traveling around the country writing about sports, leaving her alone to cut grass, shovel snow, and raise two wonderful daughters.

Doug Grow worked for twenty-eight years as a sportswriter and columnist for the *Minneapolis Star Tribune*. He now writes for the on-line publication *MinnPost*.